IMAGINE
DESIGN
CREATE

WHY DOES DESIGN MATTER?

—

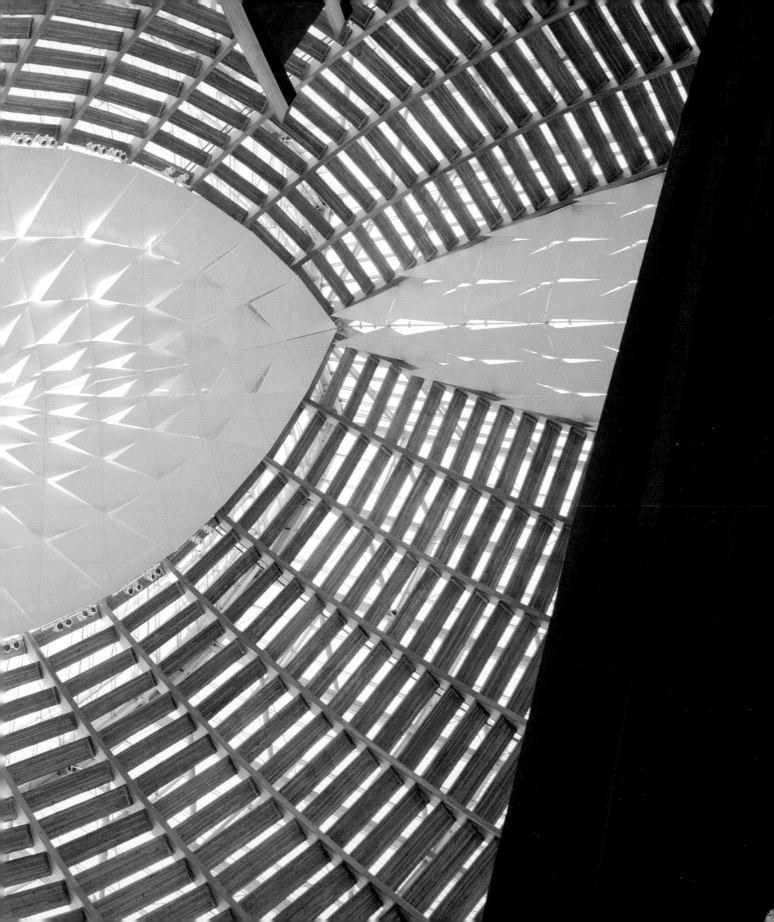

HOW DOES DESIGN INSPIRE?

HOW DO WE MAKE DESIGN?

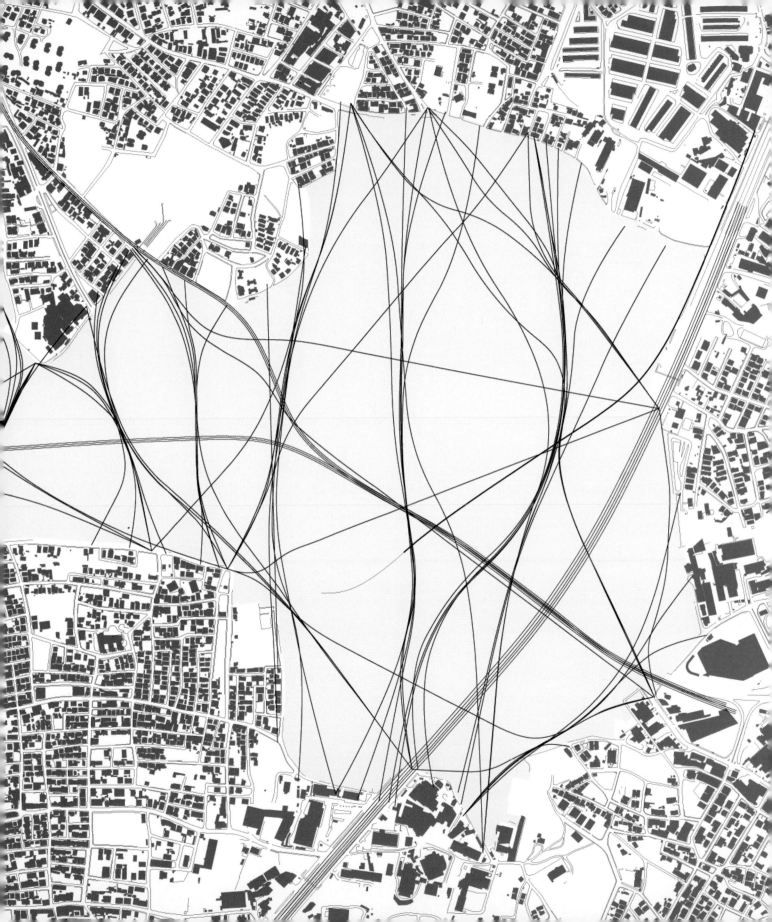

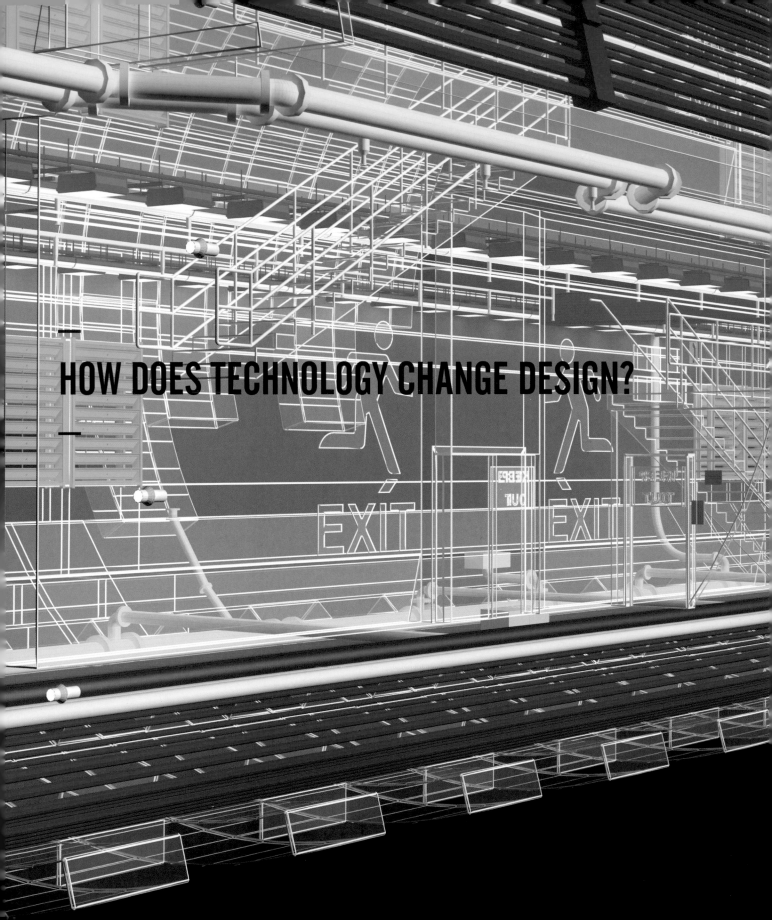

HOW DOES TECHNOLOGY CHANGE DESIGN?

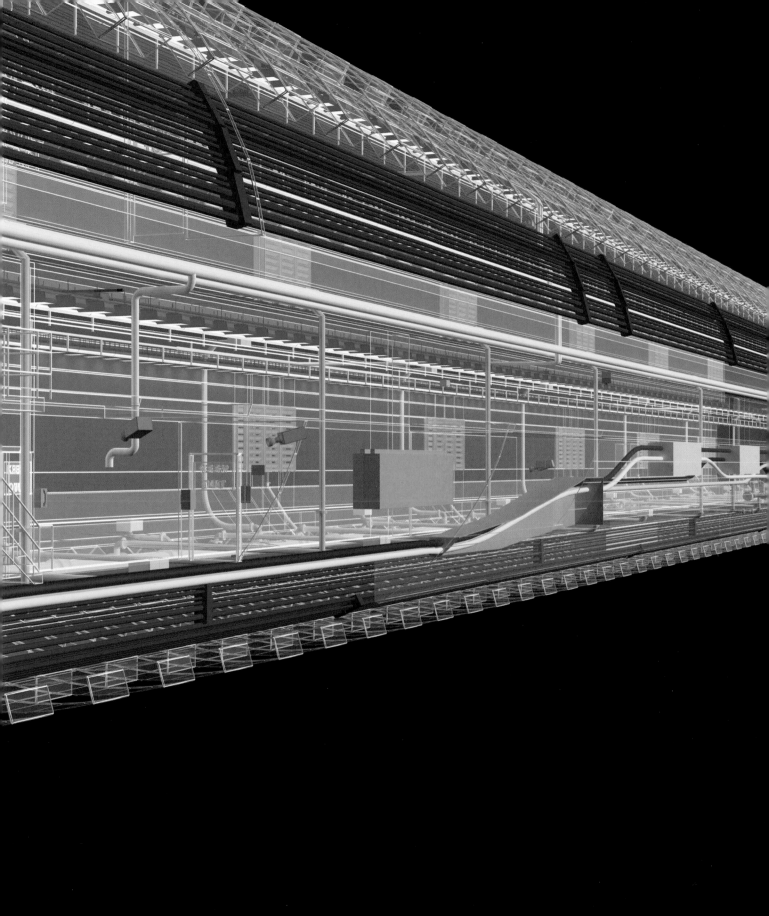

HOW DOES DESIGN MAKE US FEEL?

HOW DO WE DESIGN DESIGN?

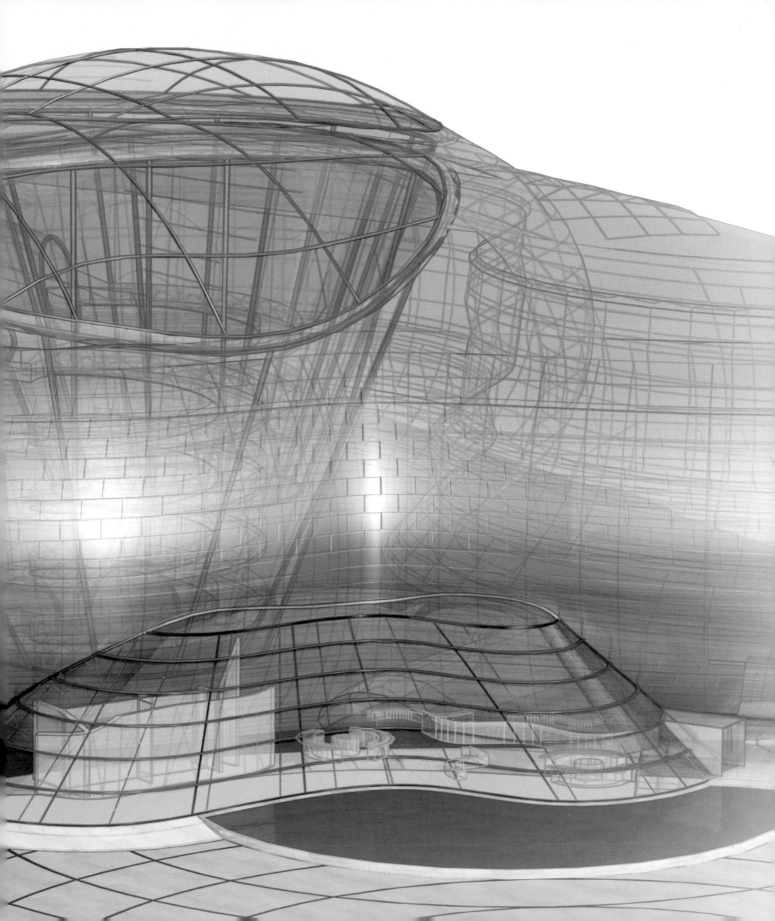

—

WHERE WILL DESIGN TAKE US NEXT?

Edited by Tom Wujec

Introductions by Warren Berger

Foreword by Carl Bass

With contributions by
Michael Behar
Amber Bravo
Alex Frankel
Suzanne LaBarre
Bill O'Connor
Bob Parks
Jessie Scanlon

Infographics by
Brian Ford and Mark Freeman

Autodesk

IMAGINE DESIGN CREATE

MELCHER
MEDIA

All proceeds from the sale of *Imagine, Design, Create* will fund grants for the Autodesk IDEA Studio, a residency program for researchers who are using design software in advanced, imaginative ways to solve real-life problems. For more information, please visit www.autodesk.com/ideastudio.

pages 2–3, Cathedral of Christ the Light, Oakland, California; pages 4–5, U.K. Pavilion, Expo 2010 Shanghai; pages 6–7, Kartal-Pendik Masterplan, Istanbul, Turkey; pages 8–9, detail, digital model of Alaskan Way Viaduct; pages 10–11, still from *Cloudy with a Chance of Meatballs*; pages 12–13, Visualization of aquarium and museum site concept, designed in AutoCAD software, rendered in Autodesk 3ds Max; pages 14–15, Ansari X Prize–winner SpaceShipOne.

Library of Congress control number: 2001012345
ISBN 978-1-59591-066-0 (hardcover), 978-1-59591-067-7 (softcover)

Produced by Melcher Media

Manufactured in China

10 9 8 7 6 5 4 3 2

HOW DESIGNERS, ARCHITECTS, AND ENGINEERS ARE CHANGING OUR WORLD

CONTENTS

FOREWORD

The impulse to design is universal. Today, design touches almost every part of our lives. From the buildings we live and work in to the machines that advance our economy, from the blockbuster movies that immerse us in fantastic stories to the everyday products that delight our senses, we live in a world that somebody imagined, designed, and created.

As technology continues to drive forward, design is reaching a new tipping point. Design, as a way to solve problems, discover opportunities, and create new objects and experiences, is reaching more people and equipping them with remarkable tools to make a better world.

With that in mind, Autodesk is delighted to present *Imagine. Design. Create.* The book offers a wide ranging look at how the creative process and the tools of design are dramatically changing—and where design is headed in the coming years. The chapters that follow are full of human stories that show how people are using fresh design approaches and new capabilities to solve problems, create opportunities, and improve the way we live and work. These stories span the business and social sectors—both of which are very much in need of better design. In fact, the whole world needs good design now, perhaps more than ever.

What's exciting to see is that emerging digital tools are actually making it possible for more people, in more situations, to design well. Those who don't even consider themselves to be designers are doing what was unthinkable a few years ago: visualizing their renovated homes, fabricating toy robots with their kids, and animating short movies. They sketch, draw, model, and animate ideas into digital forms that can be viewed, analyzed, experienced, and eventually brought into the real world.

New technologies are also revolutionizing the way creative professionals do the work of design. Next generation tools harness the power of ever-faster connected computers, providing new ways to capture and model reality, analyze structures as conceptual designs take place, and print objects in three dimensions from the minuscule to the gargantuan. Collectively, these tools help people create what was otherwise impossible: taller and greener buildings, faster and safer cars, better and more affordable products.

Because of new technologies, today's designers are able to imagine new and better possibilities. And that's important because designers are playing a critical role in addressing many of our most complex challenges. Without a doubt, technology is changing the very nature and scope of design.

Even as technology advances, good design remains a distinctly human endeavor—one that begins with the spark of creativity and is nurtured by way of a disciplined, iterative process that provides a path to innovation and progress.

I hope these stories of leading designers, engineers, and architects who are making the world a better place through the discipline of design foster and contribute to a larger cultural conversation about the critical role of design in tackling the formidable challenges we face. Ⓐ

—Carl Bass, President and CEO, Autodesk, Inc.

INTRODUCTION

WHAT CAN GOOD DESIGN DO?

WHAT CAN GOOD DESIGN DO?

Can it make a plane fly better?
Can it help people gain access to clean water?
Can it change the way we tell stories?
Or can it create a new way to play?
Or bring people in Oakland, California, a little closer to heaven?

It can do all of those things—and already has. For evidence, start by looking to Shanghai (and be prepared to look up high). There, Gensler architects have conceived a radically innovative spiral design for the 2,074-foot (632-meter) tall Shanghai Tower not just to withstand wind but to channel its power for use in the building.

For more evidence, visit Oakland, California's Cathedral of Christ the Light, where you can bear witness to design's power to create even the most sacred experiences. For yet another example of design's ability to create an immersive experience, lose yourself on Pandora, from James Cameron's *Avatar*—a film whose astonishing realism would not have been possible without revolutionary digital tools.

At the heart of each of these stories are the questions that swirl around the idea of design. How does design change our lives for the better? How is our capacity to produce good design evolving? How will the next generation of designers work—and on what? What new areas of human experience is design opening for us? And on a more basic level: What is good design? How do we define and better appreciate it, in hopes that we can encourage and nurture more of it?

At the outset, it should be acknowledged that the phrase *good design* is a loaded one. Indeed, any discussion of "design"—let alone the more subjective "good design"—must start by recognizing that the word has multiple meanings, depending on usage and context. The design scholar John Heskett memorably constructed a sentence—"Design is to design a design to produce a design"—to show how one word can alternately refer to 1) a general practice, 2) an action, 3) a plan, or 4) a finished product.

When we think of design as a noun, we often associate it with made objects—particularly with how they look and perform. But think of design as a verb and suddenly it takes on movement and purpose: to envision, to plan, to construct, to improve. As we move from noun to verb, we also move from objects to objectives. And that opens up a world of possibilities. Focusing on the action of design also reveals the range of people engaged in its practice: architects and engineers, product designers and video-game creators, contractors and highway builders, programmers and filmmakers. The *who* of design is nearly as broad as the *what*.

This expansive view of design and designers is the lens used throughout this book. It's a recognition that good design isn't limited to what we see in showrooms, glossy catalogs, and architecture magazines—those are limited, often stereotyped views. Rather, design is a powerful force in addressing complex challenges in the business and social realms. So while design is often treated as a "matter of taste," the truth is, in this larger context, it can be clearly seen as a matter of prosperity, progress, and even survival.

This is particularly true right now, when economic pressures, global crises, and environmental threats have created a massive and urgent need for innovative, considered solutions. To be blunt: The world needs good design, and needs it badly.

That's the sobering news. The good news, as many

EVEN WITH ALL THE DRAMATIC CHANGES BEING WROUGHT BY TECHNOLOGY, DESIGN REMAINS, AND LIKELY ALWAYS WILL, A FUNDAMENTALLY HUMAN ENDEAVOR, FUELED BY THE INSIGHTS, IDEAS, PASSIONS, AND TALENTS OF PEOPLE IN PURSUIT OF PROGRESS.

—

of the projects and people and ideas seen in this book attest, is that our capacity to produce good design is expanding and improving at a breathtaking pace. Technology is a driving force in this unfolding revolution. It is beginning to provide designers with tools that can enable them to take on the thorniest, most complex challenges facing business and the world at large. In the process, technology is in some ways altering the very nature of design and the role of the designer—which can be inspiring or, for some, unsettling. But even with all the dramatic changes being wrought by technology, design remains, and likely always will, a fundamentally human endeavor, fueled by the insights, ideas, passions, and talents of people in pursuit of progress.

DESIGN IS CHANGING OUR WORLD

The urge to design—to reimagine, reorder, and reshape the world around us—is deep in our DNA. History takes us back to the most primitive stone tools—which, archaeologists tell us, were not necessarily as primitive as one might presume. One recent discovery of Stone Age objects in Colorado included a set of hand tools with rounded, ergonomic handles worthy of OXO-brand peelers. Early examples of such well-planned and thoughtful creations just confirm that from the beginning, design has always been purposeful. It always had a job to do. Often, that job was to improve life in some way.

Skills were required, of course, but beyond that, the best designers had to have vision. To bring

ELEMENTS OF DESIGN
Ten essentials of good design

No simple checklist of qualities can define design. Good design emerges from the elements of the design process—design as a verb—and through considering each element of a designed object—design as a noun.

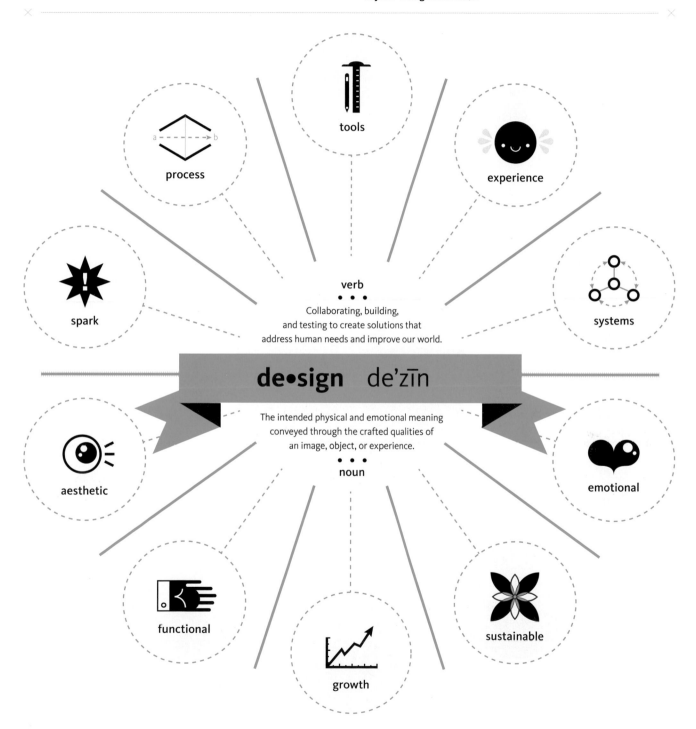

process

tools

experience

spark

verb
• • •
Collaborating, building,
and testing to create solutions that
address human needs and improve our world.

systems

de•sign de′zīn

aesthetic

The intended physical and emotional meaning
conveyed through the crafted qualities of
an image, object, or experience.
• • •
noun

emotional

functional

growth

sustainable

about improvements in the world around them, they needed to be able to look beyond the existing realities and see new possibilities—not just what was, but what *might be*. There's a philosophical aspect to the design mind, as designers grapple with the notion that *something isn't quite right with the world*. And, as experience designer and educator Nathan Shedroff relates on page 224, designers have the capacity to make it better. Designers don't just think and theorize. They model. They make. They build.

Whatever lofty visions design may sometimes aspire to, the process itself is grounded in solid principles and a bias toward action. It's a process that is, itself, designed—for the purpose of transforming possibility into reality. And while it may often begin with the vagaries of human insight and creativity, these first sparks quickly beget an iterative methodology, a process that involves exploring options, sifting through what works and what doesn't, and refining solutions.

The design process is often rigorous and disciplined. Yet design cannot be reduced to a formula. Give a hundred designers the same challenge, with the same constraints and raw materials, and chances are you'll end up with countless different solutions, including (if fortune smiles and all goes well) possibilities that no one could have predicted. Indeed, the ability to produce diverse solutions is a key driver of innovation, as designers explore multiple approaches.

Likewise, it is difficult to predict how successful these various new ideas and possibilities will be once they are actually tested in the real world—by all those complex human beings who wait at the other end of the design process. Upon interacting with the design in question, these end-users may find it frustrating or functional, confusing or refreshingly simple, mundane or inspiring. For a multitude of reasons, some of which are not easily explained, *good design*

fully lives up to that label only when people actually engage with the design and discover that "it works beautifully," or "it just feels right." In those moments, design's power to transform an everyday experience becomes evident: Suddenly, the act of listening to music, living in a high-rise, peeling a potato, engaging with a film, is entirely different and improved. And at that moment, the world—or at least one aspect of living in it—has been changed forever.

Is that change always for the good? Even as design helped tame and shrink and connect the planet, it has also played a role in cluttering, polluting, and overheating it. Some of design's greatest successes have also yielded problems we now must grapple with. And it has made us increasingly aware of the dual nature of the design challenge: Yes, it must strive to make things better, but simultaneously, and always, it must strive to not make things worse. First, do no harm.

Some recognized this dual nature of design—and the responsibility that comes with it—earlier than others. Nearly a half-century before green became fashionable in design, Buckminster Fuller urged designers to "do more with less" and to be conscious of the planet's limited resources. By the 1970s, design activists and writers like Victor Papanek warned us that designers, in the service of booming industry, were propagating far too much unnecessary "stuff," while also giving us (to use just one example) unsafe cars that fouled the environment. Papanek spoke of the moral and social imperative to use design as "an innovative, highly creative, cross-disciplinary tool responsive to the true needs of men."

Today we are seeing a new interest in design's moral and social realm. Designers and leaders such as Cameron Sinclair, Kate Stohr, Emily Pilloton, and John Cary have helped bring empowering, socially responsible design into the limelight. The idea that design—

DEFINING DESIGN
Fourteen reasons why it's important.

What is design? What is it good for? A hundred designers will have a hundred different answers. These business leaders, designers, and writers have provided some of the best definitions.

WHEN PEOPLE TALK ABOUT INNOVATION IN THIS DECADE, THEY REALLY MEAN DESIGN.
—Bruce Nussbaum, editor, *BusinessWeek*

Design should do the same thing in everyday life that art does when encountered: amaze us, scare us or delight us, but certainly open us to new worlds within our daily existence.

—Aaron Betsky, director, Cincinnati Art Museum

Design is as much an expression of feeling as an articulation of reason. It is an art as well as a science, a process and a product, an assertion of disorder, and a display of order.

—Victor Margolin, design historian, University of Illinois at Chicago

GOOD DESIGN IS GOOD BUSINESS.
—Thomas Watson, Jr., president, IBM

Design is the fundamental soul of a man-made creation that ends up expressing itself in successive outer layers of the product or service. Design is not just what it looks like and feels like. Design is how it works.

—Steve Jobs, CEO, Apple

DESIGN IS ALWAYS ABOUT SYNTHESIS—SYNTHESIS OF MARKET NEEDS, TECHNOLOGY TRENDS, AND BUSINESS NEEDS.
—Jim Wicks, vice president, consumer experience design, Motorola

Good design is a form of respect—on the part of the producer for the person who will eventually spend hard-earned cash on the product, use the product, own the product.

—David R. Brown, designer and educator

DESIGN IS THE CONSCIOUS EFFORT TO IMPOSE A MEANINGFUL ORDER.
—Victor Papanek, designer, educator, and author

Design is the term we use to describe both the process and the result of giving tangible form to human ideas. Design doesn't just contribute to the quality of life, design, in many ways, now constitutes the quality of life.

—Peter Lawrence, founder & chairman, Corporate Design Foundation

Good design is good citizenship.
—Milton Glaser, designer

GOOD DESIGN MAKES YOU FEEL GOOD...IT MAKES YOUR LIFE BETTER. GOOD DESIGN TOUCHES YOUR HEART. AND WHEN IT TOUCHES YOUR HEART, DESIGN AND DESIRE BECOME ONE.
—Robyn Waters, former vice president of design, Target

DESIGN ADDRESSES ITSELF TO THE NEED.
—Charles Eames, designer

Poor design is making something worthless. Good design is making something intelligible and memorable. Great design is making something memorable and meaningful. Exceptional design is making meaningful and worthwhile.

—Alan Fletcher, designer

DESIGN CAN BE ART. DESIGN CAN BE AESTHETICS. DESIGN IS SO SIMPLE, THAT'S WHY IT IS SO COMPLICATED.
—Paul Rand, designer

THE BAR IS RAISED. IT IS NO LONGER ENOUGH FOR DESIGN TO BE CLEVER; NOW IT MUST BE <u>THOUGHTFUL</u>. IT MUST CONSIDER, ANTICIPATE, ANALYZE AS NEVER BEFORE, TAKING INTO ACCOUNT MULTIPLE VIEWPOINTS AND HUMAN NEEDS. IT MUST TAKE THE LONG VIEW ON PROBLEM-SOLVING, RATHER THAN FOCUSING JUST ON THE IMMEDIATE FIX. AND IT MUST BEGIN TO TRAVERSE THE OLD VERTICAL BOUNDARIES AND DISCIPLINES.

—

whether architecture or urban planning or new products—can play an important role in empowering people and improving lives has captured our attention and produced extraordinary, innovative work. And there is barely a designer today who is not keenly aware of the imperative to practice environmentally sustainable design.

Having finally come to appreciate that there are consequences to design—and that they can be dev-astating—we cannot help but alter the way we define and measure "good design." The bar is raised. It is no longer enough for design to be clever; now it must be *thoughtful*. It must consider, anticipate, analyze as never before, taking into account multiple viewpoints and human needs. It must factor in all the variables that can influence how a design will perform (or fail to do so) once it is exposed to the real-world pressures—social, environmental, political, economic—that are likely to come to bear. It must take the long view on problem-solving, rather than focusing just on the immediate fix. And it must, as Papanek noted, begin to traverse the old vertical boundaries and disciplines, with designers taking a more collaborative approach.

All of this is dictated by the immense and complex challenges at hand: technological upheaval, population growth, economic instability, heightened global competitiveness, and, perhaps looming above all else, a planet in environmental distress. These grand challenges cry out for design intervention and ingenuity.

NEW TOOLS,
NEW METHODS,
NEW RESULTS

The word *innovation* is used perhaps even more loosely than *design*. Some seem to think of it in terms of inventing additional features or spin-offs that amount to not much more than new wrinkles on the old offerings. But true innovation occurs only when new ideas or inventions are brought into the world in a way that spurs *meaningful change* in the marketplace and in people's life experiences. The process of design—with its cycles of exploration and deep insights, analysis, and prototyping—can help business distinguish between new ideas that matter and those that don't. Moreover, it can take those new ideas and mold them to fit into people's lives in the most meaningful, impactful way. As such, design is the bridge between invention and innovation.

While enabling business to focus on the prize of innovation, design can also help companies see the bigger picture—by providing a systemic way of thinking about the issues and challenges that are now coming at business from all sides. Globaliza-

tion, customization, sustainability, social networking, the newly empowered consumer—these trends all present separate and distinct business challenges. Yet they are all interrelated, too. Design offers an approach to problem-solving that is not only creative but connective—one that considers the ways in which solving problem A may affect problem B, not to mention C.

This integrative thinking, a mind-set that seeks connections and the big picture as well as collaboration between people and disciplines, is essential when tackling the biggest problems in business as well as in the world. Consider, for example, sustainability—it's a global issue, a social one, and an increasingly critical business concern. And the complexities inherent in addressing this issue point to the need for a systems-design approach. For example, a company may make a commitment to using eco-friendly materials in its products, but that's only a small part of the sustainability equation. Many related factors, having to do with where those materials originate, how they're transported to the manufacturer, what happens during manufacturing, how the product is shipped, how it is packaged, what happens during its use, and, of course, *after* it has been used—all have an impact. To some extent, the company seeking to be sustainable must go well beyond designing products; it may have to *re*-design much of its overall operations to be in alignment with this mission.

In truth, *good design* should help us to not only address these issues but also anticipate them—so that designers can, in effect, solve problems before they even arise. Today's most sophisticated design processes use predictive analysis to help designers see into the future—enabling them to determine, for example, how a building that hasn't been built yet will perform, over time, in shifting weather or environmental conditions. It's a radical new approach to designing that promises to help designers preempt some of those inadequacies or unintended consequences that, in the past, would become evident only after a building or bridge was in use.

What this means is that we are now beginning to expect *good design* to predict the future and know the unknown—in addition to figuring out what we need, even though we may not realize we need it yet. We want design to do all this and, oh by the way, make it all affordable, functional, simple, scalable, sustainable, utilize that information. Good design is nourished and inspired by rich and diverse sources of information, whether it takes the form of documented human experience, lessons from nature, or mathematical algorithms—designers are apt to draw on anything and everything to solve problems.

As more information has become immediately available to designers, new technology is making it possible to connect that vast base of knowledge to the particular design challenge at hand. The result is a potential game-changer. While design, in its

—

WE ARE NOW BEGINNING TO EXPECT <u>GOOD DESIGN</u> TO PREDICT THE FUTURE AND KNOW THE UNKNOWN—IN ADDITION TO FIGURING OUT WHAT WE NEED, EVEN THOUGH WE MAY NOT REALIZE WE NEED IT YET.

—

and, of course, delightful.

That's a lot to ask of design, and of designers. Fortunately, designers have never been better armed for the task—whether they're conceiving massive machines or developing new building materials, modeling entire cities or rendering 3D worlds indistinguishable from the real thing. This has a great deal to do with the explosion of information and the development of new tools that can help designers access and essential nature and process, remains, as ever, a uniquely human activity that involves working within constraints, envisioning potential outcomes, and prototyping possible solutions, technology is having an impact at each of these stages. By enabling designers to instantly tap into vast sources of information and analysis previously unavailable or even unimaginable, technology is deeply augmenting the designer's ability to consider more possibilities, try more options, and fine-tune new ideas with remarkable levels of speed and precision.

This marks an important shift in the relationship between technology and design. In the recent past, technology's chief impact was to help designers more effectively document and visualize their plans, replacing pencil sketches and blueprints with computer-aided design. Now we are seeing the first major signs of how technology will play a much greater role in helping designers to *conceive* those plans through the development of new generative design soft-

always had the luxury of being able to explore as much as they might wish; the process of seeking out alternatives and trying multiple variations can take more time than a given project will allow. Hence, we often ended up with "good enough" design choices, simply because there wasn't time to seek out and find the better option or to test and validate the performance or function of the design. To the extent that technology can make it possible for designers to explore possibilities more quickly and exhaustively, it increases the chances that design results will progress

—

FORTUNATELY, DESIGNERS HAVE NEVER BEEN BETTER ARMED FOR THE TASK. THIS HAS A GREAT DEAL TO DO WITH THE EXPLOSION OF INFORMATION AND THE DEVELOPMENT OF NEW TOOLS.

—

ware, which can seek out and render possible design options and solutions that fit within the specific parameters set by a designer.

This is not so much about making design easier; it's more about making it *better*. Good design has always been driven by the designer's hunger to explore possibilities—and the more possibilities the designer can explore and select from, the better the result is apt to be. But in the past, designers haven't

from *good enough* to *good*, period.

Through the use of better upfront analysis—again, made possible by advanced software and the tremendous computing power that is now so cheap—designers can figure out how a particular solution will perform over time and under varying conditions. What if an earthquake hits—will the structure hold? How will it perform in changing solar or thermal conditions? Suppose the designer were to try a

WITH OUR TOOL SETS FOR DESIGN GROWING SO QUICKLY AND PROVIDING SO MANY NEW APPROACHES, OPTIONS, AND TECHNIQUES, WE NOW NEED TO THINK ABOUT UPDATING OUR MIND-SETS.

—

different material in a different configuration—might the structure perform more efficiently? Designers are in a position to tap into a knowledge base that instantly tells them what they need to know about available materials and their properties, about the experiences of other designers on similar projects, about product life cycles, or geographic or weather conditions. And if the designer wonders, *How would nature solve this problem?* the answer will soon be readily accessible from massive biomimicry databases—putting 3 billion years' worth of nature's research and development at our fingertips.

Armed with this knowledge, designers can optimize designs by way of tinkering, testing, and refining, done on digital prototypes placed in ultrarealistic simulated environments—in effect, the outside world is being scanned and brought to life on-screen (and quickly: an entire city can be scanned and digitally reproduced in a few hours). These advanced simulations not only help the designer foresee how a project will look and perform but help others see it, too. This kind of sophisticated visualization—showing people

what the future will look like before it happens—can be key to winning support for projects, particularly ambitious ones that may be difficult for others to envision. If design is, as the designer Brian Collins has defined it, "hope made visible," then visualization technology can show us hope in high definition.

THE FUTURE OF THE DESIGNER

These revolutionary changes are bound to alter the role of the designer. With our tool sets for design growing so quickly and providing so many new approaches, options, and techniques, we now need to think about updating our mind-sets. One hopeful possibility is that designers will now be able to draw less and dream more. Freed from some of the time-consuming technical burdens of modeling and visualizing ideas, designers can focus more on the exploration of possibilities. This could mean that for the designer of tomorrow, the ability to conceive and communicate far-reaching ideas will be prized

WHILE MUCH WILL CHANGE FOR THE DESIGNER, THIS DOES NOT: THE DESIGNER BRINGS TO THE TABLE VISION, TALENT, AND HUMAN JUDGMENT.

—

more than drafting skills. Put another way, what will matter is the designer's ability to grasp the big picture, though not necessarily to draw it.

Complex, multifaceted problems will also demand that design become a more collaborative profession. Web-based computing opens up new ways for designers to work together, sharing markups and edits in real time, allowing multiple and far-flung collaborators to work simultaneously on the same design. But even though technology may make it easier to collaborate, it still requires an attitudinal shift on the part of the designer: a willingness to give up some control, and maybe some of the individual creative glory, too.

And designers won't just be sharing the stage with other designers across disciplines—they'll be sharing it with the public as well. The "democratization" of design may make some design professionals uncomfortable, but it is definitely under way. The movement of such technologies as 3D printing from superexpensive tool to desktop appliance promises that just about anyone will be able to take their own designs from prototype to finished product.

Where does that leave today's designers? As the ones who will guide this new generation of citizen designers. The job of "good designers" in days ahead may well be to steer the rest of us toward good design.

While much will change for the designer in this shifting landscape, this does not: the designer brings to the table vision, talent, and human judgment. Technology may help generate a bonanza of options and possibilities—but the designer will be the moderator of these suggestions and ultimately will be responsible for the choices made.

As the designer/engineer Dean Kamen observes, it may be true that technology can help the designer do an infinite number of things, but some of those things happen to be far more important and worthwhile than others.

And so, Kamen notes, it is left to today's newly empowered designer to answer the following question, first and foremost:

"Now that we can do anything, what *should* we do?" Ⓐ

IMPACT

WHY DOES DESIGN MATTER?

DOES GOOD DESIGN MATTER? THE ANSWER BECOMES MOST CLEAR WHEN WE ARE CONFRONTED WITH THE FAILURE OF DESIGN.

—

previous spread: **Emily Pilloton's Design Revolution Road Show championed products like the LifeStraw, which puts clean drinking water within anyone's reach.**

That has always been true, of course, but it's truer now. In a world that is "smaller," faster, and more interconnected than ever before, a world that is dealing with increased complexities and pressures, there is less margin for design error and more need for considered actions that produce desired outcomes and intended results—one essential definition of design. Increasingly, we are depending on good design to deliver progress on the environment, to help businesses be more innovative and competitive in uncertain economic times, and to improve our lives as well as the lives of those in the developing world.

There is a growing recognition that design—not as an aesthetic function but as a systematic approach to problem-solving and innovation—can have a profound impact on a company's success. "Good design is good business" has been a rallying cry for designers since IBM's Tom Watson coined the phrase 50 years ago. Today, researchers see a direct correlation between design-led innovation and the vitality of national economies, and companies that emphasize design have been found to be more profitable. One important reason why this is true has to do with advanced design's power to create richer, more rewarding con-sumer experiences—witness the stories of companies like Boeing, which prove that design can be a key in differentiating products in order to gain a critical competitive edge.

Yet the impact of design extends far beyond the balance sheet. At the Cathedral of Christ the Light in Oakland, California, good design feeds the aesthetic and spiritual values of a community (while also addressing such greater-world concerns as sustainability). And as designers dedicated to humanitarian and social issues—such as Emily Pilloton—have made clear, good design can have its greatest impact where it has previously been lacking: in rural communities, developing countries, low-income neighborhoods, and all those other places that comprise what some social-activist designers have referred to as "the other 90 percent."

As we come to recognize the expanding impact of and the ever-growing need for good design, a question arises: How do we encourage more of it? It starts here: with a fundamental understanding and appreciation of design's value to us, its impact on the way we work and live, and its power to effect positive change and progress. Ⓐ

THE CATHEDRAL OF CHRIST THE LIGHT

A new house of worship in downtown Oakland put invention above imitation and illuminated the spirit of a community.

The Cathedral of Christ the Light replaced an earthquake-damaged building and reinvigorated the Catholic community surrounding Oakland, California.

A SACRED PLACE IS DIFFERENT FROM MOST BUILDINGS. Sometime during its construction, it must transform from a job site into a place of God. Three years after the Cathedral of Christ the Light opened its doors as a place of worship, there are still faint oil stains on the exposed concrete reliquary walls. There, with oil-covered hands, a priest made the sign of the cross and consecrated the space.

The Cathedral of Christ the Light, the first cathedral designed and built in the twenty-first century, was completed in 2008 on the banks of Oakland's Lake Merritt. The building draws attention as an angular and colorful structure among square, gray urban shapes. Inside, visitors find superb contemporary architecture, not an elaborately finished "churchlike" space. A visit to the cathedral raises the question of what aesthetically defines a church.

As its parishioners and guests have found since the cathedral opened, a more appropriate and important question is, "How should a church function?"

The Cathedral of Christ the Light, perhaps more than most contemporary, thoughtfully designed buildings, was built with a definitive purpose: to anchor a large religious and secular urban community and serve an important role in nurturing that community's spirit. Designing a building with such a weighty role could have easily led to a watered-down, utilitarian edifice; instead, the client and architect together achieved a remarkable final product.

The origin of the Cathedral of Christ the Light dates to October 17, 1989, when the 6.9 magnitude Loma Prieta earthquake rumbled through northern California and destroyed the cathedral's predecessor. By the end of the 1990s, a move was under way within the local diocese to design and construct a new cathedral. The Bay Area's Alameda/Contra Costa Diocese (the spiritual home of more than 600,000 Catholics) launched a major design competition. The project was eventually awarded to Craig Hartman, FAIA, and his team in the San Francisco office of Skidmore, Owings & Merrill LLP (SOM).

During the competition, the diocese presented Hartman with a series of questions that demonstrated its interest in a building designed to recast the very notion of what a cathedral should look like and what roles it should serve. "The questions they asked were sort of imponderables: How would you make a place that is both civic and sacred? How would you make a place that is both noble and soaring, yet intimate?" recalls Hartman. "It made me think about what it means to design a cathedral in the twenty-first century." Indeed, that very question was at the heart of the diocese's design prospectus.

"A decision was made to build neither in a neo-Gothic style, nor in a Mission style, nor in a basilica form, but to build something contemporary," recalls Father Paul Minnihan, who was responsible for opening the Cathedral of Christ the Light for the Diocese of Oakland. "The wisdom in that decision allowed us to create a structure that glorifies God in the twenty-

"THE QUESTIONS [THE DIOCESE] ASKED WERE SORT OF IMPONDERABLES: HOW WOULD YOU MAKE A PLACE THAT IS BOTH CIVIC AND SACRED? HOW WOULD YOU MAKE A PLACE THAT IS BOTH NOBLE AND SOARING, YET INTIMATE?"

—

first century. If we would have replicated a design from earlier centuries, it would convey the message that we don't have the tools or resources in the twenty-first century to adequately glorify God, that we have to imitate. And that is the last message we would want to send through this building."

It was important to the diocese to erect a building that would reflect not only its place in time but also its diverse congregation, which includes speakers of seventeen different languages. Hartman, a modernist perhaps best known for his design of San Francisco Airport's soaring international terminal and the U.S. Embassy Complex in Beijing, explains, "The question was, How do you make a place that has cultural and critical authenticity for today, yet still resonates with this history? That was the biggest design challenge, and inspiration, for me."

The diocese, which had stood without a true cathedral for more than a decade, sought to bring people together by building a place that would first and foremost serve its community. It wanted not just a cathedral but, in essence, a large urban mixed-use project: a two-and-a-half-acre complex with a rectory, clergy offices, a café, a book-

store, a parish hall, a conference center, and underground parking.

Hartman recalled that the Catholic Church has, throughout history, developed and utilized the newest, most innovative ideas in construction methods and technology, such as the enormous stained-glass windows of Sainte-Chapelle and the flying buttresses of Notre Dame, both in Paris.

To design a building relevant for a house of worship, Hartman found his answer in light. "What is the essence of sacred space?" he asks. "For me, that comes down to a question of the nature of light. You can see this quest for the introduction of light in all the great cathedrals."

In creating his design, Hartman's more traditional influences were Eero Saarinen's MIT Chapel and Le Corbusier's Chapelle du Nôtre Dame du Haut, both built in the mid-1950s. "Le Corbusier's building," Hartman says, "is for me one of the great touchstones of modern architecture and the way I think about design. It is about raking light across modest materials." On a trip to New York City, Hartman happened to see two concurrent exhibits of minimalist artists: Richard Serra's "Torqued Ellipses" and Fred Sandback's yarn sculptures. Serra's massive

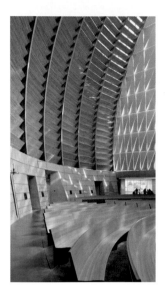

steel structures are full of force and weight. Sandback created shapes in space by simply stretching yarn and changed perceptions of space by doing so. Hartman was inspired to combine heaviness with the ephemerality of light.

Hartman's cathedral is chiefly a glue-laminated wood structure constructed of 120-foot Douglas fir beams. These beams bend toward a massive roof skylight and are knit together by a series of wood louvers. The building's foundation is a reliquary wall of exposed fly-ash concrete. The wood lattice oval structure encloses a womblike nave that seats 1,350. It has the appearance of a half-built ship turned upside down. The exterior shell is a massive glass membrane composed of more than 1,000 pieces of fritted glass panels to control UV rays and protect the exposed wood.

Hartman achieved a sacred space by designing a building illuminated by natural light and made it modern by distilling it in a minimalist way. The Douglas fir interior helped unite the two notions of monumentality and intimacy. "What I tried to do was strip away what I consider the 'encrustations' of religious iconography of the last couple of centuries—mandated artifacts that have become layered on. Strip it away and come back to fundamentals of space, light, and simplicity of materials and form."

—

"A DECISION WAS MADE...TO BUILD SOMETHING CONTEMPORARY," SAYS FATHER PAUL MINNIHAN. "IF WE WOULD HAVE REPLICATED A DESIGN FROM EARLIER CENTURIES, IT WOULD CONVEY THE MESSAGE THAT WE DON'T HAVE THE TOOLS OR RESOURCES IN THE TWENTY-FIRST CENTURY TO ADEQUATELY GLORIFY GOD, THAT WE HAVE TO IMITATE. AND THAT IS THE LAST MESSAGE WE WOULD WANT TO SEND."

The diocese had another bold goal for the cathedral: They wanted it to endure for at least the next three hundred years, to declare that it was built not for a specific generation, but for generations to come. "This is where structural design and theology overlap in a wonderful way," says Father Minnihan. "A cathedral is meant for the ages. That is why we strive to use the latest technologies to ensure that it lasts for centuries; a place where the story of Christianity continues to be unpacked and told."

The cathedral was built on a site near two active earthquake faults, so ensuring such longevity was a tall order. Hartman's

enough crane to do so.

"To try to be reductivist, to reduce it to just the essence, that is what good architecture is about. That is what this building is about," says Hartman. Sarkisian was on board with Hartman's minimalist approach; together they designed all of the building materials to unite in purpose, integrating the architecture with the engineering. "Everything that you see is basically essential. Everything visible in the space is working structurally," says Sarkisian. "It is a very honest structure. The outside shell is tied to the inner core to create greater structural depth. Even the louvers that control the

The visual focus of the cathedral is the "Omega Window," a 58-foot-tall image of Christ holding the Book of Life. Although it resembles a projection, the image is created by natural light passing through perforated aluminum screens.

—

"WHAT IS THE ESSENCE OF SACRED SPACE?" SOM'S CRAIG HARTMAN ASKS. "FOR ME, THAT COMES DOWN TO THE NATURE OF LIGHT. YOU CAN SEE THIS QUEST FOR THE INTRODUCTION OF LIGHT IN ALL THE GREAT CATHEDRALS."

—

colleague at SOM, Mark Sarkisian, PE, SE, LEED AP, director of seismic and structural engineering, solved this issue with seismic base isolation technology—essentially floating the structure on a series of thirty-six friction-pendulum base isolators that will allow the building to move thirty inches in any direction during a large seismic event. The bulk of the cathedral could be lifted from its foundation if there were a strong

light create the building's shell."

The result is organic and ever-changing; the space is spare but not industrial. "Light is never the same at any two times of the day. It changes day to day, and it changes seasonally," explains Father Minnihan. "What that illustrates is that light is not static but organic. If you consider Christ as light, then Christ is on the move. Here and now."

"LIGHT IS NEVER THE SAME AT ANY TWO TIMES OF THE DAY. IT CHANGES DAY TO DAY, AND IT CHANGES SEASONALLY," EXPLAINS FATHER MINNIHAN. "WHAT THAT ILLUSTRATES IS THAT LIGHT IS NOT STATIC BUT ORGANIC. IF YOU CONSIDER CHRIST AS LIGHT, THEN CHRIST IS ON THE MOVE. HERE AND NOW."

—

In commissioning the new cathedral, the diocese asked the architects to create a space that was both sacred and civic, noble and intimate. The result, which stands alongside Lake Merritt as a centerpiece of downtown Oakland, became an important gathering place as well as an inspirational spiritual space.

Not all people who visit the cathedral recognize or appreciate the minimalist aesthetic of the building. Yet visitors can't help but feel closer to activities in the space—either through the brilliance of the daylight illumination inside or the semicircular arrangement of the congregation around the altar.

The age-old cathedral design that enforced a sense of church hierarchy has been reduced and softened. The notion of an inclusionary space is at the heart of this design and derives not only from the wishes of the diocese but also from the Second Ecumenical Council of the Vatican (or Vatican II). This 1960s reform movement promoted the notion of gathering as a congregation, religious democratization, and a better sensibility of "the people of God."

"People, regardless of religious denomination or affiliation, find a great sense of peace here. They feel as though they can come, be still, and pray or meditate, or just be silent," says Father Minnihan. "All are welcome!"

"Architects and engineers are able to create very successful spaces that change over time and use. But this is on the extreme end," says Sarkisian. "Folks that worship there feel this is their home, a place that transforms itself during the day and at night. It is not a closed form that is artificially lit where every time you walk in you have the same feeling."

Inside the cathedral, the central figurative image visible across the space is a 58-foot-tall image of Christ that at first glance appears to be projected on a white wall. "The Omega Window," as it is known, is the cathedral's boldest example of the fusion of old and new iconography and of the innovative use of technology.

The Omega Window features an image of Christ at the end of time with the Book of Life in one hand and the other hand offering a blessing. The image derives from a twelfth-century Romanesque stone statue above the Royal Portal of Chartres Cathedral in France. A photograph of that carving was converted by SOM into a massive, pixilated three-dimensional image. Rather than using a projection, the image is created by natural light passing through angular, perforated aluminum screens.

The SOM Graphic Design Studio, led by Lonny Israel, conceptualized and implemented this awe-inspiring achievement, collaborating with Neil Katz, AIA, an architect and digital designer in SOM's New York office. The team used a variety of digital tools, including pattern-generating software usually reserved for producing frit patterns for glass, to generate the algorithm required to compose the image. The final image was created by laser-cutting 94,000 holes of various sizes and densities into the aluminum panels that compose the wall.

Father Minnihan explains, "We wanted the primary piece of art and focus to be integrated with the structure." The final product is an arresting image and, for parishioners, a focus of their worship. "The image itself is inseparable from the architecture and light," says Hartman.

The diocese faced many challenges from parishioners who questioned the new cathedral's ultimate value. "People wondered why we needed this," remembers Father Minnihan. "My response was, the human spirit needs to be lifted by beauty. If things are just reduced to a utilitarian value, I think we have lost the human spirit."

The diocese views the tangible value of the cathedral in three parts: as a house of worship, as a center for the arts and education, and as a center for outreach that includes a diagnostic health clinic and a legal center. In its short existence, the church has been host to many performing-arts events as well. "Historically, cathedrals, such as Notre Dame, were schools of the arts. We are trying to maintain that sensibility," says Father Minnihan. Regular concerts demonstrate the clear acoustics and bring in many from the local community.

"A cathedral like this is a work of optimism," says Hartman. "You can't build something without being optimistic about the future. A cathedral is perhaps one of the most optimistic acts that a group can make. It's not about commercial return; it's about creating a place of solace, of spiritual renewal, and there can be no more important building in those terms." Ⓐ

The primary function of the cathedral is as a place of worship. The Cathedral of Christ the Light has helped energize the region's Catholic community.

"YOU CAN'T BUILD SOMETHING WITHOUT BEING OPTIMISTIC ABOUT THE FUTURE. A CATHEDRAL IS PERHAPS ONE OF THE MOST OPTIMISTIC ACTS THAT A GROUP CAN MAKE."

TIM BROWN

Popular engagement with design is helping us find a balance among what's demanded, what's possible, and what works, according to IDEO's CEO.

How do you define good design?
Good design is all about successfully managing tensions. It's about successfully managing the tension between user needs, technological feasibility, and the viability of business; between desirability, feasibility, and viability; between functional performance and emotional performance. The tension between something that works well and something that connects to people in some deeper way. And it is about managing the tension between what's appropriate and able to be produced, and what's appropriate and needs to be consumed.

When you say managing tensions, does that mean there's an equal balance?
Not at all. You're looking for whatever the best balance point might be for that given situation, which, for different companies, or different markets, or different users, or different moments in time might be entirely different. The process has to include the exploration of multiple solutions.

"There is never a perfect, for all time, completely rational, simple single answer in design. That's what makes design so interesting."

—

There is never a perfect, for all time, completely rational, simple single answer in design. That's what makes design so interesting.

How has design evolved over the past decade, a time when some of your ideas about design thinking have taken root?
The scope of design has grown. Designers are now getting invited into a much broader range of conversations than we were twenty or thirty years ago, or even ten years ago. And that increases the opportunity to work on things beyond the next products and services, toward things that have strategic impact: how businesses design themselves and present themselves to their communities of consumers and customers and partners and stakeholders. That's a big change.

And the language of design is no longer the preserve of an elite priesthood, which it had been for a long time. It has begun to be popularized. Which some people don't like. But until you begin to popularize a topic, it's hard to get the kind of broad engagement that I think design needs.

You've seen some resistance to the broadening of design thinking. Where is that coming from?
It comes mostly from designers. [*Laughs*] None of us who are trying to expand the awareness of design believes that design is easy to do and anybody can do it. But I believe that it's understandable by most people, and most people can participate in it somehow.

I've always liked something the writer Virginia Postrel said: I'm an author, but I don't say other people can't write. For me, this is not about saying that there aren't truly skilled, deeply capable, elite designers who are able to design in ways that bring wonder to all of us. I think there always will be, and I think that's wonderful. But equally, there's an opportunity for many more people to participate in a design process and create value in the world.

What role do you think technology plays in letting more people participate in design?
It's making it possible for people to collaborate in new ways. Design is, in my view, a team sport. Even if individual designers have wonderful insights and create wonderful things, if they are not tapped into a network of others, then I don't see how they can possibly have the most relevant ideas, the most relevant insights. Our ability to collaborate is key to the growth of design.

We've all talked and learned about the huge challenges facing us, facing our planet. Do you think that design is going to be part of the solution?
My hope is that design is part of solving some of these complex problems. My fear is that design claims that it can be all of the solution, which of course it can't be. We have a habit as a species of dealing with complexity by getting excited about one particular thing at a time, and then we get bored with that thing and move on to the next one.

I believe that if we can tap into more of the creative potential of more of the planet, of more people, that they can make a contribution to creative solutions to problems, either at the small scale or the large scale. Because so many of these problems are fractal, right? I mean, you solve lots of

—

"We have a habit as a species of dealing with complexity by getting excited about one particular thing at a time, and then we get bored with that thing and move on to the next one."

"Even if designers have wonderful insights and create wonderful things, if they are not tapped into a network of others, then I don't see how they can possibly have the most relevant ideas."

—

things at a small scale, and you end up having an impact on a large scale.

What are some of the trends that will shape design over the next decade?
I've been part of a profession that's been extremely small. I hope we see many, many more people who think of themselves as designers in the future.

What we're starting to see now is design diversifying culturally. It's bubbling up in India, in China, and in more places where other cultural and social and business and perhaps even technological influences are coming to bear on it. It leads to more diversity of solutions.

Another thing that I think the future's about is a shift from physics to biology. Biologically inspired ways of thinking are going to grow significantly in their impact on design, whether that's the way we think about it today, in the sort of biomimetic sense, or even ultimately to the point where designers are designing living organisms.

Designers today are trained to operate in the world of physics by building things out of materials. In the future, designers will have to grow their ideas. That's an interesting shift, and one that will require the tools to shift, and one that will require the conceptual models of designers to shift, too. **Ⓐ**

Tim Brown is CEO and president of the design company IDEO.

THE DREAMLINER

Boeing's inquiry into why people fly helped shape the 787, which reimagines the modern airliner.

IN 2002, TWO UNLUCKY DESIGNERS at the Seattle-based product-development firm Teague were given a mission: fly around the world in eighteen days, traveling coach, and document their experiences and travails along the way.

As an exercise in design research, their 45,000-mile (72,400-kilometer) odyssey was grueling (nine sleepless nights and twenty-five takeoffs and landings at sixteen airports), though not particularly remarkable. But the insights it provided about air travel—including the inescapable fact that, in the words of Teague vice president Ken Dowd, "the flying experience was in trouble"—helped alter the trajectory of Teague's client, Boeing's Commercial Airplanes division, and sent ripple effects through the aircraft industry.

The timing was important. Boeing, the company that had launched the era of modern air travel in 1958 with the introduction of the Boeing 707 jetliner, was in a slump. In 2003, Airbus, its aggressive European competitor, outsold Boeing for the first time, seizing the mantle as the world's number-one airplane manufacturer.

That same year, Boeing announced plans for the 7E7, a midsized, long-range jet designed—with the aid of Teague and hundreds of other engineers and designers—to maximize efficiency and comfort. Now known as the 787, or the Dreamliner, the plane and its radical design—from its all-carbon-fiber fuselage to its oversized passenger windows—brought Boeing back from the brink and changed the engineering-driven company's approach to design. "There is a growing corporate appreciation for things you don't measure with a tape measure," says Kent Craver, Boeing Commercial Airplanes' regional director for passenger satisfaction and revenue. "Interior design is an integral part of the process of building airplanes."

Indeed. The 787 has become the best-selling new commercial aircraft introduction in history, and despite production delays that gave Airbus time to develop its own fuel-efficient competitor, the 787 grabbed about 850 orders as of mid-2010. The success of the Dreamliner reflects the degree to which good design creates value, even in an engineering-driven company and a penny-pinching industry.

Boeing's design for the 787 accomplished that, in part because the company approached its development with an eye toward features that would do more than look good. Beginning in late 1998, the company assembled a series of future-focused teams to ponder questions such as, What kind of airplanes should the company bring to market? How would it compete? What would differentiate a Boeing plane from the competition?

The team tasked with developing the differentiation strategy started with a line of inquiry that's standard for design firms but uncommon within the performance-focused aviation industry: At a deep psychological level, what does flying mean to people? How do they experience being inside of an airplane?

"That led to the idea of differentiating around the experience people have when they interact with our airplane," says Blake Emery, an organizational psychologist by training who now serves as Boeing's director of differentiation strategy. Boeing wasn't only thinking about

With some 850 orders in by mid-2010, Boeing's 787 is one of the most successful jets of all time. The plane's appeal to airlines comes in part from a number of design innovations, ranging from quieter engines to better overhead bins. Ten of those advances are detailed in the following pages.

NEW ENTRYWAY

Neither Boeing nor its airline customers can do much about endless airport lines or the dehumanizing security process. So the 787's calm, welcoming entry is designed to create a moment of transition—a clear shift from the frustrations of airport-land. Teague's Dowd says, "We wanted to use the moment of boarding as an opportunity to reconnect passengers to the magic of flight." The 787's entryway is arched to create a more open space, and the ceiling is bathed in sky-like blue light. The cabin design also includes oversized windows and wider aisles, which make the plane feel more expansive. After visiting the 787 mock-up, one potential buyer declared, "I didn't realize that the 787 was going to be bigger than a triple 7!" In fact, the new plane is 16 inches (41 cm) narrower than its older cousin.

the passenger experience but also that of the crew, the pilots, and so on. "What if a mechanic preferred to work on a Boeing airplane because he wouldn't hurt his back climbing into a space to fix something? If we could create a preference, we knew we could build value around that."

Work on the 787 fell broadly into two areas—improved experience and superior operational efficiency—that Boeing believed would appeal to cost-conscious airline fleet managers. The 787's interior development effort was driven by a multidisciplinary team of designers, engineers, and experts from

revealed specific factors that create a poor flying experience, with lack of personal space being chief among them.

To test design concepts, Boeing built a Passenger Experience Research Center (PERC) next to the company's tour center in Everett, Washington, so 100,000 annual visitors could provide critical feedback on, for example, the ideal size and height of cabin windows. "Once we did the windows research, we discovered that it was a valuable tool," says Emery. Eventually, PERC was also used to test cabin width, seat arrangements, and even the latches used to open

AT A DEEP PSYCHOLOGICAL LEVEL, WHAT DOES FLYING MEAN TO PEOPLE? HOW DO THEY EXPERIENCE BEING INSIDE OF AN AIRPLANE?

manufacturing and sales and marketing, as well as partner and vendor representatives. The group met weekly to discuss research findings, evaluate design concepts, and make key decisions. It was to give this 787 team a deeper understanding of the economy-class experience that Teague's designers made their round-the-world journey.

"Consumer expectations have continuously moved up Maslow's 'hierarchy of needs' pyramid over the past century," says Teague researcher Juliane Trummer. "We now expect products to do more than function; we want them to provide us with an experience and give us meaning." Trummer and her traveling companion, Charles Lau, discovered several things. Their research

overhead storage bins.

As the design team refined ideas, they kept in mind both passenger experience and airline economics. "Airlines want to please passengers, but they also need to make money," says Craver. "So one of the questions that gets answered in our process is, Will a certain feature add cost to the airplane or airline?" And if it does, is there an upside? The new-and-improved storage bins, for instance, had no impact on price. But larger windows add weight, making an airplane more expensive to operate. Would the improved experience they offered be worth it?

The 787 turned out to be the right plane at the right time. With air travel down after

"WE NOW EXPECT PRODUCTS TO DO MORE THAN FUNCTION," SAYS RESEARCHER JULIANE TRUMMER. "WE WANT THEM TO PROVIDE US WITH AN EXPERIENCE AND GIVE US MEANING."

—

9/11, struggling airlines were eager to boost efficiency. Airbus, meanwhile, had been distracted by the introduction of its A380 superjumbo, so it had no comparable aircraft to sell—leaving Boeing with the field to itself. But efficiency alone didn't clinch the deal. Emery also credits design advances such as the 787 cabin with helping to spur sales. "When we built the mock-up"—which gave potential customers a true sense of the 787's experience—"we wanted airline customers to walk into the mock-up and say 'Wow!'" says Emery. "That's when sales took off."

In July 2004, All Nippon Airways ordered fifty Dreamliners for a reported $6 billion, the first 787 order and the single largest for a new jet in Boeing's history. British Airways, Virgin Airways, and Air Canada soon followed, with the latter's CEO declaring the 787 a "game-changer."

The consensus is that the Dreamliner raised the bar for innovation and design that all manufacturers are now measured against. According to aviation expert Jennifer Coutts Clay, "All other aircraft development programs will need to take into account the new standards associated with this aircraft." Ⓐ

BIGGER WINDOWS

The 787 team knew from the start that the carbon fiber fuselage would allow for larger windows—but how big could they be? The designers built a mock-up at Boeing's PERC to capture the input of the center's steady stream of visitors. The resulting windows—the largest in the industry at almost 19 inches (48 cm) tall and 11 inches (28 cm) wide—even give passengers in non-window seats a view of the horizon and bring more natural light into the cabin, adding to the feeling of spaciousness. The windows also feature an innovative electro-chromatic dimming technology that replaces clunky plastic shades.

CARBON FIBER FUSELAGE

Lightweight carbon fiber covers more than half of the 787's wings and all of its fuselage. The composite material, along with more fuel-efficient engines, makes the 787 20 percent more efficient to operate than existing planes of similar size. The composite material can also withstand higher cabin pressures and higher cabin humidity than a traditional aluminum fuselage, changes which should make passengers more comfortable by reducing the unpleasant side effects (such as headaches and dehydration) of long flights.

LED LIGHTING

The initial choice to go with LED lighting was based on cost and energy efficiency: LEDs last 50,000 operational hours, much longer than traditional incandescents. But the design team also took full advantage of the unique capabilities of LED technology because, as Teague's Lau explains, "lighting has a huge impact on how you perceive and experience a space." Designers used optical tricks, such as skylike ceiling lights, to make the cabin space feel larger, and created colorful lighting modes that mimic dawn, dusk, and any time of day in between.

BIGGER BINS

Teague's designers learned quickly that personal storage space is a critical issue for cabin passengers. "We heard a lot of complaints about carry-on luggage," says Dowd. The 787's overhead bins are each large enough to hold three large carry-ons—a nicety for passengers and flight attendants, who won't have to lug the bags of late-boarding passengers up and down the aisle to find empty space. The bins pivot upward, rising toward the ceiling to create more space in the aisle. Teague's team also designed latches that open whether they are pulled down or pushed up. All those details add virtually no cost to the aircraft, but they should deliver real value by expediting the boarding process and reducing the number of passengers who need assistance.

DREAMLINER GALLERY

The multidisciplinary 787 team thought beyond the airplane itself to redesign elements of the sales experience, emphasizing customer touch points that had previously been overlooked. Traditionally, airline teams might spend up to a year traveling from supplier to supplier selecting seats, carpets, coffeemakers, lavatories, and so on, products that are shipped to Boeing for installation. As an alternative to this expensive, time-consuming process, Boeing built the Dreamliner Gallery, a 54,000-square-foot (5,000-square-meter) one-stop shop where airline buyers can view all of the available options in one place, under accurate lighting conditions, and, in some cases, within a full-scale cross-section of the plane. Like so many of the 787's design features, the Dreamliner Gallery reflects a heightened focus on serving the needs of customers.

REDUCED ENGINE NOISE

To reduce jet roar, the 787 team redesigned the standard housing around the engine (called a *nacelle*) in two ways: by adding a sound-absorbing liner to the nacelle and by serrating the rear edge where the exhaust exits. The result: Boeing claims the "noise footprint" of the 787 is 60 percent smaller than that of a similarly sized plane today. That's a boon for passengers, airport employees, and airport neighbors alike. It will likely also allow the 787 to operate late at night and early in the morning, when local noise regulations prohibit louder planes from flying.

THE DREAMLINER CHANGED THE ENGINEERING-DRIVEN COMPANY'S APPROACH TO DESIGN.

SNAP-N-GO INTERIORS

To reduce manufacturing time and simplify maintenance, the 787 design team brought together engineers and manufacturing experts to develop a standard assembly interface for interior components such as seats, overhead bins, and galleys. Typically, such components attach to the cabin structure differently and often require special tools. But inspired by the speed and efficiency of auto-racing pit crews, the 787 team developed a simple, intuitive system for all interior components. That means a damaged flight-attendant seat—which in the past might have resulted in a flight cancellation—can be replaced quickly at the gate.

SPACIOUS COCKPIT

The 787 cockpit was a design challenge: Instrument panels need to accommodate flight and navigation technology, while designers want the space to reflect the newness of the 787. At the same time, Boeing wanted "commonality"—industry jargon for cockpit configurations that are consistent across different aircraft models to reduce pilot-training costs. To strike the right balance, the 787 team relied heavily on the input of pilots themselves. The result: The cockpit borrows the arched ceilings and larger windows of the passenger cabin to enhance the feeling of spaciousness. The color scheme draws on the gray and black of titanium and carbon fiber. New ergonomic seats, a digital instrument panel with larger screens, and heads-up displays provide a more comfortable workspace. Lastly, commonality means that captains who have flown Boeing's 777 will need just five days of training to adapt to the 787.

LONGER WINGS

Carbon fiber gives the 787 wings more flex than traditional aluminum structures, and Boeing designed the wing to take advantage of that. "[The wing tip] was designed to blend in with the curve of the carbon fiber wing when it's loaded," says Emery. "It's a beautiful, beautiful shape." The beauty is heightened by the wing's dramatic length: Both 787 models have wingspans of 197 feet (60 meters)—about 25 percent longer than an aluminum-winged plane of equal size.

JOHN CARY

The social architecture leader explains how good design promotes human dignity.

What are some of the challenges that America is facing in its built environment? What power does design have to address them?

The two greatest challenges are the economy and expectations. There is some real attention being paid to some of our most challenged cities, like Detroit, Baltimore, and New Orleans. But the scale of economic despair facing those cities is pretty unprecedented.

Design in this environment can easily be seen as frivolous, as a luxury, and as nonessential. Yet this is a moment where design is needed more than ever to raise expectations; design can dignify otherwise very unfortunate conditions and human experiences.

Think about what design could do for a homeless shelter, to enhance education, to improve care and recovery within a hospital environment, to improve the quality of one's experience in virtually any and every kind of space. There's just so much need in terms of improving the quality of our built environment.

How does design dignify?

In my opening essay in *The Power of Pro Bono*, a book that represents the culmination of my long tenure as director of the nonprofit Public Architecture, I start off by painting a picture of design disparities to illustrate opportunities to dignify. Often in the same city, there are technologically sophisticated grade-school classrooms, with natural light and every imaginable accessory to enhance learning and stimulate the experience of students and teachers alike. In another school across town, there's not even chalk or Kleenex. The kids are sitting at rickety desks. There's the buzz of fluorescent lights above them. There's no technology whatsoever.

Holding images of those two environments side by side, there's no question that one will—in every way that we can expect—lead to better outcomes, better students, higher-quality education, improved literacy rates, etc. It doesn't take much effort to look at the quality of an environment that is reserved for people who can afford it versus the ones that are reserved for the rest. It's imperative that we get those more in balance.

It sounds like there is a choice, a moral choice to put human dignity at the center of the undertaking.

Absolutely. Furthermore, this is a really unique time in our country and for all strata in our government and society. Overall, I think that everyone is looking for impact. People are searching for new meaning around public life. Design can increasingly play a role in those things.

Design does that through example. Having some really successful projects and products to point to is an incredibly handy thing, and I'm not sure we had as much of that in the past. A lot of current public-interest design projects carry really compelling narratives that appeal to non-designers.

Do you have any favorite examples of public spaces with great, meaningful design?

There's a space on the South Side of Chicago that is home to an organization called SOS Children's Village Illinois. It reunites foster children with their biological parents and houses them in this community for extended periods of time. The building was designed by Studio Gang as a community center, and it truly serves as an anchor. It is a safe place while these families go through these transitions, but

> # "I think that everyone is looking for impact. People are searching for new meaning around public life. Design can increasingly play a role in those things."

—

also a really energizing and inspiring experience for people who visit.

It wasn't just Studio Gang that contributed a significant amount of their time. It was also contractors, material vendors, and others that all came together to create this very unique, really remarkable space. It's a project that serves an enormous need and also happens to win design awards. Projects like this are happening across the country, frequently under the radar. Because of the nature of pro bono work, there are a lot of people that don't, for one reason or another, feel comfortable promoting them or treat them the same way that they do their fee-generating projects.

Do you think it's possible to create a system to get these deeper values and meanings?
It's certainly possible to create a framework for it. Whether or not you can truly systematize it is another issue. One can minimally point to LEED [Leadership in Energy & Environmental Design, a green building certification system], which is itself a checklist and a points-based system.

One of the reasons that people care about LEED is because the U.S. Green Building Council wisely got the General Services Administration and other major client entities to encourage it and, ultimately, require it. Also, LEED AP became a credential that both designers and non-designers use to express their commitment to green design.

Something comparable as it relates to social value is certainly within the realm of possibility and has been explored by a small group of community design leaders over the past handful of years. I think it could potentially piggyback on LEED.

What's your sense of the future of design in the next decade?
This cleansing of sorts that we're going through in this recession can be a very positive thing. It's a very humbling thing. It is already forcing firms and individual designers to demonstrate value in new ways.

In the last economy, we leaned on exquisite materials to demonstrate value. Today, the meaning that a place can create, or can be paired with, is a better illustration of value. We've made lots of great places—I'm thinking of Jean Nouvel's Guthrie Theater in Minneapolis, one of the most beautifully detailed buildings in the world— but we've relied on spectacle that we're not able to afford any longer.

What's different today, compared with the earlier social-design movement of the 1960s and 1970s?
There used to be this idea, a very, very deeply rooted idea within the profession, that doing good was distinct from good design. In a lot of cases, community design centers and community design advocates promoted this idea that you had to turn over the design to the community. What we ended up with through that general approach is some pretty unremarkable design.

What I see these days, in the work of people like Jeanne Gang, as well as firms like SHoP and bigger companies such as Gensler, HOK, Perkins+Will, SOM, and others, is the willingness to keep design a top priority in socially oriented work. To say, "Hey, we're a professional service firm that's providing our best professional skill: design. We are committed to understanding your needs and desires, and that's part of the design process."

I don't think good design costs all that much more, so I hope that people see these examples in *The Power of Pro Bono*. Each of the more than 40 projects were completed for nonprofit clients and done on remarkably limited budgets. They illustrate that design is possible; good design is possible for good causes. **Ⓐ**

John Cary is president and CEO of New American City (americancity.org) and the editor of *The Power of Pro Bono: 40 Stories about Design for the Public Good by Architects and Their Clients*.

DESIGNING A BETTER WORLD

Emily Pilloton thinks design is useless if it only serves to make things beautiful. She's part of a movement to make design improve people's lives.

Designer Emily Pilloton's Design Revolution Road Show—housed in a converted Airstream trailer—took dozens of social and humanitarian designs on the road to design schools and other venues around the United States.

ON A FALL DAY IN 2007, the young designer Emily Pilloton found herself in a conference room discussing interior renovations the clothing retailer she worked for planned to make in several of its stores. Pilloton listened as her colleagues argued over different doorknob options. "I sat there thinking, *Are you guys seriously getting this riled up over a stupid doorknob?*" Pilloton recalls.

The next day, she quit.

At twenty-six, Pilloton had an undergraduate degree in architecture, a master's in product design, a growing disenchantment with the realities of the design industry, and a deep conviction that design could change the world. She hadn't become a designer to redecorate dressing rooms or help companies churn out redundant products—more "stuff" as she calls it. "Who the hell cares about the ornamentation on a doorknob when there are real problems to solve?" she says. "I was interested in the social side of design. I wanted to make an impact."

A few months later, in January 2008, Pilloton founded Project H, a nonprofit network of designers working on projects that improve people's lives in meaningful ways. The *H* stands for Humanity, Habitats, Health, and Happiness—four points on the compass that would guide the organization's work. In a manifesto she wrote to announce the organization's launch, Pilloton explained, "We need to challenge the design world to take the 'product' out of product design for a second and deliver results and impact rather than form and function."

By the end of that first year, Project H had raised $46,000 from individual donors chipping in $50 here, $100 there. It had attracted 150 volunteers, sprouted nine local teams, and initiated twenty-two projects, each with a budget of roughly $1,000. Project H teams have built playgrounds that help teach math and other subjects, designed products that can be produced and sold by women living in Los Angeles homeless shelters, created wall graphics for a foster care center in Texas, and crafted furniture for a school in Mexico. In addition, the organization has developed tools to help struggling students in Seattle stay focused in class, and it has developed a design curriculum for a high school in North Carolina. Project H has also earned the attention of *The New York Times* and *Forbes*, not to mention the Adobe Foundation, the Kellogg Foundation, and other supporters.

Pilloton's manifesto, meanwhile, led to a book: *Design Revolution: 100 Products That Empower People*. Published in 2009, it is both a call to action that urges fellow designers to apply their skills to social problems, and a compendium of products and tools that are already improving people's lives. The pages overflow with ingenious design concepts and products that improve general well-being; address a range of energy, food, and water issues; and spotlight smart approaches to mobility and education. Critics greeted the book warmly, with *Fast Company* welcoming it as "smart analysis about what it means to design for good."

Pilloton's focus on design for social good places her within an intergenerational tradition of design thinkers such as Buckminster Fuller, the ambitiously idealistic inventor of the

"WE NEED TO CHALLENGE THE DESIGN WORLD TO TAKE THE 'PRODUCT' OUT OF PRODUCT DESIGN AND DELIVER RESULTS AND IMPACT RATHER THAN FORM AND FUNCTION."

—

geodesic dome, and Victor Papanek, author of the 1971 book *Design for the Real World*. More recently, important groundwork was laid down by the likes of Alice Waters, the celebrated chef and local-food agitator, and Paul Hawken, an advocate for sustainable business practices. That tradition gained a new sense of urgency and—thanks to the Internet—momentum, as growing numbers of designers and creative professionals sought to integrate social responsibility into their work. Pilloton, now twenty-nine, is one of the movement's leading voices, joined by such designer/activists as Cameron Sinclair and Kate Stohr, authors of the architecture-focused book *Design Like You Give a Damn*; Bruce Mau, the force behind the book and traveling exhibition *Massive Change*; and Valerie Casey, founder of the Designers Accord, a sustainable-design initiative.

"The tide is turning," Pilloton writes in her book, in an essay clearly intended to wake designers from the haze of consumerism. "We need nothing short of an industrial design revolution to shake us from our consumption-for-consumption's-sake momentum." In making her case for a new breed of "citizen designers," Pilloton lays out the tools and tactics needed to spark her revolution, including what she calls "The Designer's Handshake." Part code of profes-

sional conduct, part blueprint for personal action, the Handshake commits those who sign it "to serve the underserved" and "to use design as a tool to empower people."

"It's time to stop talking and start walking," Pilloton urges. As if to lead by example, she has since taken off on her own at a fast clip.

On February 1, 2010, Pilloton and her partner, Matthew Miller, an architect and Project H coconspirator, kicked off a cross-country publicity tour. Rather than flying from city to city for book signings, the couple hitched their Ford pickup to a 1972 Airstream trailer rebuilt to serve as a rolling gallery for forty of the products featured in the book. Dubbing it the Design Revolution Road Show, the duo then set out on an 8,000-mile trek, stopping at thirty-five design colleges and high schools between San Francisco and Savannah, Georgia.

Pilloton eschewed the traditional book tour, in part because of her contrarian streak. "I've always associated being like everyone else as a bad thing," says Pilloton, who started a calculus club at her Northern California high school and points to guerrilla artist Shepard Fairey as a source of inspiration. But more than that, the goal of her tour—with its lectures and hands-on demonstrations of designs intended to

After leaving the corporate world of design, Pilloton and her Project H partner, Matthew Miller (top right), staged the Design Revolution Road Show—a traveling, hands-on exhibition of designs meant to improve lives. Among the featured products were, clockwise from middle right: the Whirlwind RoughRider wheelchair, which can withstand rigorous rural landscapes; adaptive-lens eyeglasses that can correct vision for nearly 90 percent of patients; the Hippo Roller water carrier; and Spider Boots, which safely raise the feet and legs of land mine clearers.

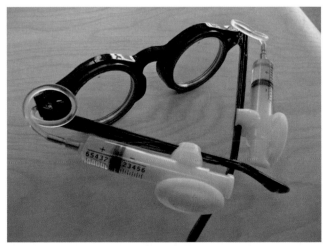

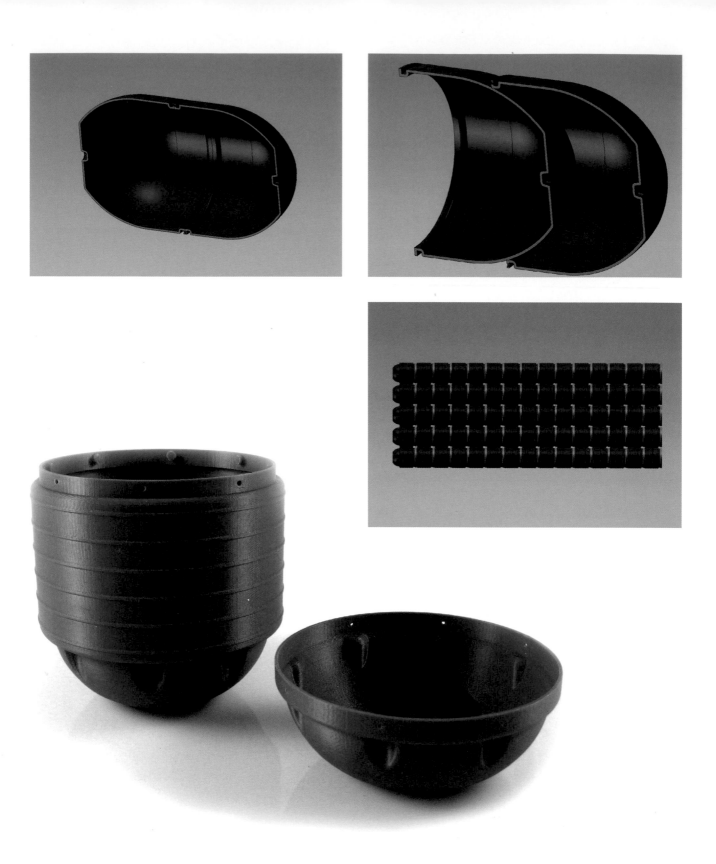

THE GOAL OF HER TOUR—WITH ITS LECTURES AND HANDS-ON DEMONSTRATIONS OF DESIGNS INTENDED TO IMPROVE THE LIVES OF THOSE WHO USE THEM—WAS TO INSPIRE THE NEXT GENERATION OF ACTIVIST-DESIGNERS TO APPROACH THEIR WORK IN A NEW WAY.

—

Pilloton's Project H took on the redesign of the Hippo Roller, a potentially significant device that was hampered by manufacturing and shipping troubles. By splitting the water-carrying drum and using an asymmetrical seam, she made transport easier and the roller much more durable.

improve the lives of those who use them—was to inspire the next activist-designers to approach their work in a new way.

For the trip, Pilloton and Miller were confined to a six-foot section at the back of the trailer, as the objects they wanted to showcase took up most of the vehicle. Every object in Pilloton's traveling road show was intended to illustrate how good design can have positive impacts. The carefully curated collection included products like the Whirlwind RoughRider, a low-cost wheelchair engineered for the often rugged environments of the developing world. The RoughRider was not just designed to better traverse uneven surfaces; its design itself is an open-source creation, with a frame and components designed so that anyone with basic manufacturing skills could produce it. In that sense, the RoughRider was designed to solve two problems at once, by both addressing the unmet needs of millions of disabled people, and by creating an opportunity for local manufacturing enterprises.

The collection also included SinkPositive, a clever add-on that saves water by converting the lid of any standard American toilet into a simple basin, so water can be used for hand-washing before it drains into the toilet's tank for flushing. Pilloton showed how hip packaging and a sleek dispenser transformed the New York City Health Department's NYC Condom campaign from a boring public health initiative into a sexy brand—and helped triple the number of free condoms distributed. She also displayed the LifeStraw, a two-dollar straw-shaped water filter that provides low-cost access to clean water for the 884 million people worldwide who currently go without.

The Design Revolution Road Show also included a Project H effort: a redesign of the Hippo Roller, a big blue plastic barrel with a lawnmower-like push handle that allows its users to easily roll, rather than carry, water from the local well.

Pilloton calls the Hippo Roller redesign a failure—a valuable failure that helped her hone her approach to design. "This was our first project, and the worst work we've ever done," she says. Although Pilloton journeyed to South Africa to see the original Hippo

IMPACT

Project H's Learning Landscapes (left) are low-cost playgrounds whose layout can be used to teach a variety of subjects through "spatialized games." The first Learning Landscape was built at an orphanage in Uganda in 2009 (below left); it has since been joined by examples in Bertie, North Carolina, and the Dominican Republic. Pilloton reports that her studio's work on a redesign for the Hippo Roller (right), seen in South Africa, was a failure—a failure that has helped focus her studio's efforts in the United States.

—

PART CODE OF PROFESSIONAL CONDUCT, PART BLUEPRINT FOR PERSONAL ACTION, PILLOTON'S "DESIGNER'S HANDSHAKE" COMMITS THOSE WHO SIGN IT "TO SERVE THE UNDERSERVED" AND "TO USE DESIGN AS A TOOL TO EMPOWER PEOPLE."

CREATING IMPACT

Project H looks beyond products to create impactful humanitarian design solutions

Emily Pilloton's Project H aims to broaden design's social and human impact. Its six tenets of design focus on solving the world's real problems and on helping to put new tools in the hands of those who need them. According to Pilloton, this requires a shift in the way designers think about their work and who it serves, leading to a broader concept of design as something that grows from the bottom up to transform lives.

There Is No Design Without (Critical) Action
● ● ●

Design with, Not for
● ● ●

Document, Share, and Measure
● ● ●

Project H
Design Principles
● ● ●

Project H's design process is built upon six core principles that enable relevant and impactful design solutions for any project.

Start Locally and Scale Globally
● ● ●

Design Systems, Not Stuff
● ● ●

Build
● ● ●

A Shift in Focus
In order to maximize the positive impact of design, fundamental shifts in focus need to occur.

From:		*To:*
designing things	------------------------------►	**designing impact**
form & function	------------------------------►	**catalysts & engagement**
design for consumers	------------------------------►	**design for humans**
clients provide funding	------------------------------►	**clients benefit most from design**
aesthetics	------------------------------►	**activism**
objects	------------------------------►	**experiences**

Creating Impact
When good design reaches underserved places and people, it creates meaningful humanitarian impact by empowering those communities.

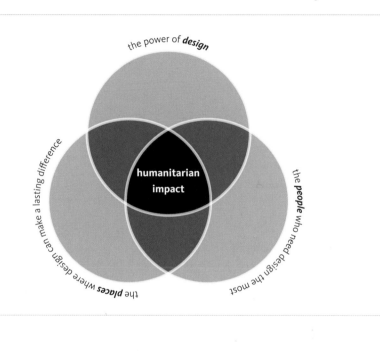

the power of *design*

the *places* where design can make a lasting difference

the *people* who need design the most

humanitarian impact

Beyond Objects
Designers should look beyond form and function to the broader human impact that design can create.

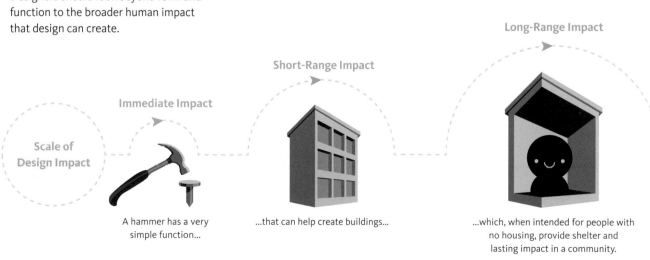

Long-Range Impact

Short-Range Impact

Immediate Impact

Scale of Design Impact

A hammer has a very simple function...

...that can help create buildings...

...which, when intended for people with no housing, provide shelter and lasting impact in a community.

Roller in use, her design work was done back home in San Francisco. "We were so enchanted by the potential of this object that we forgot about the people. It was incredibly arrogant, and it was 'design as charity,' not design as empowerment and user engagement."

Her redesign of the Hippo Roller—intended to make it easier to manufacture and distribute—was not realized. "We learned a lot from seeing it fail so terribly," she adds. Her studio now works only locally, for example. And it helped them discover and focus on their strengths as designers, such as design for public education.

Another Project H effort, perhaps its most successful to date, exhibits that focus. The Learning Landscape is a playground originally designed to teach math. Created in 2008, the Learning Landscape is a sandbox filled with a grid of partially buried tires, each numbered in chalk. Intended for use with an accompanying lineup of games that combine physical play with educational exercises, it was first introduced at the Kutamba AIDS Orphans School in Uganda. Today there are ten built and more on the way. The system is free, open source, and easily built in a day.

The Learning Landscape is a clear demonstration of Project H's core values, but over time the specifics of the organization—its structure and the kinds of projects it takes on—have evolved. Gradually, Project H shifted from an organization with international chapters and a global approach to humanitarian design, toward a U.S.-based effort with a small core group, led by Pilloton and Miller. The shift didn't represent a retrenchment so much as a refinement; Pilloton had always believed in co-creation—designing with users rather

Pilloton and Miller's current focus is "Studio H," an ambitious design education project in Bertie, North Carolina. The high school–level "design/build" curriculum is meant to spark development in the rural community through real-world projects. The studio's thirteen students learn design thinking through intensive hands-on education, as well as construction skills and critical thinking.

PILLOTON DESCRIBES STUDIO H AS "SHOP CLASS WITH A PURPOSE." "ONCE WE STARTED TALKING TO THE STUDENTS, TOGETHER WE BEGAN TO VISUALIZE OTHER PROJECTS," SHE SAYS. THE STUDENTS DIRECTED THE PROJECT'S AMBITIONS. NOW, THIRTEEN 11TH-GRADERS IN THE STUDIO ARE WORKING TOGETHER TO DESIGN AND BUILD A FARMERS' MARKET IN DOWNTOWN WINDSOR, NORTH CAROLINA.

—

than for them. She was also committed to understanding the impact of design, and that required being able to follow a project after completion by talking to users and measuring impact. Geographic distance made both difficult. "Start locally, scale globally," is how Pilloton describes her ideal.

Local for Pilloton and Miller now means Bertie County, North Carolina, a rural area 75 miles west of the Outer Banks. The Bertie landscape, and its economy, are dominated by agriculture: fields of cotton, tobacco, peanuts, corn, and soybeans stretch to the horizon. It is the poorest county in North Carolina; nearly a quarter of Bertie residents live under the poverty line.

"It's a forgotten place in a way, an extreme example of the demise of rural America," says Pilloton, who saw Bertie as an opportunity, not a backwater. If Project H's mission is to connect "the power of design to the people who need it most and the places where it can make a lasting difference," Bertie is a perfect place to be.

Pilloton and Miller came to Bertie by invitation: After reading an article about the Learning Landscape in Uganda, Chip Zullinger, the former superintendent of schools, had asked the young designers to build the educational playgrounds at four local grade schools. From there, the energetic duo redesigned and rebuilt the high school's three computer labs, developed a branding campaign to put a computer and broadband Internet access in every Bertie high school student's home, and launched Studio H—a design/build studio class that combines design thinking, vocational training, and community service.

Pilloton describes Studio H as "shop class with a purpose," and not surprisingly, she has myriad project ideas: a series of shelters along the school bus route, an open-air movie theater in an abandoned building downtown, and so on. "Once we started talking to the students, we began to visualize other projects," she says. "One

has a big family farm, for instance, yet there is no local farmers' market in Bertie." Now, thirteen eleventh-graders in the studio are working to create the farmers' market in downtown Windsor, the county seat.

Such projects are a world removed from the client-driven, form-meets-function obsessions of today's design industry. Nevertheless, Pilloton's efforts have attracted a lot of attention, which is why, on a chilly night last winter, Pilloton sat in a greenroom at Comedy Central, waiting for her turn to stride onto the set of *The Colbert Report*.

Pilloton knows how to give an inspiring talk about how design can change the world. Yet she was also astute enough to know that a satirical comedy show is no place for well-rehearsed presentations, let alone an earnest lecture on humanitarian design. By the time Stephen Colbert walked awkwardly across the stage wearing a pair of Spider Boots—a strap-on platform shoe designed to prevent injuries from land mines—Pilloton was ready to handle any comedic volleys he lobbed her way.

And come they did. Colbert asked her to discuss "the Herman Munsters" on his feet. Then he donned a pair of $10 eyeglasses that made Coke bottles seem svelte, but which allow their wearers to adjust the lenses to the correct prescription. Pilloton cheerfully explained that they were developed by a British physicist to help the estimated 1 billion people in developing countries who need corrective lenses but lack access to an ophthalmologist. Impressed by the potential size of the market, Colbert quipped, "There are billions of people in the world who don't have jack!"

The line generated laughs from the live audience, but it also underscored the scale of the design revolution that Pilloton hopes to spark. Her efforts may or may not make anyone rich, but that's not the point. What matters to her is that the opportunities for designers to meaningfully improve people's lives are almost endless. Ⓐ

SPARK

HOW DOES DESIGN INSPIRE?

MOST OF US LOOK AROUND AT THE WORLD AND SEE <u>WHAT IS</u>. DESIGNERS HAVE AN UNCANNY KNACK FOR ENVISIONING WHAT <u>MIGHT BE</u>. BUT WHAT INSPIRES THESE FRESH VISIONS OF NEW POSSIBILITIES? WHAT CAUSES THEM TO BEGIN TO TAKE SHAPE?

—

previous spread: **Inside Thomas Heatherwick's Seed Cathedral at Expo 2010 Shanghai**

As creativity expert Sir Ken Robinson reminds us, the design impulse comes from all kind of stimuli. It may begin with simple observation: A designer witnesses a human problem, and the motivation to solve it becomes the impetus that sets design in motion. It's not only problems that inspire designers, but also potential of all kinds: the potential of using new tools to solve old challenges, or of tapping into nature's wisdom to improve the man-made world. And for some designers, inspiration and drive come from the unknown, the unbuildable, the ideas we might call crazy.

The inspirational sparks that can ignite design are flickering all around us. The trick, for designers, is to be able to see them with sufficient clarity. For instance, the moment a designer *clearly* understands an existing problem—and the needs, desires, and dreams of the people involved—then he or she can properly frame that challenge and begin to tackle it.

But clarity may also come in the flash of mental connection, as when a designer suddenly realizes that a principle of nature can, in fact, be applied to a particular design challenge. For example, Thomas Heatherwick's Seed Cathedral at Expo Shanghai, which draws upon timeless, fundamental elements of the natural world to create a building that both pays trib-

ute to and lives by enduring laws of nature. Or, on the other hand, the inspirational breakthrough can occur, as Dean Kamen explains, at the moment a designer becomes aware that a newly available tool or technological capability happens to intersect perfectly with an existing need out there in the world. In these lucid, revelatory moments, a vague notion or hunch begins to morph into a vision that is more clearly defined, and therefore sharable, actionable, and ultimately possible. And business strategist Roger Martin has discussed another approach—"abductive reasoning," a "logical leap of the mind." New ideas come from a leap based on observation and experience, not from a linear process.

Can these moments of clarity or genius be encouraged? Are there ways that designers can get better at seeing, and being inspired by, the sparks all around? Technology can play an accommodating role in terms of providing the designer with greater and immediate access to more sources of inspiration. To some extent, it can bring the world—all those lessons from nature, or documented human experiences, or countless other sparks—into the designer's purview. Whether those sparks ignite anything more depends on the individual designer—and his or her willingness to observe, consider, and wonder about *what might be.* Ⓐ

SIR KEN ROBINSON

The creativity expert describes the constant creative dialogue between speculation and judgment.

What are your thoughts on the relationship between creativity and design?

I always feel it is relevant to first back up and offer definitions of *imagination*, *creativity*, and *innovation*.

To me, the fundamental capacity is imagination. It's where everything comes from—the ability to bring to mind things that aren't present to our senses, to step outside of the immediate sensory environment and to form images in consciousness of other places, other possibilities. That may be the fundamental gift of human consciousness.

Creativity is a very practical type of process. It's the process of having original ideas that have value. Innovation is putting original ideas into practice, trying them out, testing them, and applying them. I think of innovation as applied creativity.

Those three ideas are really continuous. And design, in the way it's commonly termed, is a very deliberate application. I think of design as a subset of creativity.

Is the nature of creativity changing? Or is it a fundamental of the human psyche?

I don't think the fundamental nature of creativity is changing. Yet some things are changing. There are more and more tools available for creative work. There's always been an intimate and powerful relationship between technology and creativity.

The tools themselves are always neutral. They rely on the intentions of people. It's all about the possibilities people see in them and the opportunities the tools provide for imaginative work.

I think they are changing the game in two respects. They are allowing many more people than ever before, probably in history, to be involved in creative work. These are tremendous instruments of the democratization of creativity. Particularly, I'm talking about online tools. They have a reach that is unprecedented.

Second, at the heart of these technologies is the principle of collaboration. There's a tendency to think of creativity as a solo performance, but for the most part, it's not. It's about people working together. Online tools and social media tools make available mental collaboration that has simply not been seen before.

What fosters the creative spark in the three domains that you've described, imagination, creativity, and innovation? What kills it?

The human spirit, the spark for creativity, can be sparked by absolutely anything. Anything could be a starting point, a point of entry. But there are all kinds of things that will stop it and that will prevent it.

—

"Tools themselves are always neutral....It's all about the possibilities people see in them and the opportunities the tools provide for imaginative work."

One of the things that prevents the imagination from flowering into creativity is lack of confidence. Kids up to a certain age are full of creative confidence. But beyond a certain point, people start to lose it. Many adults think that they're just not very creative. Confidence in your own creative ability is a big factor.

Institutional settings can also squelch it. If you're in an institution—and it's true of many schools—where there's a strong emphasis on conformity and on there being one answer, it's almost inevitable that the creative spirit will either get suppressed or it will start to become subversive.

People operating in the wrong field can also find their creativity suppressed. We all have creative abilities, but we all have them very differently. Very often, someone's real creative abilities are sparked by a particular medium.

Creativity is a process; it's not an event. It's not just a matter of random inspiration. It's not only about generating ideas. A good deal of the creative process is about exercising critical judgment, about testing it. Part of being creative is a kind of constant dialogue between speculation and judgment. Is this right? Does this work? Does that feel right? Does it look right?

That intertwining of critical judgment with imaginative speculation seems to me the DNA of the creative process. It's true in the arts. It's true in the sciences. Most of the things that are true about creativity are exemplified in the process of design.

New technologies have the promise of helping not only with data and computation but with conceptual work as well. What impact will machine-led creativity have on our own capabilities?

At the moment, the software is not acting intelligently. It's not exercising judgment any more than a supercomputer playing chess is. It's processing options and gathering data at a furious rate, far faster than we could do it. But you wouldn't describe it as being intelligent in the sense that it's exercising a sensibility or that it's acting consciously.

The more that the tools we use can make the job more doable, the more they can support and anticipate, the better. The thing I get concerned about is what the implications will be further down the track when—as lots of people anticipate—machines do become, in some sense of the term, conscious.

What would it mean to be a person when artificial systems of intelligence effectively replicate the primary functions of the human mind? That's a threshold that humanity

"The human spirit, the spark for creativity, can be sparked by absolutely anything....But there are all kinds of things that will stop it."

—

has never crossed. Like most technological thresholds, we'll probably just wander across it without thinking.

Are you optimistic about the future of our ability to be creative, innovative, and design-savvy?

Am I optimistic about the future? I want to be. I have confidence in the ability of human beings to solve problems. But we have an equally capacious appetite for creating them in the first place.

You only have to look in the past to see how bad our intentions have been in predicting the future that we now inhabit. Most of the problems we face are in fact the result of human imagination.

In a way, they've been brought about not by too much imagination, but by too little of it—our ability to anticipate consequences. As we approach 9 billion people on the earth, as we find ourselves being hurtled forward on this wave of technological innovation, we really have to think seriously about how to anticipate the consequences and how we prepare people to deal with them.

I was reminded of H.G. Wells's comment that civilization is a race between education and catastrophe. That's truer than it ever was. **A**

Sir Ken Robinson is an internationally renowned expert in the field of creativity and innovation.

THE SEED CATHEDRAL

Seeds and metaphor inspired Thomas Heatherwick's startlingly original design for the U.K. Pavilion at Expo 2010 Shanghai.

Chinese visitors to Expo 2010 Shanghai called it *Pu Gong Ying*—"The Dandelion"—for the quivering U.K. Pavilion's resemblance to a bursting dandelion blossom. Much like that flower's seeded strands dispersed by the wind, the thousands of tremulous "hairs" on what many others called the Seed Cathedral rustled in the breeze, creating a sumptuous display of light and motion both within and without the building.

A seed can connote many things: a token of nature, a link with the past, an impetus to preserve, a symbol of fertility and possibility. For British designer Thomas Heatherwick and his collaborators, the U.K. Pavilion became an opportunity to enact all these themes in a building and a surrounding landscape. The U.K. Pavilion stands both as a symbol for sustainability and as one of the most biodiverse structures on the planet.

First and foremost, though, the pavilion stands for the United Kingdom itself. Rather than make a pavilion that took a sweeping view of a country's qualities, Heatherwick and his team honed in on particular aspects of the state. The idea behind the pavilion was to explore the relationship between nature and cities. "In our research we found that London is one of the greenest cities of its size in the world, and we have a long history of bringing nature into our cities," Heatherwick says. "[The British] pioneered the world's first-ever public park and the first major botanical institution, the Royal Botanical Gardens at Kew."

Britain has also led the way in archiving the world's seeds. By partnering with Kew Gardens, Heatherwick was able to take advantage of the institution's unparalleled resources while promoting the Millennium Seed Bank Project, an extraordinary conservation effort that seeks to collect and preserve a quarter of the world's plant species by 2020. "These seeds have the potential to feed people," the designer says, "to clothe people, to cure diseases, to clean air, to filter water, to create building materials, to create energy, to fight climate change."

Heatherwick notes that while many people had heard of the seed preservation effort, no one had *seen* the seeds. A key gesture of the Seed Cathedral is to reveal and display them. (The Pavilion's seeds are drawn from the collection of China's Kunming Institute of Botany, one of many institutions that are part of the Millennium Seed Bank Project.)

The inspiration for the U.K. Pavilion also came from a more abstract challenge: to design a building that is both the physical and symbolic embodiment of its content. "That's something I'd never seen done before," Heatherwick says. Dandelion, cathedral, seed repository, miniature urban landscape—the Pavilion was not only one of the most popular and successful pavilions at the Expo, it did indeed succeed on both physical and symbolic levels.

Pierced with 60,000 25-foot (7.5-meter) fiber-optic filaments implanted at their tips with one or several seeds, the 66-foot-tall (20-meter) Pavilion is a striking, sometimes mind-boggling vision. In calling the bristled structure the Seed Cathedral, Heatherwick sought to play off the iconic properties of a house of worship—and play off the unique qualities of seeds, too. "When you are inside of a cathedral, you feel small," the Pavilion's lead architect,

At the U.K. Pavilion's main entrance, the diffuse, fuzzy appearance of the building resolves into the surprising reality of the 60,000 gently waving fiber-optic "filaments" that transmit light in and out of the structure and contain its namesake seeds.

—

WHILE MANY PEOPLE HAD HEARD OF KEW GARDENS' SEED PRESERVATION EFFORTS, NO ONE HAD SEEN THE SEEDS.

WHERE A TRADITIONAL CATHEDRAL UNDER-SCORES THE DISTINCTION BETWEEN HEAVEN AND EARTH WITH VAULTS AND DOMES OR STAINED-GLASS SCENES FROM SCRIPTURE, THE SEED CATHEDRAL CONNECTS US WITH THE EARTH BY ILLUMINATING SOME 260,000 INDIVIDUAL SEEDS.

—

Seeds from the Kunming Institute of Botany's collection (left) are encased at the tip of each of the Pavilion's 60,000 fiber-optic rods. Designer Thomas Heatherwick (below) was inspired in part by the symbolic role of seeds as containers of potential.

Katerina Dionysopoulou explains, "but a seed is a small thing with tremendous potential." Heatherwick echoes that sentiment, saying, "Seeds are incredible. In a tiny speck, all that power." Where a traditional cathedral underscores the distinction between heaven and earth with vaults and domes or stained-glass scenes from scripture, the Seed Cathedral connects us with the earth by illuminating some 260,000 individual seeds encased in those filaments.

Heatherwick and his team were inspired by Victorian-era efforts to integrate nature into urban spaces. That era also serves as a fitting reference due to its association with the 1851 Great Exhibition, the first-ever World's Fair, held in the temporarily constructed Crystal Palace in London's Hyde Park. (That pavilion, too, was a transparent, technologically advanced building that evidenced its own ideals of progress.)

The Pavilion gives the impression of a tightly packaged concept, but its form grew out of a highly generative process. As designer Dionysopoulou explains: "The outcome of our work is often artistic, but our process is very practical and methodological. The form of the Seed Cathedral came out of other experiments. One, in particular, experimented with the edge of the building and asked: What if a building were soft as opposed to harsh?"

THE PARK SURROUNDING THE SEED CATHEDRAL IS MEANT TO SEEM LIKE THE CREASED FOLDS OF WRAPPING PAPER, AS IF THE CATHEDRAL WERE A FRESHLY OPENED GIFT TO CHINA.

—

She is referring to the Sitooterie II, a smaller pavilion the studio designed for the National Malus (crabapple) Collection in Barnards Farm, Essex. The permanent pavilion is designed to encourage guests to "sit oot" and enjoy the grounds, and is named for a Scottish term for just such a structure: a Sitooterie. Much like the Seed Cathedral, the 25.8-square-foot (2.4-square-meter) Sitooterie boasts 5,000 hollow "staves"

ing machine), there was the added complication of embedding the seeds.

Wolfgang Stuppy, a seed morphologist and director of the Millennium Seed Bank Project, acted as a consultant for the Pavilion. He was an invaluable resource for describing the qualities and tolerances of the various seed specimens. Stuppy and his associates at Kew's sister institute in China, the Kunming Institute of Botany, set out to

—

"THE FORM OF THE SEED CATHEDRAL CAME OUT OF OTHER EXPERIMENTS. ONE, IN PARTICULAR, EXPERIMENTED WITH THE EDGE OF THE BUILDING AND ASKED: WHAT IF A BUILDING WERE SOFT AS OPPOSED TO HARSH?"

—

glazed at their tips, which act as miniature windows. The play of light extends both inward and outward. In the evening, the Sitooterie projects an array of light through its numerous staves, creating a dappled burst of color in the middle of the field.

Heatherwick's studio collaborated with Adams Kara Taylor Engineers to ensure that the arrangement of the filaments took into account the fact that they sway and quiver. This required the architects and engineers to work and communicate within a highly detailed 3D modeling system. In addition to milling the filaments and their sleeves to the exact specifications of the parametric model (which also guided the computer-driven mill-

curate a seed collection that achieved the highest possible diversity within the physical limitations of the Cathedral, including both surplus material of wild species from the Kunming Institute as well as cereals and legumes available locally. When the structure is eventually dismantled, the rods will be sent to schools in the U.K. and China.

The seed as a symbol of life could have become clichéd or overwrought. Heatherwick and his team avoided these trappings by working through an honest form-making process, and through collaborating with highly specialized consultants.

Troika, a London-based design firm, articulated some of the ideas presented in

SPARK

THE ORGANIC MATERIAL INSIDE THE SEED CATHEDRAL IS ENCASED IN SO MANY GLIMMERING, UNDULATING SURFACES THAT, AT TIMES, IT SEEMS THE INTERIOR IS COVERED IN A HIGHLY STYLIZED MOSAIC OF METALLIC TILES.

—

the U.K. Pavilion with a three-part exhibition: "Green City," "Open City," and "Living City." "Green City" is a map that isolates the green spaces of four British cities. Rendered in bas-relief Astroturf, the map adheres to the canopy of the Pavilion's entrance. Visitors then move through "Open City," in which a series of icicle-like models depicting various British buildings clings to the roof. The organic material inside the Pavilion is encased in so many glimmering, undulating surfaces that, at times, it seems the interior is covered in a highly stylized mosaic of metallic tiles. The play of reflective opacity and translucence makes the interior a dizzying array of light that feels at once fully enclosed yet discreetly linked to the outside elements. In this way, the Seed Cathedral almost behaves as if it were a living organism, interacting with its habitat. This is heightened by the fact that all of the service-related spaces in the Pavilion are tucked beneath its outer grounds. "We wanted to give the impression that everyone who visits the Pavilion has access to all spaces," explains Dionysopoulou.

Upon exiting the Seed Cathedral, visitors encounter "Living City," where they first glimpse living plants, which run along the canopy in a faultlike depression. The 30 species chosen for this display can all be used for medicinal purposes. These ancillary exhibition materials ensure that the experience of visiting the Pavilion is edifying on multiple levels, and that its organic, nature-inspired themes are presented with a fresh and sophisticated sensibility.

That these private spaces are hidden speaks to one of the unique elements of the Pavilion: Only a fraction of the Pavilion's space is taken up by the Seed Cathedral. The rest is an active, engaging landscape and popular public space. That space, like the "dandelion" sitting at its edge, is also metaphor made real. The multiplanar park is meant to seem like the creased folds of wrapping paper, as if the Seed Cathedral were a freshly opened gift to China. Ⓐ

What visitors found inside the Seed Cathedral was open to their own interpretation. The thousands of fiber-optic bristles created a dramatically lit space that was also an oasis of calm in the hyperstimulating environment of Expo Shanghai.

The Seed Cathedral was meant to provide some relief from the hubbub of the Expo. "In a sea of stimulation," Heatherwick says, "we thought that calmness would actually be the thing that would refresh you and that you might be the most thirsty for."

SPHERES OF INFLUENCE
Where do innovations come from?

All designed objects bear the traces of previous innovation, and Apple's iPad is no different. It evolved out of advances in mobile computing and interface design over the course of many years, fueled by the creative capital in the San Francisco Bay Area and a constantly evolving supply of applications, digital content, and online services.

The iPad Family Tree

The iPad has a complex family tree spanning the history of personal computing devices. These innovations have combined with one another over the past few decades.

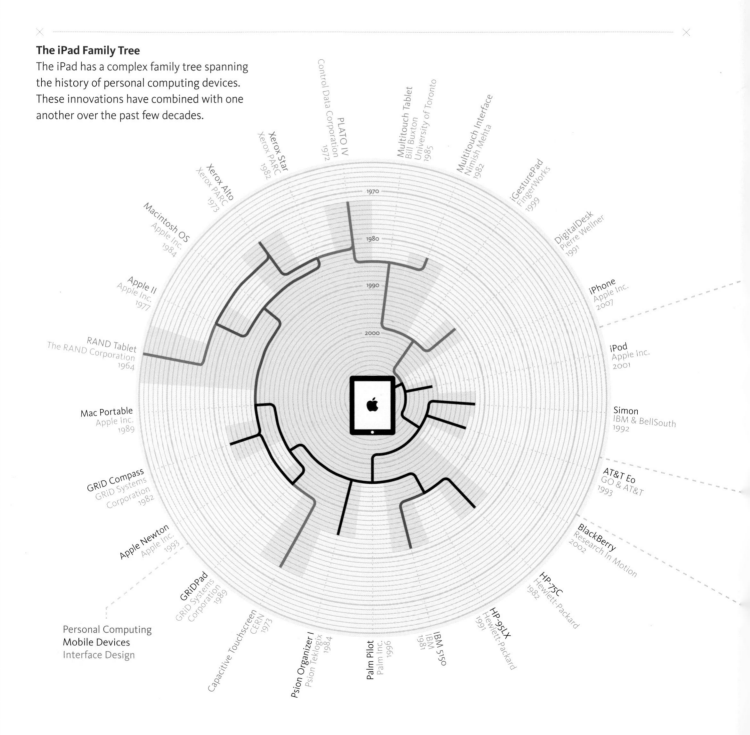

Control Data Corporation
PLATO IV
1972

Xerox Star
Xerox PARC
1982

Xerox Alto
Xerox PARC
1973

Macintosh OS
Apple Inc.
1984

Apple II
Apple Inc.
1977

RAND Tablet
The RAND Corporation
1964

Mac Portable
Apple Inc.
1989

GRiD Compass
GRiD Systems
Corporation
1982

Apple Newton
Apple Inc.
1993

GRiDPad
GRiD Systems
Corporation
1989

Capacitive Touchscreen
CERN
1973

Personal Computing
Mobile Devices
Interface Design

Psion Organizer I
Psion Teklogix
1984

Palm Pilot
Palm Inc.
1996

IBM 5150
IBM
1981

HP-95LX
Hewlett-Packard
1991

HP-75C
Hewlett-Packard
1982

BlackBerry
Research In Motion
2002

AT&T Eo
GO & AT&T
1993

Simon
IBM & BellSouth
1992

iPod
Apple Inc.
2001

iPhone
Apple Inc.
2007

DigitalDesk
Pierre Wellner
1991

iGesturePad
FingerWorks
1999

Multitouch Interface
Nimish Mehta
1982

Multitouch Tablet
Bill Buxton
University of Toronto
1985

1970

1980

1990

2000

On the Shoulders of Giants
The roots of some of the iPad's technologies reach back centuries.

1703
Mathemetician Gottfried Wilhelm Leibniz invents and publishes the modern binary system.

1783
George Atwood builds the first accelerometer in order to demonstrate Newton's first law of motion.

1820
Thomas de Colmar patents the Arithmometer, the first mass-produced portable calculating machine.

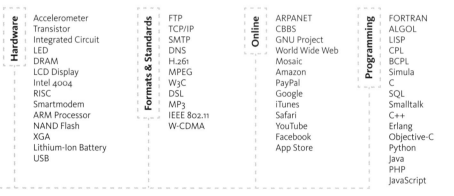

○ Personal Computing
● Mobile Devices
○ Interface Design

Mapping Tablet Innovation
Many of the creative innovations in the iPad family tree originated in North America, particularly the San Francisco Bay Area. The close proximity of so many companies innovating around similar concepts led to, and was fed by, a constant cross-pollination of ideas and personnel.

A Hardware & Software Ecosystem
The hardware advances, online services, and programming languages noted here are just a few of the innovations that were necessary in the evolution and execution of the iPad's rich digital content environment.

Hardware	Formats & Standards	Online	Programming
Accelerometer	FTP	ARPANET	FORTRAN
Transistor	TCP/IP	CBBS	ALGOL
Integrated Circuit	SMTP	GNU Project	LISP
LED	DNS	World Wide Web	CPL
DRAM	H.261	Mosaic	BCPL
LCD Display	MPEG	Amazon	Simula
Intel 4004	W3C	PayPal	C
RISC	DSL	Google	SQL
Smartmodem	MP3	iTunes	Smalltalk
ARM Processor	IEEE 802.11	Safari	C++
NAND Flash	W-CDMA	YouTube	Erlang
XGA		Facebook	Objective-C
Lithium-Ion Battery		App Store	Python
USB			Java
			PHP
			JavaScript

Apple's Hardware History
Since it was founded in 1976, Apple has released 37 portable devices, 91 laptops, and 161 desktop computer designs. Not including peripheral devices, the iPad was Apple's 289th hardware product.

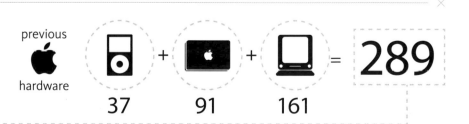

previous
 hardware

37   +   91   +   161   =   **289**

FIRST'S COMPETITIVE DESIGN
The quarter-million young robot builders of FIRST practice design as a contact sport—and learn important lessons about teamwork along the way.

KICKOFF

If you are seriously into building robots and you are between ages twelve and nineteen, then the first Saturday of January is no ordinary day: It is a day you have been excited about for months. The day marks the end of your normal sleep patterns and social engagements and the beginning of a madcap, sleep-and-eat-when-you-can, six-week robot-building race. It is the day of *The Announcement*.

It is on the first Saturday of January that the FIRST Robotics Competition announces its yearly robot game challenge. FIRST (For Inspiration and Recognition of Science and Technology) was founded in 1989 by engineer and inventor Dean Kamen and MIT professor Woodie Flowers to get young people interested in engineering and technology.

The Announcement leads to weeks of intense designing, engineering, testing, and robot-versus-robot competition, and ultimately what might best be described as design as a contact sport. With immediate feedback, the thrill of competition, and the elevating spirit of teamwork, FIRST inspires its participants in design and engineering like no other related educational process.

Today, FIRST's twenty-two thousand teams and 250,000 students compete in a range of leagues in the United States and a dozen other countries. After January's *Kickoff*, each of the three thousand teams enrolled in the FIRST Robotics Competition—the highest level of competition—has six weeks to design and build a robot that meets particular design specifications. Each year brings a new challenge: One year, robots had to lift and throw 8-pound balls; another year, they placed inflatable rings on racks.

The world of FIRST competition can seem upside down: where sometimes winning is losing, where teams often mentor their biggest rivals, and where sharing a love of robots with the teams' community can be rewarded more than on-field prowess.

The Announcement for the 2010 season was broadcast live on NASA TV. Dubbed "Breakaway," the challenge featured a 27-by-54-foot (8.2-by-16.4-meter) field with two bumps splitting the field into three zones. The zones also connected via tunnel. At the end of each field were two goals, and the field would be stocked with some twenty soccer balls. Teams would win by racking up the most points using robots to get the balls into the goals; it was a form of robot soccer.

Each year's challenge comes with its own rules. In 2010, you could never win a game alone; each match would have six robots on the field, split into two alliances. The first twenty seconds of a match were autonomous play in which preprogrammed commands could run the robot. Then three team members would take wireless control of their robots. During the final twenty seconds of the match, a team could win an additional two points by connecting its robot to an overhead tower and lifting it at least 30 inches (76.2 centimeters) off the ground. That was the Announcement—all of it.

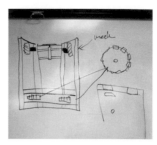

Like most real-world design problems, the limitations of FIRST's rules—and the fact that each team receives the same set of standard issue parts to build their robot—is a primary instigator for creative solutions. With Kickoff behind them, the teams were now cast into *Build Season*. Teams read lists of rules and opened up their boxes of parts. Then it was time to brainstorm and work out how they would face the challenge to design, build, and program a robot for the challenge. They hoped to build something capable of winning their regional competition, go to the national championships in Atlanta's Georgia Dome, and beat the field. That was the plan for at least two different teams in 2010—each with a varied approach.

BUILD SEASON

Oregon City is a city of twenty-five thousand just south of Portland, Oregon, and home to FIRST Team 2550, OCPRO—the three-year-old Oregon City Pioneer Robotics Organization. In January, Team 2550 hosted fifteen other teams for its annual "all-nighter," its pre-Announcement sleepover. After the Announcement, Team 2550, in typical community-outreach mode, helped some of the regional rookie teams to brainstorm before huddling around their own well-used whiteboard.

Team 2550 was founded in 2007 by Roger Collier and Sean Hally, two dads who sought an extracurricular challenge for their sons. After stumbling on FIRST's junior Lego league robotics, the dads moved to the more advanced Robotics Competition and patched together a team of students from local high schools. The dads, joined eventually by five other adults, serve as mentors and coaches to the students but take a largely hands-off approach.

In brainstorm mode, the team's concepts and designs started flowing. Each new idea brought questions that launched debates. The team began to set priorities: First they had to build a robot that would

move, then a robot that *scored*. Wouldn't it be cool to build something like a *Star Wars* AT-AT walker? What about a circular- or triangular-shaped robot? How about a monster-truck design, a lowrider, or a Formula One design? Should they try to build multiple subsystems or focus? "We had to decide if we wanted to score in every way or specialize in one thing," recalls Andrew, an eighteen-year-old team member.

Discussions on form led to questions of function. Should their robot be designed to go over the bumps or under them? That choice, they decided, would most shape their design and subsequent building. *Over*

LIKE MOST REAL-WORLD DESIGN PROBLEMS, THE LIMITATIONS OF FIRST'S RULES—AND THE FACT THAT EACH TEAM RECEIVES THE SAME SET OF STANDARD-ISSUE PARTS TO BUILD THEIR ROBOT—IS A PRIMARY INSTIGATOR FOR CREATIVE SOLUTIONS.

—

The design of each FIRST robot begins with the Announcement, which defines the playing field and goals and the kit of parts available. At left, Oregon City's Team 2550 began its design phase by surveying the playing field and sketching out parts of the drivetrain.

or under? The team wandered in circles trying to decide. "We wasted a lot of time on that," says Andrew's teammate Morgan, fourteen. "I said, 'Let's do it. It shouldn't be that hard to go over.'"

Ultimately, the robot went over, but the endless discussion "taught us how to debate, compromise, and get our point across," says Morgan. "Our main challenge in building the robot was communication." Teammate Margo, seventeen, agreed: "There's no doubt that the most learning happens in the group discussions."

Inspiration and ideas turned into robotics through software. Andrew, the team's lead designer, made a digital model of the bump in Autodesk Inventor modeling software and tried to work out the coefficient of force that the bump would exert on the robot's front wheels and the geometric dimensions necessary to get the robot over the bump without it being high-centered. His teammates Darien and Ryan used Google's Sketchup to design the ball kicker with a pneumatic-assisted surgical tube–powered lever to propel the balls. With a team history of bad luck in build-

ing robot subsystems (like arms), Andrew turned to Inventor to map out the travel of a ball punted by the team's proposed kicker arm. He sought to determine the needed force of a piston that would serve as the ball kicker and the trajectory of a ball kicked by the robot. He found it challenging due to the limits of what he'd learned in his physics class.

DESIGN REVIEW

Meanwhile, some 550 miles south, Team 604, aka Quixilver, from Leland High School in San Jose, California, held similar debates. After Kickoff, the much larger fifty-five-student team met in their school library. Some of the crew sketched out ideas with pencil on paper. As in Oregon City, the requirements of scoring and the limits of the rules sparked creative discussions. One early design called for an articulated chassis that would allow the team's robot to bend over the bumps like a centipede. Quixilver debated how best to play the game. With dozens of ideas in play, team members cast votes for the best ones.

Team 604 split into subgroups: There

The limitations of FIRST competition, including the necessary tasks for robots to complete and the stock set of parts, roughly define how FIRST robots will look. Yet those limitations are a primary instigator for the students' creative solutions. Every FIRST robot presents unique adaptations to those limits; as a group, the robots evidence the enormous creativity and effort of the participating teams.

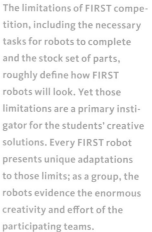

"PARENTS TELL US WE HAVE TO BE MEAN IN SPORTS, BUT HERE WE DON'T HAVE TO BE THAT WAY."

was a programming group that used Java, C++, and LabVIEW coded for the robot movements; electronics and drivetrain groups; a manipulator group; and team spirit, design, building, leadership, fundraising, business, and marketing groups. Two weeks into Build Season, Team 604 had completed the CAD for most of the initial robot design. The team and its mentors invited in local engineers for a design review. The review was a way to hear criticism that would tighten the team's design, and it followed what one mentor called a "corporate model." The visitors' concerns were primarily about the lifting mechanism. After looking carefully at the range of options for scoring points, the team decided to scrap the hanging arm mechanism and to instead build a superb kicking mechanism.

Once the team finalized general concepts, various prototypes were made to test the concepts. A select group of team members, primarily seniors James and Eugene, then worked out the details of every design and put them into a CAD program. As the digital model grew more complete, the team found some constraints it had to follow (such as limited motion of the kicker due to space constraints). The team tried to tweak its prototypes to match the model and see if they would still work. First-year students Tyler and Sebastian helped with the digital

rendering of the robot. They realized that they would need shock mounts to hold the robot's battery—its heaviest part—and Tyler ran stress tests in the CAD software to test the battery's forces and the forces on the spokes of the wheels. Tyler designed the wheels and then machined them with his dad's assistance.

Build Season was soon over, and the team had moved through a lot of ideas. Initially, the team was going to use a pneumatic-powered kicker, but it found that when prototyped, the force generated was weak compared with a superior surgical tubing–powered kicker. Originally, the

The 2010 FIRST competition (above) was a form of robot soccer, with each team scoring points for goals. In the final seconds of a match, teams could earn extra points by connecting their robots to a tower in the middle of the field (below) and having it lift itself at least 30 inches (76.2 cm) off the ground.

"I LOVE WORKING ON IT WITH MY HANDS," SAYS OREGON CITY'S OLIVER. "WE KNEW WHAT WE NEEDED TO DO," RECALLS MORGAN. "THE DESIGN FORMED AS WE WORKED."

—

team chose a six-wheel drive base, but it later discovered an eight-wheel drive to be superior. The original ball-retention device was a vacuum; however, the team discovered that the vacuum could not effectively retain the ball. The team quickly designed a ball roller, which they eventually upgraded post–Build Season. There was an early idea (never executed) to have a lid on the robot that would open up to right the robot if it flipped over.

After six weeks of build time, FIRST teams ship their robot off to the competition site. But the team kept working on redesigning the ball kicker. They discovered they had to add curvature to the kicker in order to avoid an interference problem with

the ball roller. Eugene added the curved section into the digital model of the robot, and the team's sponsor re-machined a kicker that cleared the ball roller perfectly.

CUSTOM WHEELS
Up in Oregon City, the wide-ranging debate having consumed precious design and build time, the team scrambled to build the robot in time for a pre-shipment scrimmage. At the scrimmage, the force of the bump on the front wheels shattered the plastic spokes and quickly sent the team back to the drawing board. With just a week remaining in Build Season, Andrew designed new metal wheels to withstand the bump's forces, and one of the team's mentors milled

"THERE ARE INFINITE POSSIBILITIES WHEN SOLVING A PROBLEM," SAYS TEAM 2550'S KRISTINA. "AMONG THE HUNDREDS OF TEAMS THAT COMPETED THIS YEAR, ONLY ONE TEAM CAME UP WITH THAT SOLUTION TO FUNNEL THE BALLS. THAT WAS BEAUTIFUL."

—

them out of aluminum. "Just knowing that my design was going to be cut out on a lathe was such a great thought," says Andrew.

Meanwhile, the electronics team, chaired by first-year students Oliver and Morgan, tore apart the robot. After four weeks of careful designing and building, they disassembled the frame and rebuilt it in forty-eight hours. Morgan, fifteen, saw himself as a tinkerer first, then a builder, and not necessarily a designer. "I'm not good at imagining things and getting them down on paper," he says. "I'll give input and analyze design." From an outside point of view, though, it's clear that all of the team members are deeply engaged with design—often, design as a seat-of-the-pants, learn-as-you-go operation. "I love working on it with my hands," adds teammate Oliver. "We knew what we needed to do," recalls Morgan. "The design formed as we worked."

At the Portland Regional games in early March, their shiny custom-machined metal wheels showed up just in time and fit into a newly designed chassis with a higher wheel-base. A poorly placed pneumatic solenoid was ripped off by a chain, but the team managed to quickly rebuild it.

Team 2550 landed fortieth out of sixty teams and, for a second year in a row, won a coveted Engineering Inspiration Award, which recognized the huge amount of work that the team had done showing off its past robotic creations and otherwise inspiring young people in its community. The award also qualified the team for a trip to the national championships in Atlanta. "Inspiring others," says team captain Amy, fifteen, "is part of our normal."

"What people don't really get is that it is not about crushing the opponent," says teammate Ryan. "We call it gracious professionalism." Says thirteen-year-old Kristina, "If we are in a competition here and another team needs a charged battery, and we have one, we'll hand it over." Sixteen-year-old Clarissa continues, "Parents tell us we have to be mean in sports, but here we don't have to be that way."

DESIGN AND REDESIGN

Team 604, in its first competition at the Sili-

San Jose's Team 604 earned a coveted Engineering Inspiration Award at the 2010 Silicon Valley Regional and a spot at the championships in Atlanta.

con Valley Regional, went to the semifinal round. Like Team 2550, Team 604 won an Engineering Inspiration Award. The kicker mechanism worked well in competition, scoring an average of four points per match. With another regional competition looming, the team decided it could do better. FIRST rules dictate that once Build Season concludes, teams can only work on and adjust robots during specified times before regional events. The kicker was good, but they realized that ball retention was a weak spot; a kicker was only good if the robot could control the ball before kicking it. Team 604 had two weeks to work on their robot, largely virtually, and find a way to improve the mechanism.

Pulling up their digital model, they were able to design a rebuilt ball-retention mechanism. "Because we CADed it all up, we didn't necessarily need to touch the robot," says Rohan, the team's ambassador. "At Silicon Valley the roller was only a single bar, so we redesigned it to have an additional, lower bar." Between their first and second regional bouts, the team redesigned this ball-retention device, which they called the BRD. The team prototyped a design that Eugene had sketched out during Build Season—one with two rollers that effectively pinched the ball. The prototype worked and

was then milled in aluminum.

At the UC Davis at Sacramento Regionals, the new surgical tubing–assisted ball-retention device–enhanced kicker performed well. The team's two on-field drivers, James and Elizabeth, held up under pressure with coaching from teammate Eugene. The team found it was able to drive, turn, and go backward with the ball much better than other teams could, and the ball-retention device improved the team's performance significantly.

After two days and twelve qualifying matches, Team 604 landed at first seed in a field of thirty-eight teams. The team chose two teams as its match alliance, including Team 3256, a team it had mentored all year. The three-team alliance faced fierce competition, led by Team Tater, from Boise, Idaho. The alliances dueled—604 winning one, losing one, tying one, and then finally clinching victory in its last match. The day of victory also included winning an award for the team's chief mentor and winning the Regional Chairman's Award.

END GAME

Both Team 604 and 2550 flew to Atlanta for the championships—a dizzying three days of competition featuring 345 high-caliber teams. For its part, Team 604 battled through ten qualification matches undefeated, coming out with eight wins and two ties. They made it as far as the quarterfinals in the elimination matches.

Team 2550 was hosted by a local family, and when not competing, the members took time to view other teams' robots. One team's ingenious robot used its hanging arm to retrieve every single ball reintroduced into play and send the balls directly into a nearby goal. "There are infinite possibilities when solving a problem," says Team 2550's Kristina. "Among the hundreds of teams that competed this year, only one team came up with that solution to funnel the balls. That was beautiful." Ⓐ

DEAN KAMEN

The famed innovator says invention begins with banishing the fear of failure.

How does design begin for you?
It starts with looking at a need or a problem and seeing a way to approach it that nobody else is doing. It may be a challenge everybody else has looked at before, perhaps for decades—but you look at it and maybe you see an opportunity at the intersection between a newly available technology and this old problem. And suddenly you say: "Hey, maybe we can do this differently."

Usually, for [my company] DEKA to take it on, it has to be something that will have an impact: "If I can do this, it'll improve the lives of lots of people." Then I look at the resources I have around me: Smart technology people with a broad base of interdisciplinary capability. And we'll get together and ask, "Can we collectively design a system that's likely to be accepted by the world?"

If we can convince ourselves that we can design a twenty-first-century solution to a problem that is currently being addressed with a nineteenth- or twentieth-century perspective—well, we'll give it a shot.

At those early stages, how do you gauge what's possible to do and what isn't?
That's a question I think about all the time. But you never really know the answer. Sometimes, after you've decided to take on a tough project, things start going badly. And that's when you roll around in bed at night and wonder, *Is it time to face reality and move on? Or is this one of those times where you're in a dark spot but the big breakthrough is just about to happen?* If you've had even one of those breakthroughs, I think it convinces you that you shouldn't give up. Every once in a while you succeed at something and you are chilled by the thought, *Wow, only six months ago, we were about to kill this project.* I can look at every project we're working on now and know that some will succeed and some will fail. My big frustration is not knowing which are which.

You take on a broad range of projects. What do they have in common?
People say that we work on so many different types of things—a diabetes pump or a dialysis machine, a way to make water, a way to make power. Yes, they're different, but I see them as all the same. It's about using a new approach and new technology to try to change the world in some way. Sometimes people talk about "the world of design," and it's about designers getting together at conferences and pontificating. That doesn't interest me. Instead, I think we should be focused on "the design of the world," meaning, the world is a certain way, but we want to use our understanding and whatever tools we have to try to impact that.

—

"We should be focused on 'the design of the world,' meaning, the world is a certain way, but we want to use whatever tools we have to try to impact that."

When you work with young people, how do you spark their interest in design and engineering?
I don't think you have to encourage that spark in young people, because they naturally have it. The problem is we do such a good job of discouraging it all along the way in formal education—which educates people to not make mistakes. But early on, kids are not afraid to fail, not afraid to ask questions. All you need to do is put them together with mentors and with projects, and they jump right in and start trying things. Sometimes, with older kids, you have to reignite that spark. You need to give them an environment where they know it's okay to make a mistake and to learn as they go.

What about lighting that spark for your own designers?
Actually, what I just described for the kids is not all that different from what we try to do on a regular basis at DEKA. We certainly don't like failing, but we continue to reassure people that a project can fail or an idea can fail without the person failing.

How is technology changing design?
Today, for most practical purposes, computing is free. Microprocessors with breathtaking computational ability cost a couple of bucks! Memory is free. We have sensor technologies and software capabilities that are breathtaking. With all of this happening, the design problem is no longer a question of "What can we do?" Now it's "What *should* we do?" And that is a much more difficult question. Where do we devote our resources? Should we put people on the moon, or should we make transportation here on earth easy, fast, and environmentally friendly? We need to start asking these bigger questions about where to apply our resources and technology in order to accomplish the most important goals. That question has typically not been left to the designers and engineers; it has been left to the politicians. And I think that question now needs to be part of the world of design.

How does technology change the way you design?
You have to invest a lot of time and energy in all these tools, and in some ways, it's a constraint to have to use a computer—because you're giving up that great user interface of your eyeball and your hand and a piece of paper. But the reason it's all worth it is the incredible power it gives you to take ideas and run them through a simulation—and keep changing them, modifying them, and trying new things. The

> "The design problem is no longer a question of 'What can we do?' Now it's 'What *should* we do?' And that is a much more difficult question."

—

rate at which you can parametrically vary things, optimize any one variable, and model a whole system is so powerful. Compared with the old way of constructing models slowly, one at a time, it's a no-brainer. I think we're reaching the point where it's going to be impossible to effectively compete if you can't do those simulations. I also think technology helps you identify weak designs quickly and allows you to focus on getting to the really good designs.

Speaking of good design, how do you define it?
Good design, I think, is the best compromise—and it's always a compromise—between what's currently available and the need to which it's being applied. To me, that's part of what's exciting: trying to achieve that balance between all those variables of what's available, affordable, reliable, functional. Ultimately, if the thing you deliver to the world manages to most appropriately meet the need of the people you're designing for, then that's the best design. ⒶⒶ

Dean Kamen is an inventor, an entrepreneur, and a tireless advocate for science and technology.

UGO CONTI'S SPIDER BOAT

An iconoclastic sailor draws on a lifetime of experience—and insect inspiration—to get a new species of boat afloat.

IF YOU TALK TO UGO CONTI FOR ANY STRETCH OF TIME, THERE'S ONE SUBJECT THAT'S BOUND TO COME UP: HIS PASSION FOR BOATS. And it is not a passion for simply riding in or sailing on boats, but building boats. Boats he has built serve as punctuation marks interspersed throughout Ugo Conti's never-boring life.

Until recently, boatbuilding was not Conti's profession at all. Rather, designing and building boats has served as a platform to test out ideas and experiment in a way very much his own. Conti, seventy-two, took several years to build his first boat in his mid-forties as a way to push through a midlife crisis. That boat was a one-of-a-kind 28-foot inflatable craft he sailed solo on a mind-expanding three-week passage to Hawaii, navigating with a primitive sextant. Then there was a boat he built seventeen years later to replace that homemade low-draft vessel. The most recent boat in the Conti line, *Proteus*, which he started to develop in 2002, is no doubt his boldest to date—one he considers a new form of boat species.

Whether planning new boats or tools for geophysics, Conti as an engineer and a designer is one who sees himself as working in a different manner than others. "I have to understand how things work," he says. "For instance, what is a magnetic field?" He seeks to possess an intuitive grasp of a subject, not just to understand a formula. Additionally, he eschews modeling in lieu of now-rare hands-on experimentation. Modeling, Conti believes, can sometimes limit the possibilities of a solution.

By training, Conti is a mechanical engineer. He was born in Rome, Italy, and has lived in the San Francisco Bay Area since 1965. The bulk of his professional career was spent at a geophysics instrumentation company he cofounded with a friend. In 2001, Conti sold Electromagnetic Instruments to French company Schlumberger. Although in theory he was retired, his instrument- and tool-filled double-door garage workshop beckoned.

THREE STAGES OF INVENTION

In the Conti framework, there are three stages to bringing an idea into the world. First, there's the fantasy, which is an idea not really tied to any sort of laws of science or reality. Then there's the dream, which has the possibility of coming to fruition because it is in fact grounded in reality. Finally, there is the plan that leads to reality. "The fantasy stage is something you do in your head," Conti explains. "At some point, you decide on some reason to do it, so you go into the dream stage."

At five o'clock in the morning one day in 2002, Conti lay in bed and realized it was time to push his long-held boat fantasy forward into the dream stage. He had come no closer to figuring out the steps needed for his invention, but he felt a change in mood to a state of happiness that he interpreted as a sign to press forward.

Conti's latest boat fantasy was a way for him to answer the simple question that had plagued him for years: "Is there a better way to go to sea?" As an engineer, he sought to solve

Ugo Conti pilots a prototype WAM-V (Wave-Adaptive Modular Vessel) on San Francisco Bay. A completely novel kind of watercraft, the WAM-V began from the idea of flexibility on water: "Not fighting the waves, but dancing with the waves," Conti says.

CONTI'S LATEST BOAT FANTASY WAS A WAY FOR HIM TO ANSWER THE SIMPLE QUESTION THAT HAD PLAGUED HIM FOR YEARS: "IS THERE A BETTER WAY TO GO TO SEA?"

———

the problem of motion on the sea, not just motion as the cause of motion sickness, but motion as a problem of safety and stability for watercraft. His new boat creation would be founded on the idea of flexibility in the water: "Not fighting the waves, but dancing with the waves," Conti explains.

As anyone who spends any length of time on the open ocean can tell you, the amount of pitching that a boat does in the face of wave action is significant. As a sailor for more than thirty years, Conti held an idea in his head that there had to be a better way. "The boat itself would adapt to the waves instead of fighting through or smashing them or jumping them," he says. "I kept working on this idea. When you're old, there's very little to lose."

For Conti, committing to building a new boat was a big step. Doing so meant jumping into the task head on, working 12- to 14-hour days, seven days a week. "I started thinking about ways to really go outside the box completely," recalls Conti. "When I retired, quote unquote, I just decided to go for it. My wife was absolutely resistant to another boat business, because when I build a boat, I don't exist. I'm capable of doing that because I get obsessed. Nothing else exists, and that's what I do. And at the end, you don't understand anything anymore because your brain is cooked."

The morning decision to turn a fantasy into a dream led Conti (and his wife) to found Marine Advanced Research, undertake four years of initial boat development, raise more than $500,000, and build three separate prototype boats within eight years.

"I think if you go down deeper," says Conti, "the motivation is to create something that doesn't exist. There's an attraction to that. It's not something I'm copying. I'm doing something completely new."

In the Conti way, when you are building things that don't exist, modeling on a computer is not the fastest or least expensive approach. Modeling, beyond being slow and expensive, often stifles experimentation. With boats—and planes, for that matter—there's a problem with modeling and scale, says Conti. "You know those little airplanes that they make out of balsa wood? They put an engine on them. They go like hell because it's not linear; it doesn't scale."

As Conti shared his nascent idea of the Wave-Adaptive Modular Vessel (or WAM-V) with experts and colleagues, he was advised to use computer models. But what he wanted to make had no easy computer model solution, because there was no precedent for a flexible boat. In a world that runs heavy on computer-aided design, Conti is a rare breed in that he prefers to

Insects such as water striders (top right) were another inspiration for Conti, who was attracted by their flexibility on water. It turned out that his craft's flexibility needed to be controlled; modeling in Autodesk Inventor (bottom right) helped turn Conti's ideas into a buildable, sailable boat.

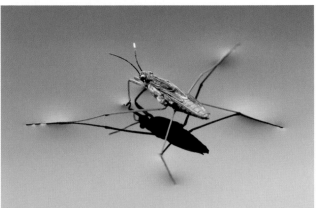

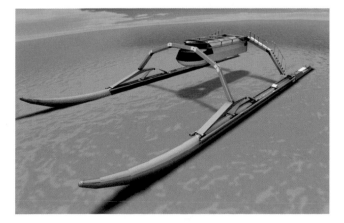

"I THINK IF YOU GO DOWN DEEPER, THE MOTIVATION IS TO CREATE SOMETHING THAT DOESN'T EXIST. THERE'S AN ATTRACTION TO THAT. IT'S NOT SOMETHING I'M COPYING. I'M DOING SOMETHING COMPLETELY NEW."

—

work with his hands. "I'm an old-fashioned experimentalist," he says. "I stick my fingers in stuff."

Conti finds it easier to model things in his head and build with his hands. "I see things in 3D, and I can turn them around and feel if they work or not," he explains. "I can think of what to do physically. I'm not a computer person anyway, so I have to make it, because I have to see it, touch it, drive it." (As it evolved and neared production, the WAM-V was brought into Autodesk Inventor 3D modeling software.)

Conti is unique—an inventor who spends time thinking about how his ideas are born and what genre of invention they will fall into. There are three types of inventions, he says. A "one whammy" is a better mousetrap, and it has a good chance of success. A "double whammy" is not only a new thing but something that people will have to learn before they can use, which often poses too great a threat to any sort of adoption or sale. A "triple whammy" is something new that you have to learn, but "it's a fantasy that catches the imagination. It's a new species."

"Working without knowledge" is

something Conti talks about a lot. "I have an intuition, and first they tell me that I'm crazy. Then I solve a problem that they have been working on for months without knowing what the hell it is. And I solve it, just out of intuition."

For Conti's new boat idea—building a boat that would be suspended above waves like a four-wheel-drive Jeep over rocky roads—the model he would build was 50 feet long. He called it POF, for "Proof of Feasibility." Built out of carbon fiber with manufacturing defects, it failed during an early test—which seemed to prove his critics right.

"I started with completely flexible legs, everything flexible. It didn't work. I actually built a prototype, and I went out in the San Francisco Bay and tried it. You can say, 'Well, wasn't that a little stupid?' because it cost money and effort—tremendous effort on my part. For physical reasons, it's not that simple. It has to be a certain size to try.

"The error was this idea of complete flexibility. I was studying insects. They're extremely efficient, and they're flexible. But they're also controlled. So if you have flexibility without control, it doesn't work."

Conti says that making the WAM-V was more like building a car than a boat, because it has components that move in relation to one another.

THE BOAT ITSELF WOULD ADAPT TO THE WAVES
INSTEAD OF FIGHTING THEM.

After the 50-foot boat was launched, tested, and failed, Conti and his team started building a larger prototype that they dubbed *Proteus*. Like the boat before it, *Proteus* was a way to prove the overall concept. Explains Conti: "*Proteus* is a platform to test the ideas in a real environment—not in a model, but in a real environment. And it works very well for that."

Proteus was built on Washington State's Puget Sound, and after it was launched on its maiden voyage, Conti felt it was very easy to maneuver using the differential steering system. "But then when we went out to sea, it was evident that there was some motion," he recalls. "There was some stuff that was not right, but it took us a couple of years to really understand what was wrong and what had to be done." After spending many hours at sea staring at the boat's movements in waves, Conti recognized that he had to make the hull more rigid and that the inflatable hull could not be a structural member.

Still, how to coordinate the hulls and their connection to the cabin and one another was not yet clear. One afternoon, Conti's assistant (and CAD designer), Mark Gundersen, brought a box of LEGO bricks to the office. Playing with the tiny modular pieces finally showed them the way. "We realized that 'Oh, look, this has to move that way, and this has to move that way,'" recalls Conti.

After a few hours in his workshop, Conti had perfected the expanded hinging system for the next iteration, which would allow the hulls to work independently of one another and limit the boat's overall flexibility. "The main thing that we wanted to test with the LEGO bricks was, 'Do I have too many degrees of freedom? Will the thing collapse?'" Conti and Gundersen realized that they could have just one single place per hull where it could move.

In its short life span, *Proteus* has drawn sponsorship from HP and Autodesk, among other companies. It has toured Italy and been to the Cannes Film Festival. The Navy has evaluated it for transport uses, and NASA has considered it for capsule recovery. Today, Conti and company are focused on building a 12-foot unmanned vehicle for military use that draws on the Lego-hinging system and that can be collapsed easily and stowed in a box for transport.

To be sure, Conti has finally achieved a solid "triple whammy" with his WAM-V. "Fortunately—and this is really the secret to happiness in life—I ended up doing what I'm very good at." ⒶnA

PROCESS

HOW DO WE MAKE DESIGN?

TO SPEAK OF DESIGN IN TERMS OF "PROCESS" IS TO INVITE DEBATE. WHILE THERE ARE THOSE WHO VIEW DESIGN AS SOMETHING THAT OCCURS METHODICALLY, IN AN ORGANIZED SEQUENCE OR SERIES OF STEPS, OTHERS SEE IT AS A VERY DIFFERENT PHENOMENON—ONE THAT RESULTS NOT FROM FOLLOWING A PRO-CESS BUT RATHER FROM THE UNIQUE VISION AND TALENT OF THE INDIVIDUAL DESIGNER. WHO'S RIGHT? UNDOUBTEDLY, BOTH SIDES ARE.

—

previous spread: **Zaha Hadid Architects' Chanel Mobile Pavilion, whose form evolved from spiraling shapes in nature**

Individual talent and vision are what make a great designer great and enable him or her to see the world differently and imagine uniquely brilliant possibilities. But even the most talented designers rely on process to carry them the great distance from possibility to reality.

Of course there is no single, universal design process; the steps taken and the order of those steps vary from one designer to the next. But there are common elements and principles at work: Somewhere along the line, good designers tend to apply holistic thinking, design research, collaboration across disciplines, the iterative use of prototypes, refinement based on feedback, and the measure of results and experience. If all goes well, a process that begins in fuzzy ideation concludes with impeccable execution.

Many of the basic elements of this process have been constants for years, but this does not mean it is immune to change—in fact, technology is having a great impact upon it, in some cases inverting some of the steps and sequences. Whereas a designer following a more conventional working model would be likely to come up with a concept, create a model of it, and then begin to analyze that model to determine what needs refining, technology is now enabling the designer to proceed in a different order: Rearranging the sequence, the designer might first specify the functional parameters or requirements of a given design project (the torque capacity of a gear, the wind load of a building, etc.) and have a computer then generate a series of options that meet those parameters. In this new version of the design process, analysis happens sooner, not later, and that opens up more possibilities that can lead to more innovative design—as evidenced in this chapter's story about the design of Shanghai Tower, a skyscraper whose shape represents maximum efficiency. Another story examines how the avant-garde firm of Zaha Hadid Architects harnesses computing power to lead the movement toward parametric design. And at Marriott, the adoption of digital prototyping—a shift in practice happening for many designers—transformed both process and product.

But even as technology alters some aspects of the design process, it doesn't negate the need for that process—in fact, it could be argued that process has never been more important in design than it is now. Having an understanding of advanced methods of problem-solving, and a systematic approach to applying those methods and principles, is critical for designers to be able to tackle the tough, complex problems of today and tomorrow. As designers venture into new territory in trying to solve these problems, the design process can serve to guide them through uncertainties and keep them moving ahead, step by step. Ⓐ

SHANGHAI TOWER

Gensler's performance-based approach to designing China's tallest building kept the focus on efficiency—and resulted in the spectacular.

WHEN THE SHANGHAI TOWER TOPS OFF IN 2014, it will be the tallest building in China and the second-tallest building in the world. At 2,074 feet (632 meters), it will outclimb the Shanghai World Financial Center, the city's current titleholder, by nearly 500 feet (152 meters), its glass skin twisting through the clouds to a blunt taper. It will be the third in a cluster of super-spires planned for a new business district that twenty years ago was abandoned farmland. Gensler, the architects of the Shanghai Tower, like to describe their building in terms of its neighbors. The Jin Mao, designed by Skidmore, Owings & Merrill, represents the past; the bottle-opener-shaped World Financial Center, finished by Kohn Pedersen Fox in 2008, the present; and the Shanghai Tower the future.

Designing for the future is no small task; it requires a suite of technical, financial, and collaborative acrobatics. There are the obvious challenges of building in a part of the world where the natural forces of everything from earthquakes to typhoons challenge brick and mortar. Raising the bar further is an aggressive sustainability agenda—the tower is slated for a LEED Gold rating and the equivalent three-star rating from China Green Building.

The architects turned to Building Information Modeling (BIM) for performance-based design—a loosely defined term for when you pin down what you want to achieve in a building and then measure whether you've achieved it. At its simplest, this kind of design involves plugging variables—like energy usage, fire and earthquake safety, and even aesthetics—into software to generate precise 3D models. The models then become the building. "Nowadays, we have better tools that can simulate these performance objectives," says Ken Sanders, a managing director at Gensler and the chief of its virtual design and construction practices. "In the old days, architects would develop a building concept, and then mechanical engineers and structural engineers would get involved. Now, from day one, we're identifying specific performance objectives and collaborating with our partners to ensure we are getting it right."

The vision for the Shanghai Tower was simple: Create a building for Shanghai. Gensler drew inspiration from traditional lane houses found in Beijing's *hutongs* and Shanghai's *shikumen*, where families live in small dwellings and share communal space. The tower's take on that is nine sections stacked one on top of the other, each its own mini skyscraper, with separate public atriums, or "sky gardens."

In renderings, the tower looks like a glass tube spiraling ever so slightly toward the sky. On closer inspection, it's a double-skin facade, with a cylinder inscribing a rounded prism; if you sliced through the building horizontally, you'd see a circle inside a guitar pick. There is parking, shops and restaurants, lobbies, conference centers, standard offices, boutique offices, a hotel, and, at the top, an outdoor observation deck—the highest of its kind in the world. The sustainability features include the best practices of the day: rainwater collection, green roofs, wind turbines, water-efficient fixtures, lighting control, geothermal heating and cooling, and an intelligent skin. The architects liken the whole thing to a vertical city. The

The distinctive spiral shape and long notch in the 2,074-foot (632-meter) Shanghai Tower emerged from a performance design analysis. The notch breaks up the force of the wind, and the twisting sheds it—dramatically reducing structural loads.

The Shanghai Tower is divided into distinct "vertical neigh-borhoods," each anchored by a sky lobby at its base. The light-filled lobby spaces will create a sense of communities within the large skyscraper.

GENSLER DREW INSPIRATION FROM TRADITIONAL LANE HOUSES FOUND IN BEIJING'S <u>HUTONGS</u> AND SHANGHAI'S <u>SHIKUMEN</u>, WHERE FAMILIES LIVE IN SMALL DWELLINGS AND SHARE COMMUNAL SPACE.

—

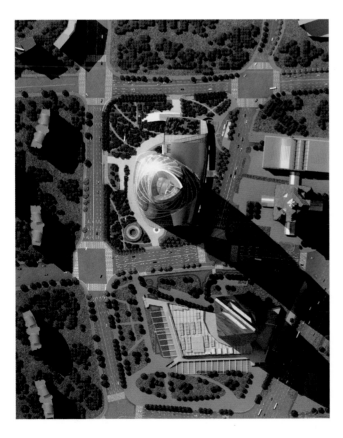

client—a consortium of three state-run entities—calls it a symbol of "a nation whose future is filled with limitless opportunities" and a celebration of "China's economic success."

Gensler could seem an unlikely candidate for the job. The largest architecture firm in the United States, it has plenty of high-rises to its credit, but its tallest building to date is the fifty-four-story Ritz-Carlton Hotel & Residences and JW Marriott at L.A. Live; the Shanghai Tower will rise 121 stories. In 2008, the forty-five-year-old firm won a competition to design the Shanghai Tower, beating out a field of major firms all eager for this opportunity. "We wanted to create something unique, beautiful, and appropriate for Shanghai," firm founder and chairman Art Gensler says. "And we had the most successful design solution." Gensler also has a pragmatic approach to design that informs everything from its giant interiors practice to its skyscrapers. Consider the firm's Workplace Performance Index, which gauges the link between employee productivity and corporate office design. Gensler tackled the Shanghai Tower the same way: performance first.

It's a method that cuts to the very geometry of the building. From bottom to top, the tower rotates 120 degrees, tapers, and has a long notch up its back that looks like the seam of a twisted stocking. "The notch breaks the force of the wind, and the twisting sheds it," says Gensler. "By incorporating those features into the design, we were able to reduce the structural loads dramatically." These measures slash material costs as well as wind loading.

You can imagine the kind of gusts you get at the top of a 2,074-foot (632-meter) skyscraper surrounded by other skyscrapers. Now imagine the skyscraper in a typhoon. But why not a 90-degree rotation? Or 210 degrees? Why not a pinpoint taper? Or no taper at all? By modeling various options in 3D software and then conducting wind-tunnel tests, the design team discovered that a 120-degree twist and 55 percent taper combination reduced wind

Digital models (right and following page) represent, from left, the tower's structure, composite floors, inner skin, hub-and-spoke supports, outer skin, and the complete composite building.

The tower will complete Shanghai's "super-high-rise precinct," next to the Jin Mao Tower and the bottle-opener-shaped Financial Center. The trio symbolizes Shanghai's past, present, and future.

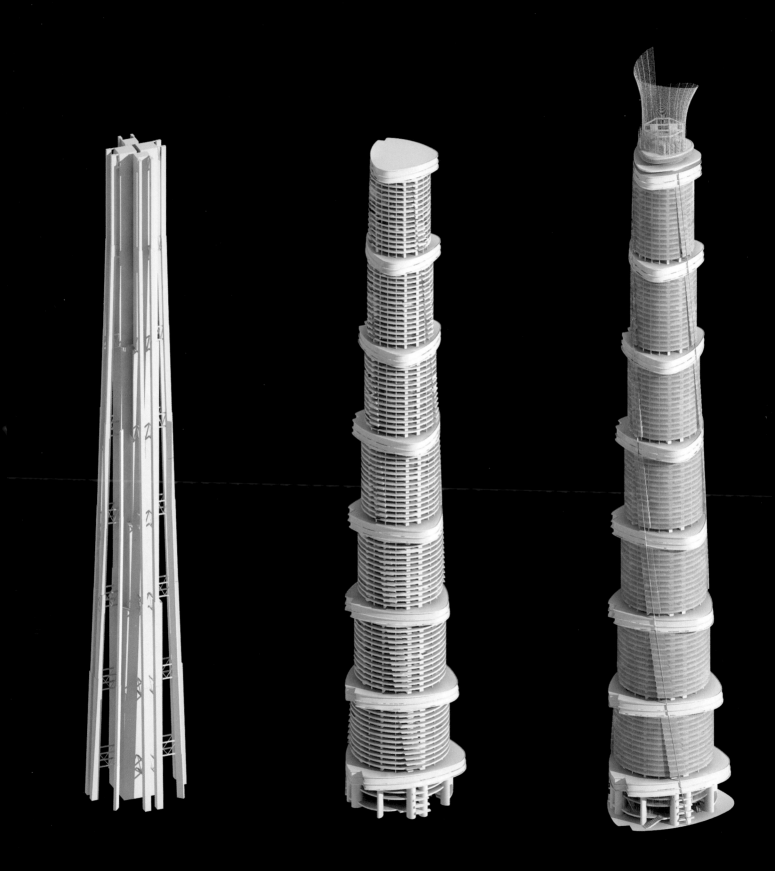

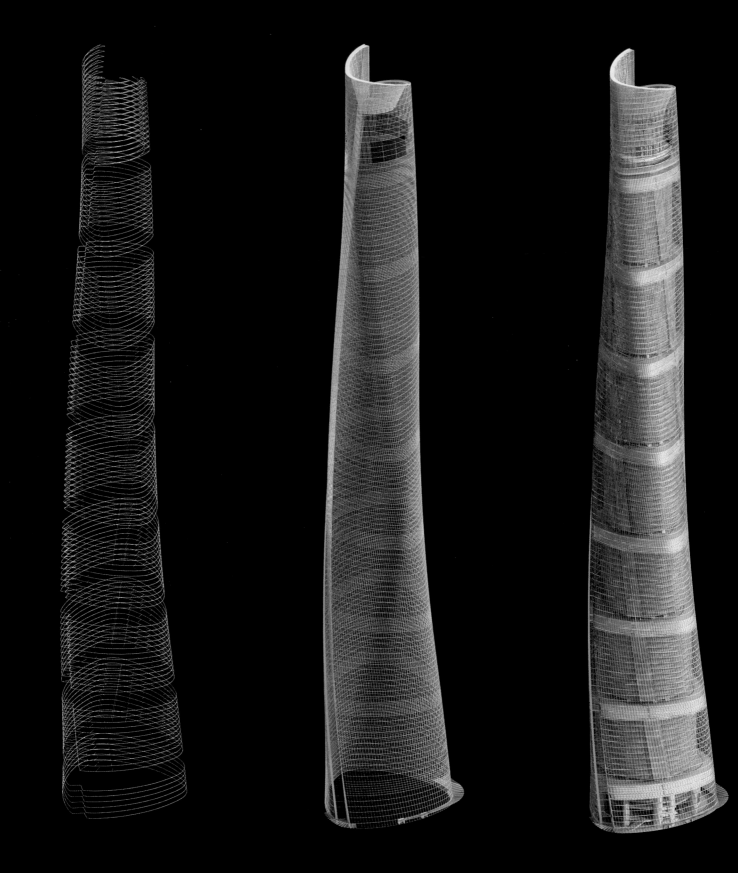

BY MODELING VARIOUS OPTIONS AND CONDUCTING WIND-TUNNEL TESTS, THE DESIGN TEAM DISCOVERED THAT A 120-DEGREE TWIST AND 55 PERCENT TAPER COMBINATION REDUCED WIND LOADS BY 24 PERCENT AND MATERIAL COSTS BY $58 MILLION.

—

The Shanghai Tower broke ground in 2008. By the summer of 2010, the skyscraper's mat-slab foundation was poured (following pages), surrounded by a temporary slurry wall.

loads by 24 percent and material costs by $58 million. The seam, for its part, buffers against wind vortices. If they had rotated the tower another 60 degrees, they would have further trimmed loading (by an extra 9 percent). But then the building would have skewed too much and resembled a "wet noodle." "That was not a desired look," notes Gensler associate Michael Concannon. It was a rare concession to form over function. In nearly every other respect, the building squarely trains its sights on efficiency.

Case in point: the structural system. The engineers, Thornton Tomasetti Associates, have to steel the building against not just wind but also an active seismic zone and soft clay-based soil that makes it tough to build pretty much anything, let alone a super-skyscraper. Using an intelligent 3D model created through BIM, the engineers tested several different earthquake scenarios against the soil conditions. Then they compared the data with China's seismic code. The structural skeleton has a set of statistics that an engineer can

love: a 20-foot-deep (6-meter) foundation, with 2,500 friction piles buried 262 feet (80 meters) in the ground; a 9,687-square-foot (900-square-meter) concrete core; a megaframe; supercolumns; outrigger trusses; double-belt trusses; and the list goes on. The point is that the engineers knew how they wanted the building to perform and had the software to simulate it. "BIM is giving us tools to facilitate analysis," Thornton Tomasetti managing principal Dennis Poon says.

For Cosentini Associates, the mechanical, electrical, and plumbing (MEP) engineers, "performance" had everything to do with shrinking the building's carbon footprint. Transporting water and energy up a skyscraper—against gravity—is a mammoth drain, and the taller the building, the bigger the drain. So Cosentini broke up the tower's guts into manageable pieces. Each of its nine zones has its own mechanical floor that houses assorted ventilation, water, and electrical systems. By drawing up the spaces in Autodesk Revit MEP design software, they could map out exactly where to put

SOFTWARE HAS PROVED ESPECIALLY INTEGRAL TO THE FACADE. IT'S A DESIGN CHALLENGE UNRIVALED ELSEWHERE IN THE BUILDING, TASKED AS IT IS WITH NEARLY EVERY PERFORMANCE GOAL IMAGINABLE.

—

An elevation (far left) reveals the relative sizes of the three super-high-rises. The Shanghai Tower's dual-skin facade (left) creates an interstitial volume large enough to be used as interior atrium spaces at the base of each "neighborhood." These sky gardens will improve air quality, create visual connections between the city and the tower's interiors, and allow visitors and tenants to interact and mingle.

the equipment. It seems like an obvious point: The mechanical engineers should design around the structural elements. But when you're talking about a 2,074-foot tower in which no two floors are the same and in which there are nine mechanical floors, plus assorted chiller rooms, cogeneration facilities, and more, it becomes exceedingly difficult to manage all the pieces. "The shapes are not regular on this building, and it's hard to visualize," says Douglas Mass, president of Cosentini. "So we used BIM software. Because of the complexity, it was the only way it could've been done."

Software has proved especially integral to the facade. It's a design challenge unrivaled elsewhere in the building, tasked as it is with nearly every performance goal imaginable. It has to withstand earthquakes, wind, lightning, and fire. It has to be transparent enough to fulfill the client's wish for a symbol of Chinese openness, and opaque enough to not annoy light-sensitive neighbors. It has to be energy-efficient. Its profile had to change at each floor because of the twist and taper as well as the program. (That particular challenge was met with the help of Revit plug-ins.) And, of course, it has to be beautiful. To hear facade designer Aleksandar Zeljic tell it, the outer skin underwent at least twenty iterations.

The biggest obstacle: reducing light pollution. When the glittering World Financial Trade Center went up in 2008, residential neighbors started complaining about the glare. They filed lawsuits; the building's owners racked up huge fines; and before long, Shanghai was working out a strict new light-pollution code. Gensler's approach was to analyze two different ways of arranging the glass: in steps and flush against the structure. Through light studies in Autodesk Ecotect Analysis green-building analysis software, the designers found that the stepped glass had a lower reflectance rate (i.e., less glare). It became their recommen-

dation. The tiered facade gives the building an engineered, almost businesslike look. It's the face of efficiency.

In February 2009, halfway through the design process, a blaze in Beijing changed everything. Wayward fireworks set a high-rise—the CCTV Tower's companion hotel—on fire, reducing it to scaffolding and ashes. The clients of the Shanghai Tower soon asked for a radically altered fire-safety apparatus for the building. The 3D models and the huge amount of information they already contained helped facilitate a complete redesign of the facade to meet rigorous new standards. It was done collaboratively and quickly. "In the architecture and engineering industry, we're always burdened by change," says Mass. "BIM makes it easier to react."

The Shanghai Tower is about leveraging advanced digital tools and massively collaborative work to engineer the best, most efficient building money can buy. That isn't to suggest that the building values economy over people. Gensler was hired to fit out the interiors, and we can expect that the firm, with its forty-five-year history of dressing up corporations everywhere, will turn this vertical city into a people's city. "We hope Shanghai Tower inspires new ideas about what sustainable tall buildings can be," says Art Gensler. "We've lined the perimeter of the tower, top to bottom, with public spaces, and we've integrated strategic environmental thinking into every move. The tower is a stage that comes to life through the presence of people." Ⓐ

"IN THE ARCHITECTURE AND ENGINEERING INDUSTRY, WE'RE ALWAYS BURDENED BY CHANGE," SAYS COSENTINI'S DOUGLAS MASS. "BIM MAKES IT EASIER TO REACT."

HUGH DUBBERLY

A design innovator argues that design learning is a prerequisite for design thinking.

You have said that design is stuck. What do you mean?
Design practice does not learn. As a profession, we don't even know *how* to learn.

We're stuck. Trapped in the past. Unable to move forward. Unclear on what forward might mean. Lacking mechanisms to build and share knowledge. Lacking even a model of design knowledge.

In fact, the problem is so structurally embedded, so pervasive, so deep, that we don't see it.

Can you give an example?
In 1985, in Boston, the AIGA held its first national conference; speakers included Nicholas Negroponte (a famous technologist) and Milton Glaser (a famous designer). Twenty years later, the AIGA conference returned to Boston and again included Negroponte and Glaser.

In his 2005 speech, Negroponte talked about the One Laptop Per Child project. Glaser showed some beautiful posters and talked movingly about human rights.

What struck me was how much things had changed in Negroponte's world and how little things had changed in Glaser's world.

During the intervening twenty years, computing power, storage capacity, and network speeds doubled more than ten times, while costs remained roughly the same. Personal computers grew from toys to necessities. Mobile phones, the Internet, and social networks arrived.

During the same twenty years, the big changes in design were not about design; they were about technology—computers and the Internet. Changes forced on Glaser's world by Negroponte's world.

The world of computers evolves. Like the worlds of biology and physics, it has learned how to learn. It bootstraps existing knowledge to create new knowledge. That's what academic disciplines do, but it rarely happens in design.

Why not? What's holding design back?
The short answer is art schools. Most design programs are housed in art schools. And art school teaching still follows a medieval model: master and apprentice.

Studio courses are mostly about socialization—sharing and creating tacit knowledge through direct experience. Students learn by watching one another. Teachers rarely espouse principles. Learning proceeds from specific to specific. Knowledge remains tacit.

Practice is much the same as education. Over the course of a career, most designers learn to design better. But what they learn is highly idiosyncratic, dependent on their unique context. The knowledge designers gain usually retires with them. Rarely do designers distill rules from experience, codify new methods, test and improve them, and pass them on to others. Rarely do designers move from tacit to explicit.

—

"Drawing and form-giving are *not* the essence of design. Seeing patterns, making connections, and understanding relationships are."

But aren't things changing?

Slowly. Publishing has become a requirement for tenure in design programs at major universities, but studio work remains the overwhelming factor in tenure decisions.

Publishing matters less in second-tier universities and independent art schools. And it is almost a black mark in for-profit design schools, where practical experience remains the main criterion for hiring.

Making things worse, art school tenure committees include non-design faculty, with little appreciation of design research.

The focus on design research at a few top schools is a positive development (e.g., IIT Institute of Design, Carnegie Mellon University, North Carolina State University, Royal College, Delft). Journals such as *Design Issues*, *Visible Language*, and *Interactions* publish interesting articles. But design journals are not widely read. And design research rarely affects practice or teaching. A few design blogs are widely read, but they aren't building lasting knowledge.

Why isn't design research making a difference?

Design doesn't have feedback loops that include funding, research, publishing, tenure, and teaching. These feedback loops ensure quality. Without them, design will remain stuck.

In contrast, engineering, medicine, and biology have strong feedback loops. Government and industry fund research, which leads to military, health care, and commercial applications. Peer reviewers look for breakthrough papers and filter out those that tread old ground. Tenure can be awarded on merit. And graduate students and professors are able to attract VC funding, start companies, and apply their ideas (e.g., Sun, Netscape, Yahoo, Google).

Setting up strong feedback loops for building design knowledge will be difficult. Existing institutions are unlikely to change. We need new ones.

What's the solution?

Visually oriented design programs should be left to do what they do well. Design should move out of art schools and into its own professional schools, alongside schools of business, law, and medicine.

Drawing and form-giving are *not* the essence of design. Seeing patterns, making connections, and understanding relationships are.

Modeling, mapping, and visualizing information should replace figure drawing. Systems theory and process manage-

"Increasingly, design is concerned with systems— and now systems of systems or ecologies."
—

ment should replace 2D and 3D foundation courses. Social sciences and communications theory must be part of design curricula—for example, ethnography, cognitive psychology, economics, rhetoric, semiotics.

Instruction should shift from an emphasis on making to a balance of making, observing, and reflecting.

The case-study teaching method works well in law, business, and medicine. We need to write and teach design cases. We need to integrate design cases and other research into studios.

Why does it matter? What are the practical consequences?

Value is created by developing new products and services. But we don't really know how to design products, services, or organizations. That great products occasionally emerge is something like magic. Design thinking remains a special form of this magic.

Product management is not yet a discipline. It isn't taught in design schools or in business schools. We have no theory of product management. We don't even have a theory of products.

Those are giant holes.

What's more, design is no longer concerned only with things. Increasingly, design is concerned with systems—and now systems of systems, or ecologies.

In a sense, these systems are alive. They grow and co-evolve. Designers and product managers cannot always control them. Instead, they must create conditions in which they can emerge and flourish.

All this requires new thinking and new knowledge. It requires design practice to learn.

Hugh Dubberly is a design planner and teacher, and the founder of Dubberly Design Office.

SIX DESIGN PROCESSES
Diagramming the ways we design

These illustrations represent the most common design processes. Some are suited to solo or small-team projects, while others are tailored to large, complex projects with multiple stakeholders and outcomes.

Diverge & Converge
At some point, most design processes incorporate this fundamental archetype of analyzing a question, expanding on possible solutions, then synthesizing those possibilities down to an optimal solution— even if that solution is another question.

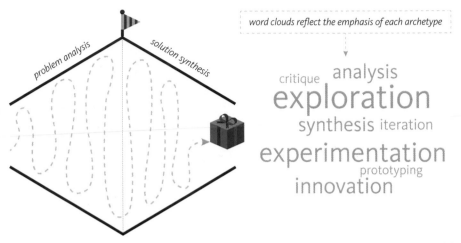

word clouds reflect the emphasis of each archetype

critique **analysis** **exploration** synthesis iteration **experimentation** prototyping **innovation**

Waterfall
In this archetypal linear process, a design project moves from one distinct phase to the next only after the previous one is complete. This approach, which is commonly used in software design, often focuses on implementing variations of previously tested design solutions.

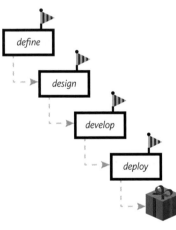

innovation experimentation **analysis** **critique** iteration collaboration exploration synthesis prototyping

Cyclical
The cyclical process emphasizes prototyping, testing, and reflecting on results before beginning the cycle again. This process is suited to incorporating feedback at each step on the cycle, which can keep the design user-focused.

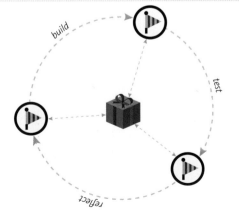

exploration **iteration** **prototyping** analysis **synthesis** **innovation** collaboration **critique** **experimentation**

Discovery

The least structured design process is about broad exploration, a multitude of prototyping methods, outside-the-box thinking, and discovering design problems and solutions in unexpected, unlikely places.

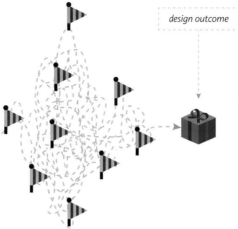

design outcome

innovation
experimentation
iteration   critique
prototyping
collaboration
exploration
analysis synthesis

Complex Linear

Complex linear design processes involve projects where multiple designers may be creating multiple outputs at various stages, which impact the outputs of other designers. Projects that depend on this process often have many stakeholders and designers moving toward a common goal.

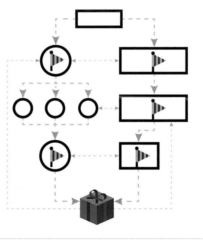

innovation
iteration analysis
experimentation
collaboration
exploration prototyping
critique
synthesis

Matrix

The matrix process is common on large projects that require multiple teams to collaborate while working in parallel. Communication through regular small-group meetings and occasional all-team meetings is key to making this process successful.

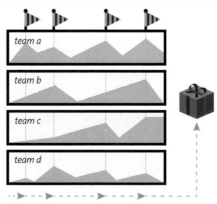

team a

team b

team c

team d

collaboration
innovation iteration
analysis prototyping
synthesis
experimentation
critique
exploration

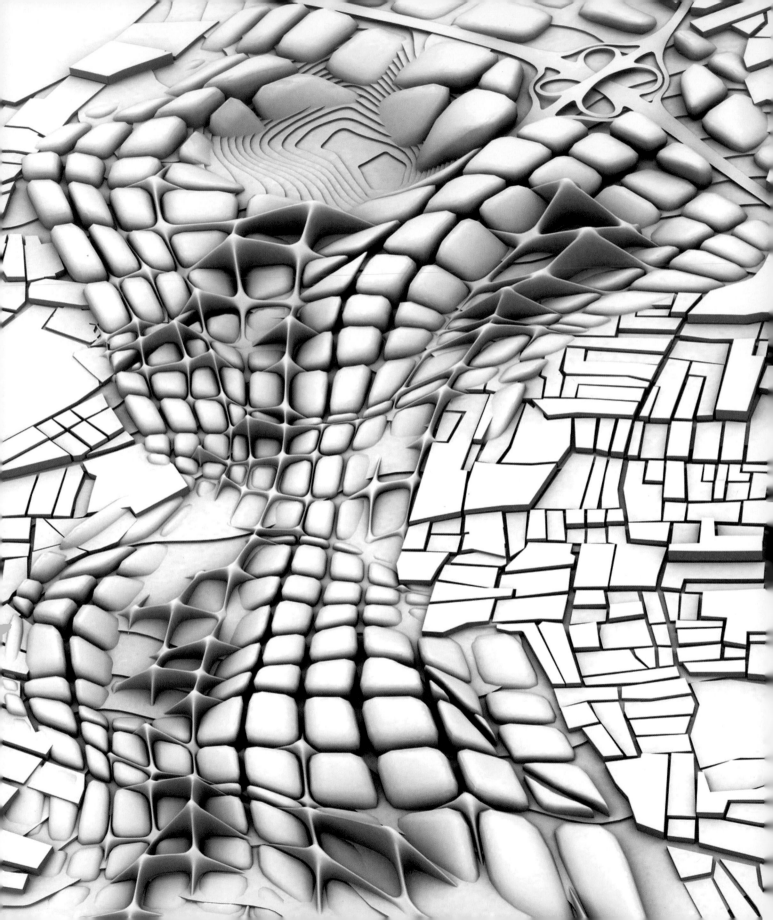

ZAHA HADID ARCHITECTS

Zaha Hadid's algorithmically controlled design opens up new possibilities for architecture.

THE QUESTION PROVOKED BY THE WORK OF ZAHA HADID IS THIS: WHY LIMIT HOW FAR THE ARCHITECT'S CREATIVE HAND EXTENDS INTO A PROJECT?

In the traditional architectural model, that hand was relevant primarily in the first phase of the design process. Beyond that, the practicalities of structure and building could compromise the original art of the architect.

Zaha Hadid and her studio have pioneered a technological and aesthetic approach that can free architects from the encumbrances of the traditional, linear design process. The resulting shapes and formations are radically unconventional solutions, but they satisfy clients because of their structurally sound underpinnings.

At the core of the dynamic design approach of Zaha Hadid Architects (ZHA) is parametricism, a style in architecture based on parametric modeling and design. That method begins with certain data—parameters based on engineering, fabrication, construction, even aesthetic and social factors—and uses algorithms and digital tools to create computer-rendered designs. At ZHA, Autodesk Maya animation software is a primary tool for creating parametric designs, which are later fleshed out into architecture in AutoCAD software.

Patrik Schumacher, partner at ZHA and one of the most vocal proponents of the approach, explains that "parametricism has become the dominant, single style for avant-garde practice today." Since its introduction, most contemporary architects have used parametric modeling to facilitate their design practice. Some, like Hadid, Schumacher, and Nils Fischer, an associate at the firm, see its capabilities as a means to create bold and distinctive new forms. Sometimes known, in variant forms, as generative design or computational design, parametric design allows architects to use instant feedback to continually recalibrate the design. Flexibility and the ability to generate a multitude of design alternatives from a set of original parameters are the hallmarks of the process. "It allows us to keep the design in flux as long as possible, and then freeze it at the very last second," explains Fischer. "That's the ideal vision: that up until the point that you actually need to bring the project to site, you are still able to re-form the entire model."

Like previous movements, parametricism has recognizable formal attributes and a set of ideological taboos. It eschews classical, Euclidean geometry—straight lines, rectangles, cubes, cylinders, spheres—and instead employs such dynamic, adaptive, and interactive forms as particles, bundles, networks, fields, swarms, blobs, waves, shells, and cocoons. These shapes and systematic formations interact with one another via scripts and allow for the creation of densely layered architectural and urban schemes.

The computing power that makes parametric design possible allows architects to explore solutions that would otherwise require too much labor. In that way, parametric design allows for and encourages complexity, rather than simplicity.

In a burst of contemporary creativity, ZHA has exploited the capabilities of parametric rendering tools to create progressive buildings and whole cityscapes. Urban areas literally bend to the will of pedestrian traffic; a skyscraper wends and rotates skyward to best capture solar gain.

Zaha Hadid Architects' Kartal-Pendik Masterplan of 2006 redeveloped a former industrial area on Istanbul's Asian side, a 65-million-square-foot (6-million-square-meter) site with suburban towns bounding it on all sides. The architects aimed to incorporate preexisting lines of circulation through the site and into other sections of the surrounding sprawl, which the new masterplan would catalyze. In ZHA's parametric model, these circulation patterns became an important input for generating the urban geometry of the site. To create a deformed grid without a single center, the studio employed a software feature in Autodesk's Maya that is normally used for manipulating hair. The resulting bundle of incoming paths was integrated into larger roads—a main artery spliced with a number of subsidiary parallel thruways.

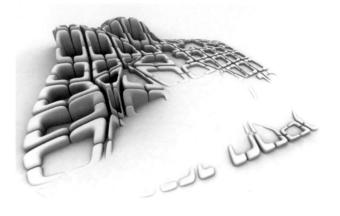

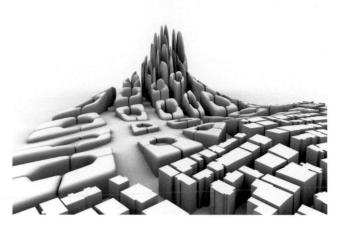

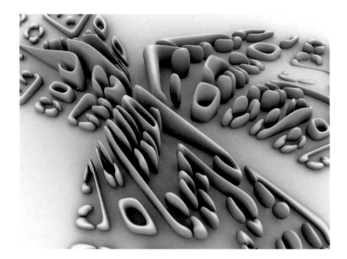

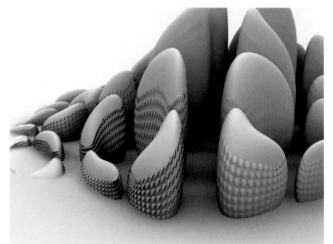

"WE STRONGLY BELIEVE THAT THE NUMBER OF ITERATIONS IS ESSENTIALLY DRIVING THE DESIGN QUALITY."

—

To design perimeter blocks and towers to mark crossing points of subsidiary paths, the team created genotypic scripts that allowed for phenotypic variation. The towers mimic the archetypal form of a cross-tower; on perimeter blocks, courtyards morph into internal atriums as sites get smaller and blocks get taller.

Parametric modeling and in particular the way it allows for design exploration until the last possible moment drives the ZHA studio's process. "We have a lot of internal competitions for ideas or solutions," says Fischer, "and it's usually something that gains in quality with the number of iterations we can run. We try to keep as many ideas alive as long as possible."

Fischer likens using the software to manipulating "a big box of clay." When architects input pertinent information, such as parameters and connections between different information nodes, they can quickly reconfigure the model in real time. "What is really important is the intuitiveness of the feedback," he says. "We really try to develop knowledge platforms that allow us real-time feedback from the design environment."

Computer scripts, using the parameters as inputs, produce a variety of forms. "Architecture is always hundreds or thousands of parts, of different materials, and they need to be coordinated," Schumacher says. "They need to come together. You can only solve this in scripting logics." The number of cycles the scripts can move through is essentially unlimited. "We strongly believe that the number of iterations is essentially driving the design quality," says Fischer.

In the case of the Kartal-Pendik Masterplan, a 136-acre (55-hectare) mixed-use urban field with 65 million square feet (6 million square meters) of buildable surface area on Istanbul's Asian side, ZHA's objective was to redevelop a former industrial zone, link it to surrounding suburban towns, and, ultimately, relieve the city's congested historic center. The parametric model was able to render the preexisting site and conditions and build into this data an entire cityscape.

Aside from rendering buildings around main arteries, the architects also made scripts for building types able to be replicated throughout the site and be appropriate in the variety of urban zones that make up the natural fabric of a city. "Hard and rigid approaches to movement through space are very much driven by the way we like to organize things, but not necessarily by the way we like to use things," Fischer explains. "Rather than having an artificial insert with a clear boundary, we found a strategy that makes the new insert appear to have grown organically." By "calligraphic scripts," ZHA is able to draw thruways and buildings throughout a master plan that simulate a more humanistic and organic architectural field. "The soft grid virtually allows us to negotiate between existing conditions and then, as a result, create spaces in that grid that all have their kind of relative, unique identity," Fischer says. "They're of course similar, because they're a result of a uniform approach, but, at the same time, the resulting geometry is varying at each point."

The more layers of information input into a model, the more dynamic the result. According to Fischer, "the ability to manage or interweave more and more complex data into a clear solution is a kind of key to success for high-quality design." For Spain's Zaragoza Bridge Pavilion, ZHA created a hybrid pedestrian bridge and exhibition space that spans the Ebro, one of Spain's most voluminous rivers. The resulting 886-foot (270-meter) passageway comprises four "pods" that act as both structural support and shelter for exhibition-goers. The firm's most recent bridge project, the Zaragoza Bridge Pavilion required both sophisticated engineering systems and a sensitively designed interior experience. The structure withstands the force of the river while the interior and exterior traverse it, defining the form of the bridge/pavilion.

According to Fischer, this approach requires both a facility with increasingly complex modeling systems and strong management skills: "Technology makes available more and more parameters, so we have to judge the relevance of data and strategize at a very early point in time." Sixty percent of ZHA employees have basic programming knowledge, and there are managers who help shepherd the design process. The studio also employs a couple of programmers who are able to develop tools to bring more and more data into the architects' repertoire.

Instead of feeling overwhelmed by the glut of information, Fischer and other architects who use parametric modeling use their increasingly content-rich data sets, visualized and understandable in highly intuitive 3D environments, to get ever closer to design. And for a firm like ZHA, the real-time feedback regarding economic, structural, and environmental viability enables the studio to find clients who will sign off on seemingly inconceivable programs.

Whether used for a traveling building, like the Chanel Mobile Pavilion, or an entire cityscape like the Kartal-Pendik Masterplan, parametricism changes the manner of construction and level of efficiency. "I think a key part of our work is to demonstrate the viability of our designs, because at the end of the day, if we can't sell it, it's not architecture," says Fischer. With great accuracy, ZHA can assure clients at a very early stage of the process that their parametric models are buildable in ways that, ten years ago, would have seemed completely unfeasible to the average client. **Ⓐ**

For the Zaragoza Bridge Pavilion in Zaragoza, Spain, ZHA researched the potential of a diamond-shaped section that would offer both structural and programming opportunities. The diamond structure is able to distribute force along its surface while maintaining a triangular pocket of space beneath the structure, which can be used for exhibition space.

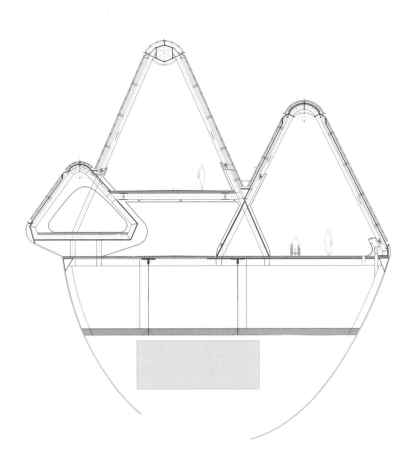

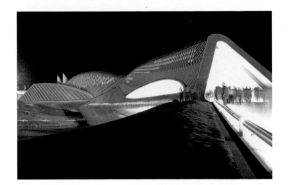

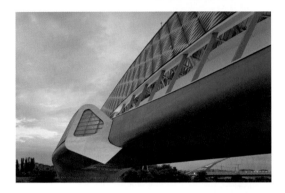

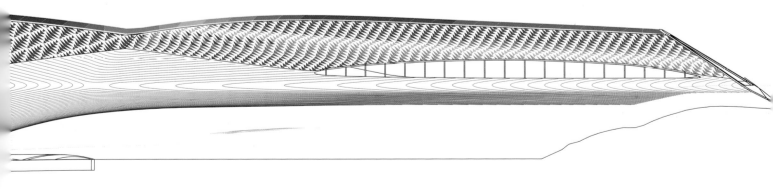

—

FOR A FIRM LIKE ZHA, THE REAL-TIME FEEDBACK REGARDING ECONOMIC, STRUCTURAL, AND ENVIRONMENTAL VIABILITY ENABLES THE STUDIO TO FIND CLIENTS WHO WILL SIGN OFF ON SEEMINGLY INCONCEIVABLE PROGRAMS.

"She is the first architect to find a way to part with the all-dominating post-Bauhaus aesthetic. The value of her designs is similar to that of great poetry. The potential of her imagination is enormous," Karl Lagerfeld said of Zaha Hadid, explaining Chanel's decision to hire ZHA to design the Mobile Art Pavilion, which launched at the 2007 Venice Art Biennale.

The Pavilion's appearance and overall structure were modeled from the parametric distortion of the torus, which creates a continuous variation of exhibition spaces as it expands outward toward its circumference. At its center, a 700-square-foot (65-square-meter) courtyard replete with natural lighting offers an area of natural confluence, where organizers can host events and visitors can congregate. The layout also allows for a highly visible viewing experience.

Set to travel over three continents, the Pavilion structure is easily broken down into reduced arched segments—each measuring no wider than 7.4 feet (2.25 meters)—which facilitates handling and shipping the Pavilion across the globe. The segment seams also become a strong formal feature of the exterior facade and reflect the seams in Chanel's iconic quilted bag, which is the formal inspiration for both the Pavilion and the artwork showcased within it.

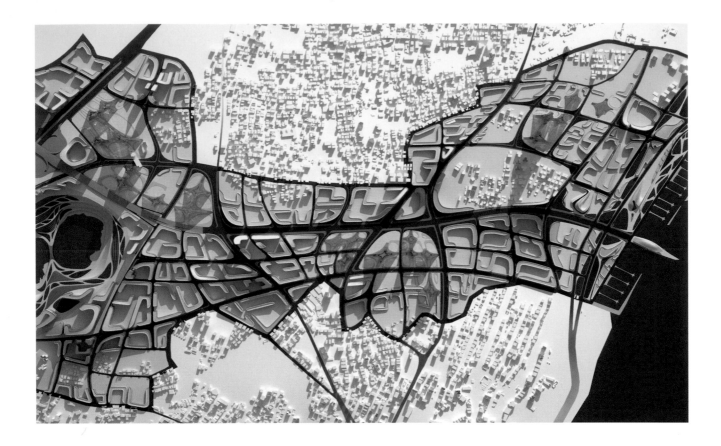

—

IN A BURST OF CONTEMPORARY CREATIVITY, ZAHA HADID ARCHITECTS HAS EXPLOITED THE CAPABILITIES OF PARAMETRIC RENDERING TOOLS TO CREATE PROGRESSIVE BUILDINGS AND WHOLE CITYSCAPES.

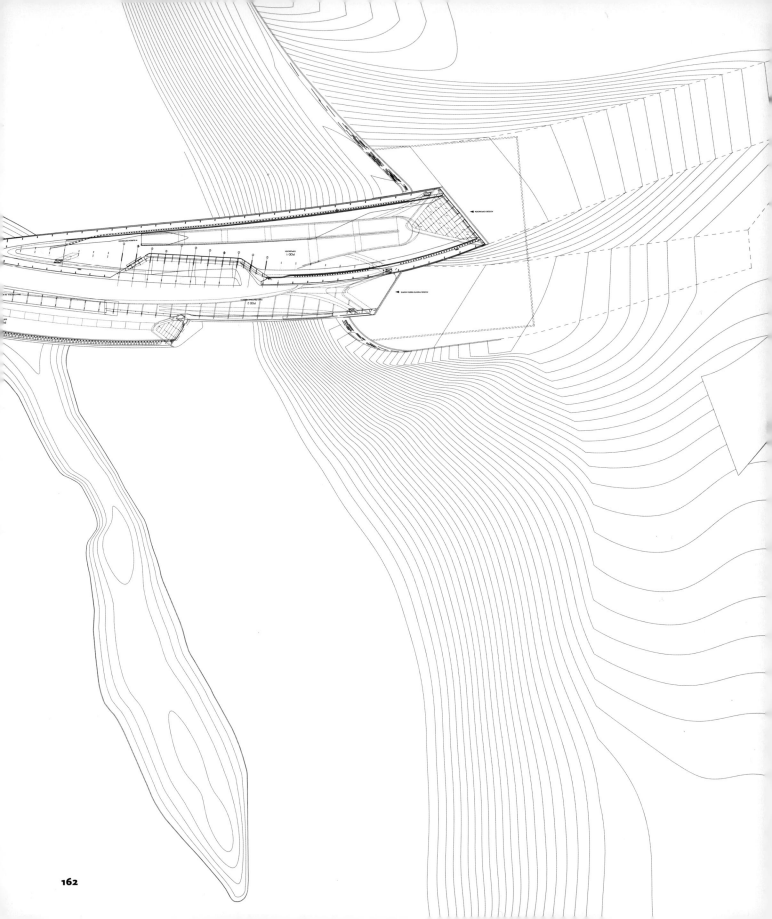

With the aid of parametric modeling, the architects were able to extrude the diamond sections along a slightly curved path, generating four separate "pods" or service sections within the Pavilion. The variable stacking and interlocking truss systems allow for architectural variety within the interior while composing a sound structural system for the bridge, which spans the Ebro River, one of Spain's largest tributaries. The pods are stacked so as to reduce the Zaragoza Bridge Pavilion's section along the 509-foot (155-meter) span from the island to the middle of the river to the right bank and enlarge it across the 410-foot (125-meter) span from the island to the expo riverbank.

The Bridge Pavilion is enveloped in a permeable skin, which offers protection from the elements while offering visitors views of the natural surroundings. An internal microenvironment requires a minimal heating and cooling infrastructure. The designers also looked to naturally occurring forms for inspiration. For example, the exterior skin is modeled after shark scales, which can easily wrap complex forms with a simple system of rectilinear elements. The skin comprises two elements: a lower deck of structural metal plates and an upper deck clad in a system of glass-reinforced concrete panels composed in a gradient of white to black.

ROBERT AISH

A computing leader describes emerging tools and processes for design.

Design computation, the use of computing to generate and analyze form and performance, seems to mark a change in the way designers think. What is significant about design computation?

Until recently, the majority of design tools used computer-graphics technologies to mimic the way users interact with existing design media. The engagement between the designer and subject, as mediated through these design tools, is very similar to the designer interacting with the original physical media.

With design computation, designers have the possibility to create a framework within which they can generate and explore different design alternatives.

What's different about using design computation in practice?

I would characterize the difference between a regular design application and a design computation application as the difference between a word processor and a spreadsheet.

Let's say I'm working out my mortgage. With the word processor, I can make a table of numbers and add them up.

The numbers might not add up properly, but the program doesn't know that. I am not constrained: Anything goes.

With a spreadsheet, you define relationships. You set up rules for the mortgage calculation. Here I want to be constrained to the underlying mortgage calculation, because I want to play "What if?" What if I buy a bigger house or the interest rate goes up? It may not be worthwhile to use a spreadsheet for a single calculation, but if you anticipate exploring alternative scenarios, then you understand the value of designing your own spreadsheet. Once you've done that, you can play "What if?" And you get, potentially, much more interesting results.

It's up to you to build the model that works for you. With the spreadsheet, as with design computation, you have to spend some time setting up the rules that you think are important. Then you can play "What if?" on two levels. You can play within that one set of rules, or you can change the rules and play within a different set.

How does one approach design using a framework?

The designer is creating a framework within which he can make a "design exploration" by generating and evaluating alternatives. To do that, he has the opportunity to reformat the design process into a system with inputs and outputs.

What are the input or "driver" variables that will be used to generate the alternative design solutions? These might include aspect ratio, floor-to-floor height, column spacing, percentage glazing, etc. What are the measures that will be used to evaluate and predict the different alternatives? These might include energy consumption or structural efficiency, but we should not forget other measures, such as comfort, that will relate to how the design is actually experienced. What may also be important is how these different performance measures are combined and translated into some composite economic indicator, like cost per square foot or value for money.

This actually opens up further possibilities. Because the design is controlled by a limited number of driver variables and can be evaluated by a limited number of performance measures, there is the possibility that we can automate the generation and evaluation—and, hence, the optimization—of the design.

How does the use of design computation differ from the use of existing design applications?

The "anything goes" versus "What if?" dichotomy has its equivalent in the world of design tools. In a traditional design application, the designer can model any geometry and has complete freedom to change any geometry created. But there are many situations where creating and editing geometry through direct manipulation does not allow the designer to create the subtlety of result that may be desired.

Imagine that the designer is working on a complex, doubly curved roof that will be realized as a series of panel components. For the subtle designer, there may be some interesting concepts in play, some formalisms that he wants to use to characterize the whole design. For example, he may want to explore the balance between *commonality* and *variation*: Which aspects of the panels are common and which aspects are unique? Perhaps the unique aspects of the panels are determined by their position in the overall roof configuration. He may also be interested in *transitions*: how the panels gradually change from one side of the roof to the other. The creative designer might argue that part of his originality is to construct—and apply—his own design rules to play his own "what ifs." The last thing he wants to do is to be forced to manually draw all the panels. That would be exhausting. The designer would never have the time or effort to explore the subtlety of this concept.

With design computation, the emphasis is on the designer constructing and tuning the design rules generating the model, propagating these rules through to the detailed design of each roof panel.

I don't want to give the impression that design computation precludes user interaction or direct manipulation. Instead, I want to encourage the designer to use direct manipulation in a truly form-generating way—for example, changing the underlying roof surface geometry and watching all the roof panels automatically update. Now we have this amazingly powerful combination of logic and intuition. The designer is manipulating the surface geometry intuitively and interactively, but what is being regenerated is the unique design logic that he has originated.

That sounds like a very different approach to design.

Yes, designers won't directly design the building. They will design the framework, which will generate different alternative designs for them. Design computation is helping the designer to reengineer the process of designing.

Understanding how to harness the new process and how to build computation design models may require a new way of thinking on the part of the designer.

Design computation is changing the design process, from creating a single design solution to stepping back and asking, "What is the fundamental basis of this design?"—not just this particular design alternative, but a whole family of designs. ⓐ

Robert Aish is director of software development at Autodesk.

—

"The emphasis is on the designer constructing and tuning the design rules generating the model."

MARRIOTT: THINKING FASTER INSIDE THE BOX

Feeling pressure from the changing market, this leading hospitality brand went into design overdrive with the aid of 3D prototyping.

Digital prototyping was a revelation for Marriott and its property owners, bringing profound changes to the hospitality giant's long-standing design process. The result was an accelerated move from digital design (top) to physical construction (bottom).

IN THE YEARS AFTER J. WILLARD MARRIOTT OPENED HIS FIRST HOTEL in Arlington, Virginia, in 1959, his guests—chiefly a pioneering group of business travelers—came to expect one thing from the expanding chain of Marriott hotels: uniformity of appearance and experience. The room design, the look and feel of Marriott hotels, and the building architecture were a matter of strict consistency. In those early days of the modern hotel, there was a lot of value in offering travelers a predictable and high-quality experience.

Fifty years on, Marriott International owns or manages some 3,500 properties in the United States and sixty-nine other countries and territories and stands as one of the world's most recognizable hotel brands. In fact, Marriott is no longer just one brand but eighteen, including Marriott Courtyard, Fairfield, Residence, Springhill Suites, and Towne Place Suites.

Marriott may have once been largely about creating a consistent image—but consistency is now simply an expected quality. Today, the interior design of hotels—chiefly lobbies and guest rooms—has become more important to the average consumer. People expect diverse designs and contemporary and fresh-looking spaces. The increasing prevalence of boutique hotels like those built by Ian Schrager has pushed interest in design into the far reaches of the lodging industry. Guests have been influenced by a spate of interior-design television shows and designer furniture to the point that many have come to expect creative and contemporary designs at the hotels where they stay.

Instead of consistency, the challenge for Marriott is more often about presenting a variety of designs and being able to change designs in a fluid manner. "Originally we wanted to be the same thing to everybody, everywhere," says John Bauer, director of design management at Marriott. "Now, with each brand, we're really looking at experiences that are more unique, and we're expanding into different markets and in different areas. Now it's not so much about frequency as it is about creating more variety across the portfolio."

As tastes shifted, Marriott found that its guests' needs and demands were changing faster than it could react. The company needed a new process that allowed it to move faster in exploring new design ideas, getting them approved, and bringing them to market.

At the most basic level, a hotel room is a box filled with a fairly typical set of items—a bed, a lamp, and a television. (In the shorthand used by procurement professionals, these are FF&E, or furniture, fixtures, and equipment.) Though basic on paper, for a visiting guest these items—as well as a host of other specific décor choices—play an increasingly important role in determining the quality of a visit. The rise of boutique hotels has cranked up hotel visitors' expectations and sent leading hotel brands like Marriott into design overdrive.

"ORIGINALLY WE WANTED TO BE THE SAME THING TO EVERYBODY, EVERYWHERE. NOW, WITH EACH BRAND, WE'RE REALLY LOOKING AT EXPERIENCES THAT ARE MORE UNIQUE, AND WE'RE ALSO EXPANDING INTO DIFFERENT MARKETS AND DIFFERENT AREAS."

—

"Over the past few years, owners, franchisees, and especially guests have become far more design savvy, as they've digested it through magazines, popular media, and television shows," says Bauer. "Our hotels have had to be far more sophisticated in their approach to design. We've really had to amp up the amount of design that goes into our hotels."

Almost all of the hotels in Marriott's large portfolio are not owned by the company itself but by separate hotel owners or franchisees. These owners turn to Marriott initially to brand their properties—and then to continue to change and upgrade them over time with Marriott's focus group– and research-driven new ideas. A typical hotel sees a "soft" upgrade every three years and a larger-scale "hard" upgrade or renovation every six years—such are the demands of the industry for change.

These days, Marriott is essentially an innovation company in which a constant loopprocesses consumer research and yields new and different hotel alterations. In recent years, for example, this has included transforming once bare lobbies into more engaging spaces. With each innovation comes a slew of concepts that need to be vetted by a range of interested parties, including Marriottexecutives and the owners of the many hotels.

With the rising importance of design, old ways of working hindered Marriott's forward progression, cost it a lot of money, and slowed down its time to market with new concepts. All of this has meant that time-tested techniques for altering and modernizing hotel interior design had to be streamlined and made more efficient. Across the board, Marriott has turned to a range of sophisticated technologies to address change in its products—from lamps to entire lobby redesigns.

Listening to executives from Marriott's broad design team discuss the changes that have swept the company, one hears a constant refrain of "in the past" versus the present. Thanks in large part to the implementation of Autodesk software, workflow has been quickly migrating from 2D to

High-resolution 3D rendering of new rooms—created to address rising competition within the industry—not only helped owners buy in to new design approaches but also got them excited for the changes.

3D, with the company barely stopping to look back.

"We need to share our latest designs with the hotel owners for renovation projects and new builds," explains Karim Khalifa, senior vice president of architecture and construction at Marriott. Adds COO Arne Sorenson, "The biggest advantage we're finding is in the use of technology. In years past, to take an idea about what a hotel ought to look like and make it a reality for our owners and franchisees would have required us to go through the architecture process, the design process, and the build process in order to show them what we were thinking about. By doing that faster and through digital imaging tools, we have a much higher level of confidence that what we ultimately turn around and build is what we want."

Dave Lippert, vice president for procurement for Marriott's Architecture and Construction group, tells the story of a lamp design process at Marriott: "About three years ago, we had a major new lamp

that we had implemented in our full-service room hotels. Everyone was interested in it, from our owners to our designers. What was that lamp going to look like? What capabilities was it going to have? Would it fit in the room? Every time we got a new sample in, it would get passed around the building, and it would be sent to other buildings for people to review it. Everybody would make changes to it. Then we'd send it back to the vendor, give them the feedback, and ten or twelve weeks later, they'd come back with another sample. It would go through the same process." Today, things have changed in that the lamp vendor designs the lamp and then provides it to Lippert and his team in a digital format, so that they can provide direct feedback on things like shape, color, and dimensions. Now the design cycle of such a lamp can be crunched from six months to six weeks.

"In our new design process, we have the ability with technology to go through rapid iterations of designs that we want to review,

to make sure that they are appropriate for the goals of the initiative," says Deborah Huguely, vice president of product development. "With a quick click of the button, you're testing out fabrics, patterns, colors, architectural features, and lighting styles."

Huguely was one of the Marriott executives in charge of proving the concept of using 3D visualization to approve new ideas and room designs. The big idea was that instead of actually building new rooms and lobbies to gain consensus and approval, such "building" would happen on the computer. Large photos could subsequently be printed and hung to give a sense of the actual scale of the new environments. It was a bold idea with the potential to save a lot of time and money—but it was also a big change.

Huguely and her group created a 3D model of a guest room that happened to be one built in Marriott's corporate headquarters and that all the participating executives knew well. "We did a review of

that 3D model for our senior executives and presented the photographs," she explains. "Those photographs represented the room, as well as how we would see it in advertising. We showed them to the executives, but did not tell them that it was the 3D model. They said, 'Oh, this is great. Now show us what you can do with 3D modeling.' And we said, 'Well, you're looking at it,'" says Huguely. "We said, 'Aha!' We had broken through. We could move forward with getting reviews from our owners, our franchisees, and our senior executives on design and innovation."

Visualization, or digital prototyping, in essence replaces the centuries-old process of model building, material selection, and drawing. In the past, Marriott used AutoCAD for just building and design documentation. Now, designers at the company are using AutoCAD software to make vivid 3D renders and photorealistic depictions of guest rooms and lobbies. One example of the new process is a recent décor

Marriott's designers presented new room and lobby visualizations on life-sized walls, allowing property owners to experience the designs in full fidelity and in a way they were comfortable with from past design reviews.

"WE SHOWED THEM TO THE EXECUTIVES, BUT DID NOT TELL THEM THAT IT WAS THE 3D MODEL. THEY SAID, 'OH, THIS IS GREAT. NOW SHOW US WHAT YOU CAN DO WITH 3D MODELING.' WE SAID, 'AHA!' WE HAD BROKEN THROUGH."

—

IN THE PAST, THE TEAM WOULD CREATE A PHYSICAL PROTOTYPE, WITH LIGHTING, FABRICS, AND FURNITURE, AND DISPLAY IT IN AN EXISTING HOTEL LOBBY. TYPICALLY, THIS PHYSICAL PROTOTYPE COST $250,000 AND GREATLY DISTURBED HOTEL GUESTS.

—

Using digital prototypes has provided cost savings in the hundreds of thousands of dollars compared with Marriott's traditional approach of building full-size physical prototypes.

initiative for a hotel lobby. In the past, the team would create a physical prototype, with lighting, fabrics, and furniture, and display it in an existing hotel lobby. Typically, this physical prototype cost $250,000 and greatly disturbed hotel guests. A hotel had to be chosen, and then, upon completion of the prototype, large groups of stakeholders would fly in to discuss the project in person.

"With the advent of Autodesk 3ds Max three-dimensional design software, we've been able to take our two-dimensional hotel designs and put them in three dimensions, allowing our owners to see the designs in a realistic format before the hotels are actually built. It's a real cost savings for our owners. And it's really helped us articulate our design prior to document-

ing it," says Thomas Kelley, design manager for Marriott.

"We just did a lobby mock-up based on virtual modeling that we executed for just a few thousand dollars. Compare that—a lobby that's done virtually for a few thousand dollars—with $100,000 or $500,000 for a lobby that's fully built out and ready for someone to walk through. We got to the point where, in the same place folks were approving it, they were saying, 'Great, let's go forward with this. Let's move.' That was a huge win for us," says Bauer. Ⓐ

TOOLS
HOW DOES TECHNOLOGY CHANGE DESIGN?

THE IMPACT OF TECHNOLOGY ON DESIGN OVER THE PAST HALF CENTURY HAS BEEN UNDENIABLE. BY AUGMENTING HUMAN SKILLS AND, IN PARTICULAR, BY AUTO- MATING SOME OF THE MECHANICAL ACTIVITIES ASSOCIATED WITH THE DESIGN PROCESS (SUCH AS SKETCHING AND MODELING), NEW TOOLS HAVE ENABLED DESIGNERS TO WORK FAR MORE EFFICIENTLY. BUT EFFICIENCY IS ONE THING AND EFFICACY IS ANOTHER. ARE THE TOOLS OF DESIGN ACTUALLY HELPING TO PRODUCE BETTER DESIGN?

—

previous spread: **Parsons Brinck- erhoff built a complete 3D digi- tal model of its SR 520 Bridge replacement near Seattle.**

What's abundantly clear in these stories of how new tools are influencing the work of design leaders is that technology is playing a central—and increasingly creative—role in the design process.

In the recent past, as designers transitioned from pencil sketches and blueprints to the use of computer-aided design, the chief benefit was to help them better document and visualize their plans, and to do so more quickly. But new digital tools are moving well beyond documentation and representation; they are enabling designers to explore more possibilities, to try more variations and iterations on a particular idea, and to conduct analysis on designs much earlier and more exhaustively.

Is there a downside to the continued rise of sophisticated design tools? A danger, perhaps, that the machines may begin to dictate design choices and directions? What seems clear at this juncture and for the foreseeable future is that human judgment will continue to prevail; technology will offer up more options and choices than ever before, but the designer will make the final call. This is not to say, however, that designers won't be influenced by tools and technology. The new tools of virtual cinematography helped shape James Cameron's *Avatar*, for example, just as much as Autodesk Revit software guided how the architecture firm KieranTimberlake went about making the Loblolly House.

As advanced tools make it possible to get to prototype faster, the designer may find there is less time for applying the considered eye. And as designers rush to take advantage of the most compelling and popular new capabilities on the computer, there is always the danger they will be influenced by some of the same sources—which could result in less-distinctive work.

But designers demonstrate every day that there is always room for the unique stamp of creativity to shine through. Indeed, in many ways design tools can free up the imagination of the designer to explore and try more ideas—including more unusual or fanciful possibilities. Those enhanced tools may also encourage designers to tackle the toughest challenges and problems—which may begin to seem slightly less daunting to a designer who's better equipped for the task. Ⓐ

AVATAR AND THE BIRTH OF VIRTUAL CINEMATOGRAPHY

How James Cameron's new, high-tech approach to filmmaking created a fresh and powerful journey to another world.

ANYONE WHO HAS SEEN *AVATAR* IS NO DOUBT AWARE of some details of how it was made. We know about director James Cameron's financial gamble—how he turned the biggest budget in Hollywood history into the biggest hit of all time. And we know about the groundbreaking experimental tools he used to turn the movie into a sort of R&D lab for Hollywood effects. A facial tracking system turned the actors' performances into preternaturally expressive animated characters. Prototype 3D cameras helped push the 3D format across the novelty threshold into a respected creative medium.

Yet the most profound technology to come out of *Avatar* is a good deal less famous and less understood. It's the virtual camera: a modest-looking gadget with a small video screen, a joystick, and a few buttons that allow makers of computer-generated films to immerse themselves inside an artificial world, adding cohesiveness and artistic control in ways that were never before possible in digital film.

Until recently, computer-generated film sequences had been plagued by synthetic-looking cinematography—a by-product of a production system in which directors handed off visual-effects sequences to animation teams. The director would tell the effects specialists what he wanted, wait weeks or months for the result, and then make a few small revisions before generating a final print. The process was laborious and disjointed, and it allowed for precious little of the spontaneous trial-and-error direction that's so common in live-action moviemaking. Although visually impressive, the finished products tend to remind viewers that what they're seeing is artificial. "Too often we get live-action parts that don't allow enough time or space for a computer-generated creature, so it ends up as a rushed scene or something that feels squished," says *Avatar*'s animation supervisor, Richie Baneham.

In *Avatar*, 80 percent of the film would be computer generated, with many scenes that involved taut, emotional interchanges between 9-foot-tall blue people. Motion-capture systems would enable real actors to provide a lifelike foundation for characters' movements and facial expressions, but Cameron wanted *Avatar* to feel absolutely real. That meant he needed a way to direct the actors in each scene using traditional filmmaking techniques, such as finessing timing and positioning to amplify the texture of emotional exchanges.

The virtual camera made that possible. Put simply, it's an innovative device that allowed Cameron to shoot footage inside a virtual world as if he were walking through a real space with a traditional film camera. Though it looks nothing like a traditional camera, the virtual camera provides most of the features and functionality of a traditional camera—as well as the familiar Hollywood motorcade of cranes, dollies, and platforms. In a single device, Cameron was able to re-create an entire suite of tools from an earlier era of filmmaking—a time when

Performance capture and state-of-the-art CGI helped create the luminous Na'vi in *Avatar*. But it was virtual cinematography that brought Pandora's people to life.

CAMERON WANTED <u>AVATAR</u> TO FEEL ABSOLUTELY REAL. THAT MEANT HE NEEDED A WAY TO DIRECT THE ACTORS IN EACH SCENE USING TRADITIONAL FILMMAKING TECHNIQUES, SUCH AS FINESSING TIMING AND POSITIONING TO AMPLIFY THE TEXTURE OF EMOTIONAL EXCHANGES.

—

the essentials of a scene were just a director, a camera, and an actor. That, in turn, enabled Cameron to bring a more human touch to his computer-generated film.

"When you see photos of Cameron on the set of *Avatar*, you might think of those shots of Cecil B. DeMille shouting through the megaphone at his actors," says film professor Bob Rehak of Swarthmore College. "In some blockbusters, you know the director is in there somewhere, but you know others supply the razzle-dazzle. Cameron's system puts him back into the filmmaking process, so we understand him to be the author of the film—not just a cog in an elaborate production."

The virtual camera was a relatively late addition to *Avatar*'s production process, and it started out as a clever hack. On a cue from his friend Rob Legato, the visual-effects supervisor from *Titanic*, Cameron started looking for a device that would help him control the camera movement in *Avatar*. His production team had already designed an entire Pandora world of plants, trees, and animals, rendered in

low-resolution 3D inside its computers. The trick, as Cameron envisioned it, would be to create a device that could capture a camera-like view of this world in a realistic way.

Cameron asked Hollywood camera and prop expert Glenn Derry to build something that might get the job done. A relentless tinkerer, Derry had worked on the animatronic dinos in *Jurassic Park* early in his career, and he now runs Technoprops, a small electronics-prototyping workshop in Los Angeles. "The only resources I had at my disposal were Jim, who pushed the concepts, and the software coders, who connected it to Autodesk MotionBuilder [animation software]," Derry recalls.

Derry started by modifying a traditional camera. He hollowed out the film mechanism, removed the eyepiece, and replaced it with a small video screen. A piece of software called Overdrive recorded the camera's moves through the virtual space, while engineers at Derry's shop prototyped hard nylon buttons for zoom, film speed, and other controls and then coded the electronics to talk to the software. Covering

Making *Avatar* involved several layers of action. Actors worked in a performance capture studio to create one layer; their performances appeared in computer-rendered 3D scenes. Cameron could then freely move the virtual camera through those scenes to fully frame and direct the action. Eventually, the scenes would be rendered in high-resolution.

Following pages: Two finished scenes from *Avatar* reveal how completely action was rendered in the world of Pandora. At left, Jake Sully explores Pandora's jungle soon after arriving on the planet. At right, Sully pilots a Toruk after he has joined with the Na'vi tribe.

the camera with reflective markers made it possible for a motion-capture system to track its exact position in the room and re-create the operator's movements inside the 3D world of Pandora, so that the camera's tiny screen showed a real-time view of Pandora's synthetic world as the camera operator moved around the space. Finally, with the device on his shoulder, Cameron wandered around the giant empty room of the motion-capture soundstage. But inside his viewfinder, he saw something very different: the lush terrain of Pandora, through which he could navigate and shoot as if it were a physical set.

To make the virtual camera easier to hold, Cameron and Derry eventually decided to abandon the traditional camera shape and turn it into a steering wheel–type gadget with a screen in the middle. That, too, proved cumbersome, so Derry installed a center-mounted LCD screen with a counterbalancing system that ensured the screen would always face the camera operator, no matter at what angle the camera was held. Whether he held on to it by its side

handles, swung it over his head to get a high shot, or lowered it to the floor, the operator could still see the screen. Additional tweaking enabled MotionBuilder to zoom out or close in to change the camera's perspective, so the director could pretend he was standing on a 60-foot platform above the action. The virtual camera not only replaced a traditional camera but also a cumbersome array of cranes, dollies, and platforms.

As shooting progressed and Cameron became more comfortable with the virtual camera, its enormous ramifications became clear. The virtual camera enabled the director to shoot *Avatar* as if it were a live-action film, even when all the actors were portraying scenes in an otherwise-empty motion-capture room. Actors' movements were tracked by more than 100 motion-capture cameras suspended from the ceiling; and with banks of computers working hard behind the scenes, their performances could be realistically translated into those of 9-foot-tall Na'vi characters in real time. The renderings weren't final—images seen through the virtual camera tend to look

INSIDE HIS VIEWFINDER, HE SAW SOMETHING VERY DIFFERENT: THE LUSH TERRAIN OF PANDORA, WHICH HE COULD NAVIGATE AND SHOOT AS IF IT WERE A PHYSICAL SET.

—

like sophisticated video games rather than photorealistic movies—but nevertheless, the virtual camera could grab their performances from any direction and provide a useful perspective on how the finished scene would look.

With the new equipment in place, the shooting schedule proceeded like no animated film before. First thing in the morning, before the actors arrived for work, Cameron would walk around the motion-capture soundstage with the virtual camera, scouting Pandora for appropriate locations for the day's shoot. Handmade plywood platforms matched the terrain of the virtual world, reproducing the alien planet's bumps and valleys exactly. Later, the actors—say, Sam Worthington (who played Jake Sully) and Zoe Saldana (Neytiri)—would arrive on the motion-capture stage covered in reflective dots. They would play the scene using the powers of imagination to envision themselves as 9-foot-tall blue creatures, surrounded by Pandora's exotic plants, vines, and ferocious beasts. But as seen through Cameron's virtual camera, the scene unfolded with all those features in place as he established the exact camera angles he wanted to use in the film.

Feature films are typically shot using both wide and tight camera shots in the same scenes to provide a variety of perspectives on the actors' performances. To do that for *Avatar*, Cameron waited until the end of the day, when the motion-capture room was empty. Alone again in the space, he would replay the scenes that had been captured that day—including the actor's performances and the 3D backgrounds—through the virtual camera, so that it looked as if the scene was unfolding right in front of him during a live-action shoot. He could walk around this world, picking new camera angles for additional shots or reshooting the original camera work from the live performance. "We always shot in real time, but whether Jim chose to use that camera move was up to him," says Derry. "Typically, Jim wanted a more refined camera move, so he would look for something better later."

When he was satisfied, Cameron's work with the virtual camera captured a final scene that functioned as the template for the way it would look in theaters. From there, the template was shipped to animators at Weta Digital, who replaced the relatively crude, video-game-style backgrounds with high-resolution art and digitally manipulated the characters' gestures to enhance their subtle facial expressions. For anyone who saw *Avatar*, the intricate detail and verisimilitude of the final product are unforgettable.

Handheld virtual cameras allowed Cameron to direct performers at the same time as he manipulated the rendered, virtual scene within the computer.

AS CAMERON BECAME MORE COMFORTABLE WITH THE VIRTUAL CAMERA, ITS ENORMOUS RAMIFICATIONS BECAME CLEAR. THE VIRTUAL CAMERA ENABLED CAMERON TO SHOOT <u>AVATAR</u> AS IF IT WERE A LIVE-ACTION FILM.

—

Indeed, on the heels of *Avatar*'s success, virtual cameras are now being used—with Cameron's blessing—on productions all over the world, and other directors are developing their own ways of using the virtual camera. For the fall 2011 animated film *Tintin,* Steven Spielberg asked Derry to shoot with the virtual camera almost entirely in real time as actors ran through the live scene. To do that, Derry set up two virtual cameras that ran simultaneously on set to capture both wide and tight shots. Although *Tintin* is animated, "Spielberg literally shot it like a movie," Derry says. "We'd do a setup, point the virtual camera at it, get a take, get another take with a closeup, and move on to the next scene."

For director Shawn Levy's fall 2011 *Real Steel,* in which giant robots hold boxing matches over Detroit and other cities, Derry used a more evolved version of the virtual camera that was introduced at the tail end of the *Avatar* production. To shoot scenes that mixed live-action and computer-generated images, Cameron and Derry built a souped-up virtual camera called the Simulcam that lets a camera operator see animated characters interacting with live actors in the frame. "In *Real Steel,* we can

see the robots out there duking it out, and it's working pretty well," says Derry. "Luckily, I was able to prototype stuff on the most expensive movie ever made, so now I get to go out on a film with a $100 million budget and use the same tools."

Gradually, the virtual camera is becoming a fixture in Hollywood, and that's good news for computer-generated films in general. In an age when the vision-driven cinematography of film auteurs was in danger of getting swallowed up by high-tech production systems, the virtual camera is reestablishing the director's ability to give computer-generated film a more human feel.

"All this stuff gives us back the filmmaker on the set having very intimate directing moments with his actors," says Swarthmore's Rehak. "It helps contradict the typical complaint about digital processes—that cameras are going away and film is going away, so that reality itself disappears into pure simulation." *Avatar*'s virtual camera may reverse that trend by giving directors a more hands-on tool they can use to enhance the illusion of reality even when films are almost entirely digital. Ⓐ

PETER SKILLMAN

The product-design veteran discusses the origins of the design impulse—and the next step in the evolution of our design tools.

Where does good design originate for you? How do you lead and foster the design spark outside of yourself?

I took a class from a Bay Area figurative painter, Nathan Oliveira, many years ago. He was part of the Bay Area Figurative Movement that included David Park, Elmer Bischoff, and a number of other people. We were in the studio, and he had just painted this incredible abstract expression of a hawk's wing. It was from a series of paintings he did based on found objects. I asked him whether he had just created it or whether there had been a big process that had resulted in it—and does the process matter?

His answer has really influenced my thinking about process and how you manage design, how you can influence it, and how you inspire people. He said it doesn't matter if you implement a structured process or if, in a flash of inspiration, you just create something without any process at all.

People in business school have been trying to train and manage creative people for decades. It usually fails, because it's so unbelievably difficult to manage the process of creativity. It was Linus Pauling who said, "If you want to have a good idea, you have to have thousands of ideas." And Einstein said that if an idea doesn't sound absurd at first, then there's no hope for it.

You have to let this messy process go on, sometimes in the absence of process, and just trust that creative people—with the right amount of support and input and even critical design reviews—can do something great. Then you have to find out which people would benefit from process and which people are better left alone.

What can spark good design is often letting go, and other times you need to micromanage it. And the genius in managing great design is in deciding when to apply the right rules based on your empathy for the problem and the individuals and teams involved.

That sounds like it's more of an art than a science.

What Nathan Oliveira said is that it doesn't matter. As long as a solution is great, it doesn't matter how you get there. In the context of what I learned at IDEO, originally it was enlightened trial and error succeeding over the lone genius. But I've since learned through many examples that another completely valid way to manage or inspire people is the lone genius succeeding over enlightened trial and error.

Dennis Boyle taught me that a picture is worth a thousand words, and a prototype is worth a thousand pictures or ten thousand words. Nurturing those vulnerable things is really important. I also think that communities and teams benefit from diversity, and in my experience, teams with women are always better than all-male teams—and cultures for that matter.

Another thing that is important in making good design happen is that you must connect to how things are made. That concept is really being challenged with the rapid loss of manufacturing to Asia. If you don't connect to the processes of how things are made, you really lose your ability to design effectively.

—

"Ultimately, tools and technology can give you the power to create mediocrity on a vast scale."

Some things that you haven't mentioned are technology and the tools that enable people to create. What do you think the evolving technology is doing for design?

There are a couple different views on that. If we start with the more curmudgeonly view, I think the ultimate example of this is Paul Rand. In his book *Design Form and Chaos*, he decried the computer as this evil and extolled students to draw more.

If you look at the advent of desktop publishing, which pushed tools upon people with little experience, it resulted in flyers with 15 different fonts. Ultimately, tools and technology can give you the power to create mediocrity on a vast scale.

The upside is that this democratization of tools results in really broad education that refines everyone's tastes and skills by raising a level of sensitivity across the board. So I don't think it's all a bad thing, but it can be really scary. Beware of the lollipop of mediocrity. You lick it once, and you suck forever.

What do you think is the future of design? What's next?

I think that the technology that helps frame learning is the next big phase shift in tools. User behavior such as click flows can enable intelligent agents to guide people toward really good solutions. Tools move from the language of production and instead are entering a world of creativity as an adjunct or as a tool for more than just executing tedious jobs. They are also becoming effective principal players.

Technology shouldn't be a hindrance to invention but rather a link between your mind and your work. I think the key here is that technology at its best is an extension that allows you to more deeply connect your mind and your work. At its worst, it's a barrier.

The UI [user interface] and the user experience of how you manipulate these tools are the most fundamental things that are going to drive this. The direct manipulation UI that's modeled on the physical manifestations of how people live spatially is really key. The Windows-mouse-pointer interface is likely going to move away. All you have to do is look at John Underkoffler's work in the future of gestures. He's the guy who did the UI for the film *Minority Report*.

He says that in five years you're going to see special UI exploding on the scene, making design tools even more democratized. The technology will become more transparent so that the user interfaces reflect more how people think spatially. The tools themselves become an extension of and expand your creative potential rather than interpreting what you're trying to do.

> "The upside is that this democratization of tools results in really broad education that refines everyone's tastes and skills by raising a level of sensitivity across the board."
>
> —

All of those design principles will embody themselves in tools that make technology more accessible to people so that they can do more creative things. So I'm actually not in the Paul Rand camp. I am really optimistic about how the technologies are going to extend what people are going to be able to do.

Agents need to be intelligent enough to guide people toward solutions. But nothing is more dangerous or pisses people off more than an intelligent agent making the wrong choice for you. **A**

Peter Skillman is a vice president of user experience at Nokia.

FORD'S VIRTUAL TEST TRACK
Ford's new design process uses digital visualization tools to save time, reduce cost, and create more beautiful vehicles.

THE DESIGNERS WORKING ON THE NEXT-GENERATION FORD EXPLORER WERE FEELING THE PRESSURE. Concept cars are easy to sketch, but it's much harder to reinvent an icon. The Ford Explorer was the quintessential SUV of the late 1990s—a vehicle that could simultaneously seat a family of seven comfortably, pull a 20-foot boat down the road, and dominate sales across the entire auto industry. But nearly a decade later, the Explorer had become a period piece, selling a tenth of the units it did during its heyday and drawing jeers from the automotive press.

At the time of the Explorer redesign in early 2007, the fight to modernize the SUV reflected a larger struggle to save Ford. Heavily in the red, Ford implemented a bold new product design process that was viewed as an essential part of the automaker's turnaround plan. Traditional automotive design techniques used time-consuming hand-drawn illustration and clay models to represent vehicle forms, but Ford's new process, which was first introduced in 2005, provides a more sophisticated way to respond to competitive market changes—or completely rethink a design midstream—without missing a beat. Digital visualization technology is the key; Ford designers now generate design concepts using high-resolution digital concept drawings that they can share on a giant screen, and even take for virtual test-drives in video-game landscapes.

Ford's new virtual design process emphasizes the use of computer-generated vehicles, which allow Ford's multidisciplinary product teams to refine vehicle designs quickly and efficiently. The process has already generated clear results, yielding a string of successful vehicle makeovers such as the 2010 Taurus (sales up 99 percent), 2011 Fiesta (a popular global model redesigned for the U.S.), and 2011 Explorer (which became a darling of the auto critics, even months before its consumer introduction). The process has also helped Ford cut its development time dramatically since 2005 and contributed to the $2.3 billion profit Ford earned during the first half of 2010.

Within Ford, employees see a direct connection between the company's current winning streak and its new design process. "Visualization technologies allow us to generate more ideas. Then you can focus those ideas quickly," explains Jeff Nowak, a Ford chief designer and manager of digital design tools. "That buys you more time to refine so you get a better product at the end of the day."

The genesis of every new Ford vehicle takes place in the digital world and evolves via high-definition video displays that are an integral part of the company's product development process. Ford calls them "Powerwalls"—large-screen displays illuminated by Sony projectors that generate images almost four times more detailed than high-definition TV. The digital sketches shown on Powerwalls gradually become a master data set of schematics that can be experienced right down to individual screwheads. Along the way, the visual file that represents a new vehicle reaches all corners of the company, from safety engineers to

At Ford's virtual-reality lab in Dearborn, Michigan, the Programmable Vehicle Model (PVM) has sped up the design process, allowing every detail of a vehicle to be experienced long before it is built.

TOOLS

manufacturing experts. Engineers use them to adjust early prototypes. Interior designers use them to test cockpit ergonomics. Market researchers don virtual-reality helmets to evaluate their appeal.

In the case of the 2011 Explorer, the process began with four designers sketching on tablet computers and then meeting to compare notes in a room called the Advanced Visualization Center. Superficially, the Advanced Visualization Center looks like a typical conference room, with a couple of meeting tables, a phone, and a big screen at one end. But when the lights go out and the Powerwall lights up, the space is transformed into a large-scale virtual-reality chamber for visualizing vehicle designs. "As designers, we knew we had to reinvent the Explorer for the twenty-first century," says Mel Betancourt, exterior design manager for the 2011 Explorer. "We tried to look at how we could modernize things to appeal to a younger demographic."

For the 2011 Explorer, Betancourt's team created digital sketches of a vehicle with distinctly muscular details, such as a sporty bump in the hood above the engine that's called a "power dome." To give the Explorer a more modern feel, one designer suggested blackening out the structural pillars on each side of the windshield so that at a quick glance, the roof looks cantilevered. But would those ideas look right on a family vehicle? The Powerwall enabled designers to judge for themselves by looking at high-def models of the new concepts and a dozen other variations. Ford's design team looked at new grilles, new body colors, competitors' vehicles, and even competitors' vehicles that morphed into their own prototype—all while working with images that were nearly indistinguishable from photographs, even

FORD'S VIRTUAL DESIGN PROCESS HAS HELPED DESIGNERS MOVE ULTRAFAST, PRODUCING A STRING OF SUCCESSFUL NEW MAKEOVERS.

—

though the vehicle itself was three years away from seeing any steel.

The digital designs don't just stand still. Ford's designers also use a software tool called Bunkspeed Drive that instantly transforms any 3D vehicle file into a drivable animation. The images still look cartoonish, but the system makes it possible to add any Ford paint color to see the optical effects on a car while it goes for a spin. "To a designer, cars are more interesting as active things than static things," says Nowak.

They're also more interesting as physical objects, which is why, when Ford's designers settled on a few versions of the Explorer they liked, a huge 54-ton milling machine at Ford used the 3D vehicle file to fabricate four full-sized clay models of each theme. The "clays" were then positioned in the Ford design studio, a giant room where natural light streams in from a wall of windows so designers can best experience a vehicle's subtle contours. Betancourt says Ford's digital tools give designers more time to sit with the winning designs and think them through. "We're always looking for a process that gives us more time where it counts. For me, that's more time to explore every single avenue to make sure the final design is the one we all think is the best," he says.

Simultaneously, as themes are established and described in digital models,

Ford's engineers analyze the new body shapes with an eye toward practical mechanics and manufacturability. In Ford's Human Occupant Package Simulator, for example, an engineering team adjusted a real-time mock-up of the Explorer SUV in their lab to study ergonomic issues, such as a driver's ability to climb in and out of the new doorway. Over the years, the team has observed that humans naturally break down into three groups: those who enter a vehicle head first, those who enter feet first, and those who enter backside first. With the Explorer, researchers tracked the movements of test subjects in all three entry scenarios with motion sensors to give the design team summaries of any likely human-factor problems.

Of course, as with any vehicle design, there are theoretical human-factor considerations, and then there is the actual experience of being inside a vehicle surrounded by glints of chrome and leather trim. For example, the old Explorer had a glaring problem: The door handle was awkwardly positioned too far forward, or "incomprehensibly placed below the door-opener," as one *BusinessWeek* story described it. To avoid such mistakes, Ford now uses a Virtual Reality Lab, where human subjects wear virtual-reality glasses to experience realistic renderings of proposed vehicle interiors—and answer questions that only

TOOLS

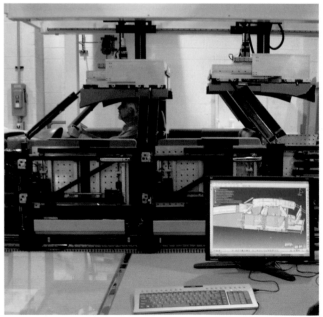

"VISUALIZATION TECHNOLOGIES ALLOW US TO GENERATE MORE IDEAS. THEN YOU CAN FOCUS THOSE IDEAS QUICKLY. THAT BUYS YOU MORE TIME TO REFINE SO YOU GET A BETTER PRODUCT AT THE END OF THE DAY."

—

Ford's Human Occupant Package Simulator (top) uses motion-capture techniques pioneered in gaming and film to help analyze ergonomics and safety. Motion capture is also used to simulate the process of manufacturing vehicles (bottom left). The Programmable Vehicle Model (bottom right) helps designers establish proper interior dimensions. Following pages: The CAVE (Cave Automated Virtual Environment) brings together several virtual-reality technologies to create an immersive car simulation.

come up when you physically interact with a design. "You might have a beautiful design on at 4,000-pixel wall," says lab founder Elizabeth Baron, "but what's it like to be inside the vehicle? Are you comfortable? What's the reach to the glovebox?" In the new Explorer, Baron made sure that the door handle was both ergonomic and attractive. (The handle is now located above the arm rest, as in a conventional sedan.)

When all the pieces come together, designers get ready for the drumroll moment when they reveal their design themes to senior managers such as Ford executive vice president Mark Fields. But here, too, the experience takes place digitally, and for the Explorer, it happened in a theater called the Electronic Design Presentation Room—a large visualization space where three Powerwalls are linked together to show virtual designs that move across a photogenic landscape.

To place the models in realistic settings, Nowak's team uses a camera that shoots a 50-megapixel spherical image in settings such as Las Vegas or a car dealer's showroom. When a vehicle design is inserted into

an immersive photo, a powerful rendering system calculates how each beam of light would bounce off the SUV in every direction. Nowak thinks that by helping managers, engineers, and others across the organization experience the designs in a realistic and visceral way, designers have a better chance of keeping their creative vision intact. "If a designer makes a case to spend another nickel on a nice finish material for the interior, a paper sketch won't do it justice," he says. "High-quality imagery helps galvanize everyone around the design team's vision."

The money-saving benefits of the computer-based visualization are difficult to overstate. Even the cost of paint drops dramatically with digital visualization. When designing the old Explorer, for example, workers literally took a dozen generic steel bodies and painted them in all of the vehicle's proposed colors—the process took a week and cost tens of thousands of dollars. But for the 2011 Explorer, each color was tested via software, with enough sophistication to include special effects such as a tricolored finish that subtly shifts

"HIGH-QUALITY IMAGERY HELPS GALVANIZE EVERYONE AROUND THE DESIGN TEAM'S VISION."
—

hues across three shades of color depending on the viewing angle.

Of course, the most important test will take place in the showrooms, when the Ford Explorer arrives. That's when Ford will at last learn if enough consumers gravitate toward the new vehicle to again make it a best-seller. Yet even after the launch, Ford's digital renderings will continue to represent the essence of what the new Explorer is about, by appearing in billboards and magazine ads that will be seen by millions of potential customers. "Our computer-generated images look better than a photo," admits Nowak. "The reflections and highlights are better, so we use those images to show the vehicles in their best light." Few potential car buyers will ever know that they are looking at a vehicle that doesn't

actually exist in physical form. Fewer still will understand that the digital images represent the final stage of Ford's digital design process. But if Ford is right and the Explorer's bold design plays a role in making it a hit, few are likely to care. Ⓐ

Though the 2011 Explorer began with a concept sketch, high-quality digital renderings were a driving force through its many iterations on the way to market.

JAY MEZHER

Parsons Brinckerhoff's design visualization guru describes how large-scale projects are changing with the introduction of new digital modeling tools.

How does Parsons Brinckerhoff use large-scale 3D models? How did your practice with them evolve?

The largest two projects that I've worked on are the Alaskan Way Viaduct Replacement Project (AWV) in Seattle and the SR 520 Bridge Replacement and HOV lanes, between Seattle and Bellevue.

When the design process was initiated, Parsons Brinckerhoff supported the AWV project with visual simulations that showed the visual effects of the proposal in the Environmental Impact Statement (EIS). Our approach was model-based, so we created a 3D model of the proposed design. Because it's an infrastructure project that impacts the whole region, we have to model the proposed design, the supporting road networks, the building context, and the city. As we were building the model, the tools continued to evolve to the point where we were getting greater capability to handle higher geometry count and attribute data.

The more context we added—the terrain in 3D, the road networks, the traffic, the different design options—the more it contributed to the design process. It also was used to effectively engage the public and the stakeholders, communicate the alternatives, analyze performance, and compare the designs visually and analytically.

For the SR 520 floating bridge, we've built the entire Seattle and Bellevue region in 3D and then added the different alignments to show the varying impacts of the proposed designs. Along with the San Francisco–Oakland Bay Bridge and the Presidio Parkway in San Francisco, those four mega-infrastructure projects were pilot projects for the application of virtual design.

How do these new tools affect the way engineers and designers at Parsons Brinckerhoff work?

Just having access to all this information in one database has been the most significant change. It used to be that if you wanted to know anything about the project, you'd have to go to 2D plans, profiles, or elevations, or have someone generate cross-sections to evaluate what the impacts were, or to look at conflicts. These virtual modeling tools and building information models gave us access to any piece of information that we wanted without going back to the drawing board.

The other thing we did was model all of the underground utilities along the alignment of the Viaduct. Adding all this existing information to the current model has been a great communication tool to show the public and project stakeholders where the project is located and how it would work.

This building information modeling approach serves the

different interests of the project team. When I work with civil engineers, they're interested in their civil design and utilities. The public is more interested in what the design's going to look like and what the visual impacts are. Traffic engineers want to see their networks, etc. The model becomes a database for the entire team, which means the project design development becomes a much more integrated and collaborative process. As a manager for these tools, you have to be well integrated with the design team, otherwise it won't work.

By building our models and bringing all that data together into one central database, it becomes the hub that everyone reaches out to for critical information. It gives the engineers access to information and additional time to decide on the best solution for a particular problem.

Once you use this model-based approach and compare it with the traditional design process, you find that the benefits outweigh the investment; it accelerates the design process and makes it much more efficient.

What does an engineer see now? What kinds of questions can you answer with these new tools?

I think you need to look at the big picture, because these are mega-infrastructure projects. There's a long, complex process to get to a final design. The first step is the environmental review process. With our model-based approach, we're supporting the NEPA (federal) environmental impacts statement by providing tools for analyzing the visual impacts, noise, lighting and glare, and shadow studies. The model proved to be an effective tool for communicating complex information to a nontechnical audience.

—

"I think you get far more effective design using these tools. If you can build it virtually, then you can build it in real life."

When you start the design process you leverage the model. Working in this virtual environment allows you to create multiple alternatives and enables the project team and stakeholders to make informed decisions. Then you move into adding details and attribute data to the model. You can then use it for different purposes, such as looking for potential design interferences, clash detections, and construction sequences.

We use the model extensively at our collaborative meeting space. We call it the CAVE—Computer Analysis Visual Environment. It has large, screen-based back projections with all the virtual design tools and multiple networked smart boards providing access to the model and all its associated data in real time. When the engineers want to have a working session, we all meet there. There's a model manager who can open the model and give us access to any project information we want.

These are able to address 90 percent of the questions. Something that would have required extensive work in the past we were able to fix in a shorter amount of time. But often there were minor questions that helped most. "Can you move this a little bit? What if we modified that? What if we changed this to that?" We were able to get consensus that this was going to work. After the meetings, we used the model to digitally mark up all the changes and then e-mail the outcome along with the list of action items to all the stakeholders. Using this approach assured the team that it has a coordinated design that is going to work.

Has the technology allowed you to take different routes or make better predictions?

I think you achieve far more effective design using these tools. If you can build it virtually, then you can build it in real life. If you can build a project virtually with no design conflicts, I don't see why you can't build it without any RFIs [requests for information] and change orders in the real world.

I think you're going to have more and more information integrated with these models, to the point where you can know anything that you want about the project by accessing it from your computer. This will allow the designers and stakeholders to make informed decisions in a more timely manner and select the design that will work best. **Ⓐ**

Jay Mezher is a manager of design visualization and virtual design and construction at Parsons Brinckerhoff.

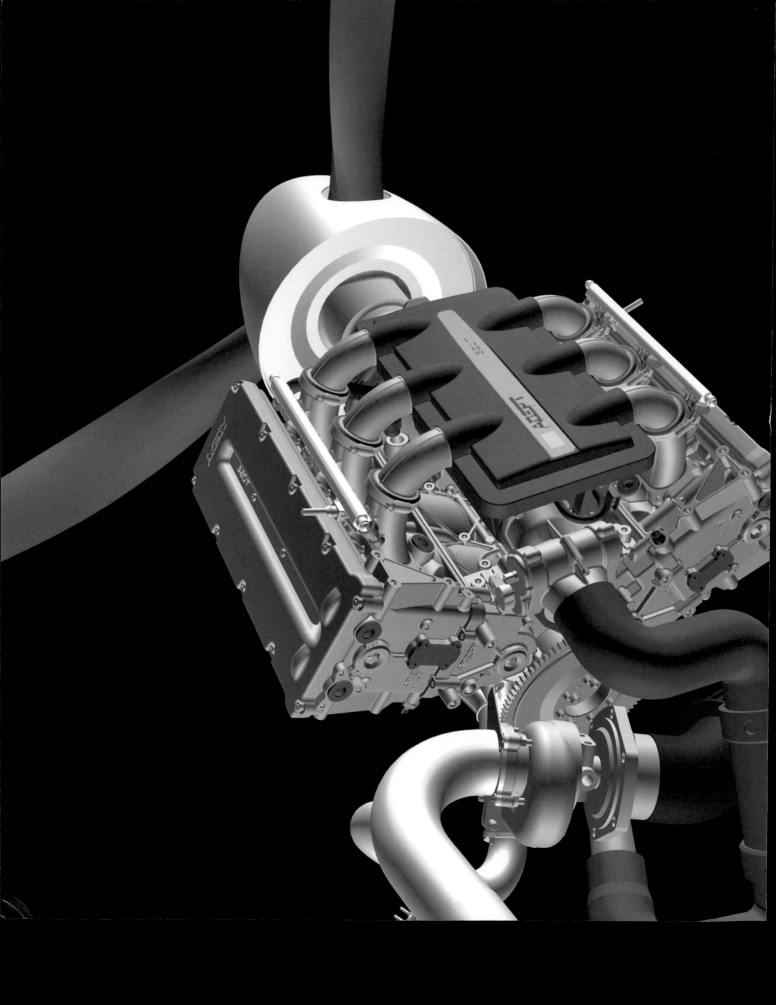

A THOROUGHLY MODERN AIRPLANE ENGINE

ADEPT Airmotive's 320T brings innovation to an industry slow to change.

SEVENTY YEARS AGO, IMPROVEMENTS IN AVIATION ENGINE TECHNOLOGY WERE STEADY AND SIGNIFICANT. Driven by competition and by the grim demands of the Second World War, European and American engine designers raced to surpass one another, attempting to outpace their automotive counterparts with bold innovations and new designs. German engineers led the way, inventing and improving engines made by Heinkel, Messerschmitt, Daimler-Benz, and others.

Yet by the 1960s, advances in the industry had slowed to a crawl. Most modern airplanes found themselves equipped with engines which, while respected and ultimately dependable, were also eventually outdated: heavy, expensive, unimaginatively designed, and not fuel-efficient. They remained the industry standard for the next fifty years.

In 2003, ADEPT Airmotive, a small South African company, was founded with the mission of developing the most technically advanced and efficient aviation engines available for general aviators. ADEPT perceived a clear moment for innovation.

And ADEPT entered the aviation engine fray just as new tools were transforming industrial design and manufacturing. Advances in CAD technology, digital prototyping, materials, and manufacturing capabilities, as well as a maturing global consciousness around environmental responsibility, all stood to radically alter the marketplace for aircraft engines. For the next five years, ADEPT and its small team of engineers and designers set and met their goals, establishing a milestone in aviation engine evolution and accelerating an idling industry into a full-throated roar.

"Our engine is modern in every respect," says Raymond Bakker, ADEPT's technical director and a designer on the project. Fierce and compact, the turbocharged, 320-horsepower, 120-degree V-6 engine, dubbed the 320T, balances unprecedented power-to-weight ratios and exceptional fuel economy with low vibration, high performance, and all the requisite reliability, structural integrity, and safety features necessary to power a modern general-aviation aircraft. "The entire philosophy behind it is very different to the traditional engine," he continues. "We recognized from the outset that smaller lightweight components are far more efficient, and that they reduce the loads on adjoining components and they reduce vibration. A traditional aircraft engine has a large amount of mass on its crankshaft to reduce the effects of vibration. The bearings have got to be able to take those higher loads; the casings have got to be more robust to contain those loads. That translates into further weight and robust engine mountings. The ADEPT engine's architecture is inherently smooth; that allows everything to be more compact and lightweight."

The 320T's maiden flight occurred in July 2010, delivering on many technological promises. Thirty percent lighter, 30 percent more fuel-efficient, and able to use alternative fuels like biofuel, liquid petroleum gas, or standard unleaded gasoline, the engine set a new

The 320-horsepower V-6 ADEPT engine, seen here as a digital prototype, represents a major advance in an industry that had not changed much since the 1960s.

"IT'S DIFFICULT TO IMAGINE HOW DESIGNERS USED TO GO ABOUT IT FIFTY YEARS AGO. YOU'D BE DRAWING SOMETHING ON A PIECE OF PAPER, AND THEN A PATTERNMAKER WOULD BE TRYING TO INTERPRET IT TO CREATE A CASTING."

—

standard for general aviation.

The seven years of development and testing may have been grueling, but nothing compared with what the process would have been using older tools. "It's difficult to imagine how designers used to go about it fifty years ago," says Bakker. "You'd be drawing something on a piece of paper, and then a patternmaker would be trying to interpret it to create a casting."

As a new company pioneering a fresh approach to aviation engines, ADEPT was at a disadvantage. It couldn't purchase off-the-shelf components or adapt older designs. Every component had to be designed, and every component's tooling had to be designed. In addition, with a lean development budget, ADEPT had to keep its costs low. The key solution was to develop a digital prototype that would let the company test and refine every element without expensive tooling changes. "You can test an idea very quickly," says Bakker. "Digital prototyping allows us to see exactly what we want out of a component."

The first indications of ADEPT's new

ways of thinking and its prototype-focused approach lie in the engine's weight. At less than 350 pounds—130 less than similar-sized engines—its smooth architecture necessitates compactness. Inside, everything weighs less: A shortened crankshaft tips the scale at just over 24 pounds; pistons are

Digital modeling, prototyping, and aerodynamic simulation were used at each step of ADEPT's process to increase performance while sticking to a budget.

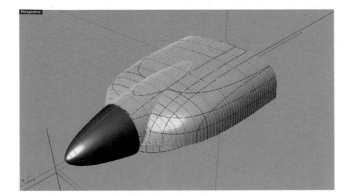
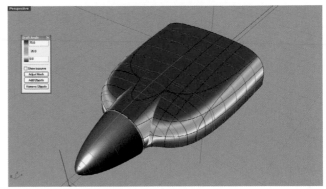
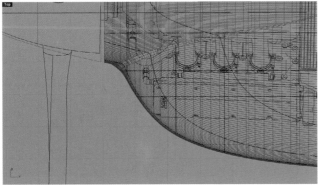
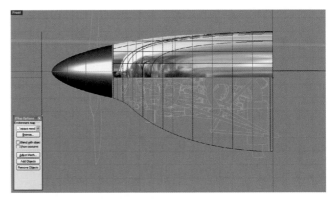
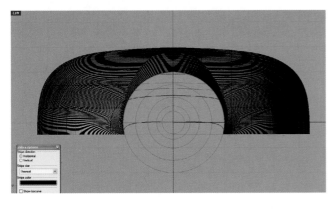
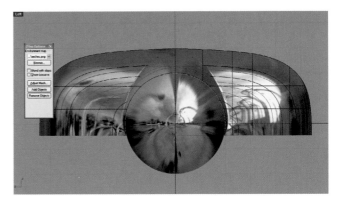
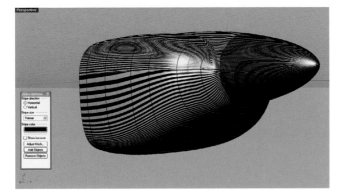
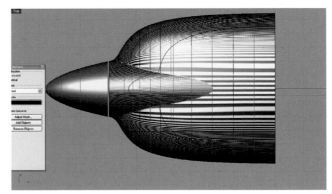

TOOLS

THE SALIENT DIFFERENCE IN THE ENGINE'S DESIGN, HOWEVER, LIES IN ITS SUPERIOR FUEL EFFICIENCY. DESIGNED FOR AN ERA OF VANISH-ING RESOURCES, HIGH OIL COSTS, AND GLOBAL WARMING, THE 320T CONSUMES ABOUT 30 PERCENT LESS FUEL THAN ITS COUNTERPARTS.

After seven years of development, the 320T took its maiden flight in July 2010 in a Ravin 300 aircraft.

lighter, too. The resulting reduction in rotating mass means the 320T's bearings and casing are under significantly less load.

"Light weight gives you performance advantage; smoothness gives you safety and efficiency," Bakker explains. "They reduce the loads on adjoining components and reduce vibration."

The salient difference in the engine's design, however, lies in its superior fuel-efficiency. Designed for an era of vanishing resources, high oil costs, and global warming, the 320T consumes about 30 percent less fuel than its counterparts. Moreover, the 320T is calibrated to run on multiple fuels: traditional Avgas 100LL—an environmentally unfriendly aviation fuel in ever-shrinking supply—as well as standard

automotive gasoline and even biofuels.

As a company, ADEPT is nearly as lean as its flagship engine. Digital design and prototyping tools allow for an efficient workflow. "Everyone on the team is responsible for designing the components *and* the relevant tooling for the parts that they're modeling," notes Bakker. "That really helps to alleviate misinterpretations of the design by outside toolmakers. We make sure there's nothing lost in translation along the way."

The pre-visualization afforded by 3D tools also aided a nontechnical aspect of the project: Investors could see the progress being made at each stage, long before there was a physical project. This built confidence that helped get this aviation revolution off the ground. Ⓐ

THE EVOLUTION OF CAD

Increasingly advanced CAD capabilities enable more-complex design processes.

Fueled by constant increases in processing power and the falling price of hardware, each progressive era of CAD evolution builds on the capabilities of the previous ones, enabling designers to create designs at higher fidelity, model expanding amounts of context around a design, and bring more imagination into reality.

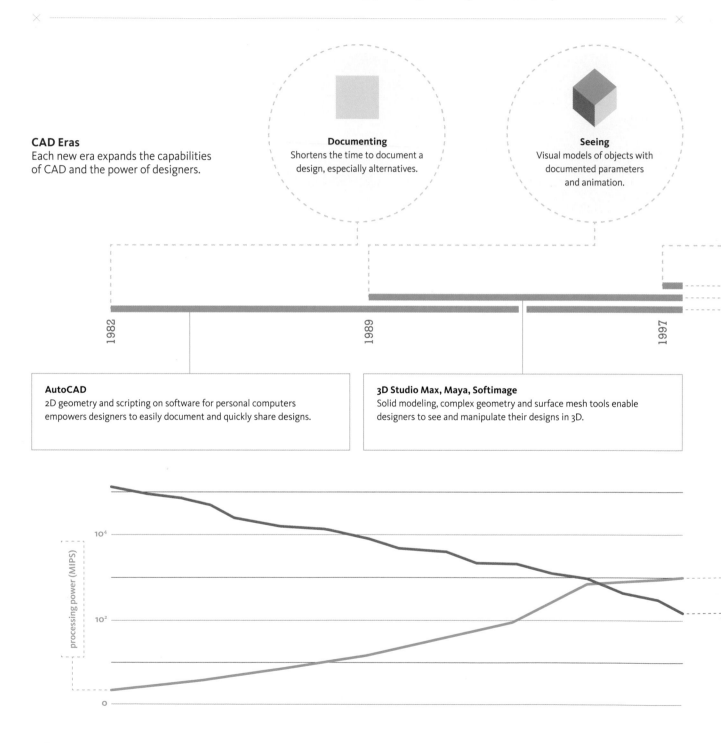

CAD Eras
Each new era expands the capabilities of CAD and the power of designers.

Documenting
Shortens the time to document a design, especially alternatives.

Seeing
Visual models of objects with documented parameters and animation.

1982

1989

1997

AutoCAD
2D geometry and scripting on software for personal computers empowers designers to easily document and quickly share designs.

3D Studio Max, Maya, Softimage
Solid modeling, complex geometry and surface mesh tools enable designers to see and manipulate their designs in 3D.

processing power (MIPS)

10^4

10^2

0

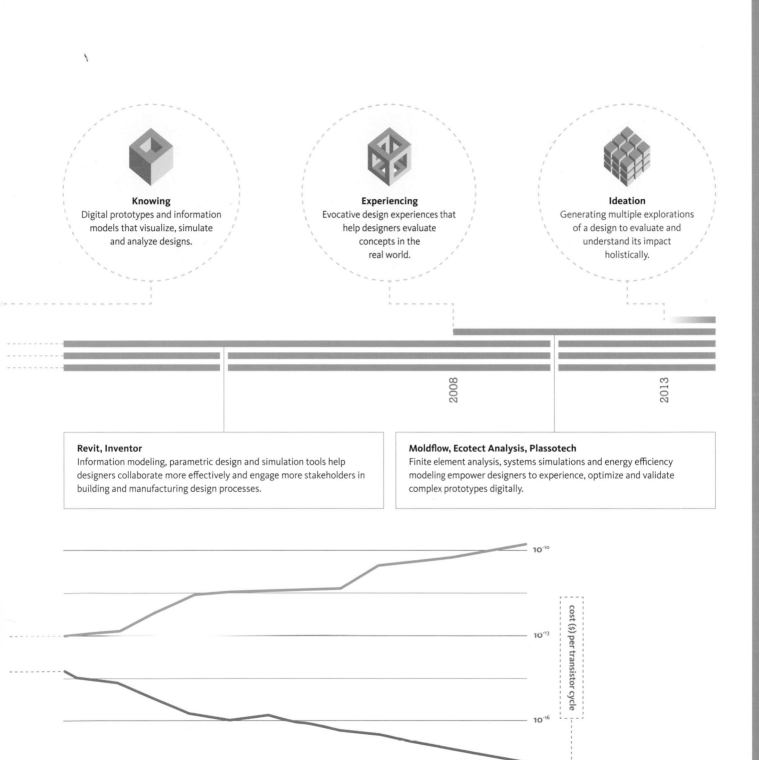

Knowing
Digital prototypes and information models that visualize, simulate and analyze designs.

Experiencing
Evocative design experiences that help designers evaluate concepts in the real world.

Ideation
Generating multiple explorations of a design to evaluate and understand its impact holistically.

2008

2013

Revit, Inventor
Information modeling, parametric design and simulation tools help designers collaborate more effectively and engage more stakeholders in building and manufacturing design processes.

Moldflow, Ecotect Analysis, Plassotech
Finite element analysis, systems simulations and energy efficiency modeling empower designers to experience, optimize and validate complex prototypes digitally.

cost ($) per transistor cycle

10^{-10}

10^{-13}

10^{-16}

KIERANTIMBERLAKE'S LOBLOLLY HOUSE
Building Information Modeling and a desire to explore the possibilities of prefabrication produced a waterfront home of uncommon beauty.

FOR STEPHEN KIERAN AND JAMES TIMBERLAKE, the National Design Award–winning architects who are partners in the firm KieranTimberlake, an unfortunate consequence of modernism was the gradual segregation of the designer from the maker. Despite advances in building technologies, the process of design and construction has changed little since the Renaissance. What's more, the role of the architect—once revered as a Master Builder—has diminished. Today, an architect provides a poetic and pragmatic ideal, which is often misinterpreted as it undergoes the construction documentation and fabrication process. Poetry is won over to logistics and structural demands, and artistry is lost in translation.

But what if the architect's vision were expressed as an exact simulation of the built form, right down to the bolts and mechanical and electrical innards? What if that simulation, or model, was smart enough that it removed the chance and play that lies between architectural thought and the general contractor's expression?

For decades, engineers working in the automotive, aeronautical, and shipbuilding industries have integrated that kind of simulation as a means of gaining precision and a higher level of craftsmanship. Kieran and Timberlake see no reason why this technology shouldn't apply to architecture, thereby uniting the architect with the contractor and the materials scientist with the product engineer in a process of simultaneous prefabricated design and construction. It is through the auspice of Building Information Modeling (BIM) that they envision the reemergence of the architect as Master Builder, a designer as skilled in the artistry of design as he is in the craft of making.

The architects set out to test their argument in the field. They found an ideal client in Stephen Kieran and his family, who used their land on Taylor's Island on the Chesapeake Bay as a test site for their prototype. The resulting Loblolly House, which is named for the distinct species of pine that populates the area, is, in many ways, the physical manifestation of the promise of BIM, as Kieran and Timberlake see it, but it's also a home that meaningfully evokes the splendor of its surrounding landscape.

"Loblolly House was an effort to really push the boundaries of what was possible. It didn't make economic sense to only look at it in isolation as a small house; we had to see it as an experiment," explains Kieran. "It was the first project we comprehensively designed with Autodesk Revit (which has since become the baseline platform at our office). At the time there were all sorts of things that hadn't been figured out yet with BIM. We were sort of guinea pigs. It was an ideal project to experiment with: It was small and had a very understanding owner."

KieranTimberlake's main objectives with Loblolly House were to create a dwelling that

The Loblolly House—named for the type of pine trees native to the area—was meant to evoke its natural environment without compromising it.

THE PRECISION OF THE JOINERY NOT ONLY ALLOWED FOR THE TIMBER FRAME TO FIT TOGETHER SEAMLESSLY, IT ALSO ACCOUNTED FOR THE CONNECTIONS BETWEEN THE TIMBER FRAME AND THE SCAFFOLDING SYSTEM.

—

evoked the natural environment without compromising it—and to achieve this goal through the use of parametric BIM modeling and off-site fabrication. "It's a very fragile wetland site," explains Kieran, "and the less time we had to spend building it, the better." BIM enabled the architects to build virtually within highly specified parameters before any physical construction began. Simply stated, BIM enables architects, engineers, manufacturers, contractors, and clients to communicate and share information through a highly sophisticated, multidimensional model. That model

simulates everything from geographic and site specifications to geometric and spatial relationships. Individually manufactured components can be rendered within the overall model, allowing designers to project every element of a building's potential life cycle. BIM also allows collaborators to extract and share information regarding materials and assembly sequences, and can generate precise information for material and permit submittals.

For example, Loblolly's off-site fabricator, Bensonwood Homes, was able to cut the timber frame to the exact specifications

Having the model of the house in Autodesk Revit allowed the architects to diagram the sequence of assembly—planning the complicated choreography of parts arriving on-site.

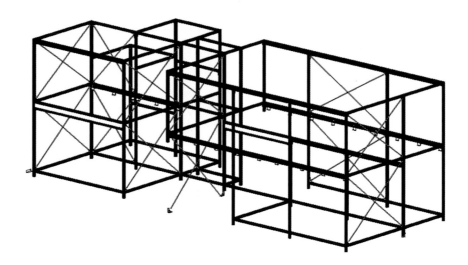

of the model with their Hundegger machine, a computer-driven milling device. The precision of the joinery not only allowed for the timber frame to fit together seamlessly, it also accounted for the connections between the timber frame and the Bosch aluminum-strut scaffolding system, which was used to frame the larger portion of the house. This eliminated the rejiggering and waste that often results from a structure built from a two-dimensional plan. Wall and floor sections, which KieranTimberlake called "cartridges" and which were fully outfitted with insulation, electrical wiring, and plumbing connections, were then plugged into the scaffolding system. The on-site plumber need only "stub up" his connections and tie into the valve for the plumbing and radiation systems to be up and running. In a standard stick-frame building, this would happen in a step-by-step linear construction process—framing, sheathing, insulation, electrical, flooring, tiling, and plumbing—requiring hours of time allotted to each individual subcontractor to perform his job in a set order. Never mind the issues that arise when there is a delay within one element of the sequential system.

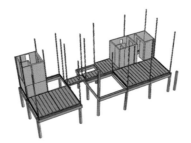

TOOLS

This is perhaps BIM's most important feature: the ability to mitigate the loss of information between the architect, construction crew, manufacturer, and client, and to promote simultaneous construction process. Of traditional design and construction processes, Kieran and Timberlake wrote, "If we are lucky, we get to keep ourselves on the job all the way through construction, acting as interpreters and arbiters of what we really intended but neither foresaw nor conveyed. All the while, as the instructions that lie between intention and outcome become obscure, we bemoan the ongoing decline in productivity, quality, and control."

Contrast that degradation of communication with the fidelity of BIM. Because communication happens within the form of a model, it isn't necessary to translate information from one format to another. Structural and mechanical drawings are no longer distinct from architectural drawings; each collaborator contributes to a unified design scheme, and the architect's vision remains intact. At Loblolly House, Kieran explains, "we could go directly from our digital models to fabrication equipment and drive that equipment from the digital models."

In adopting off-site fabrication and parametric modeling, KieranTimberlake looked to the automotive, aeronautical, and shipbuilding industries for guidance. As car manufacturing evolved, for example, a car console that was once composed of two hundred separate parts is now collapsed into one integrated piece. Similarly, Boeing engineers have long used parametric models to develop highly sophisticated building plans for their aircraft. The simulative models achieved with BIM provide a complete three-dimensional structure as opposed to an interpretive two-dimensional drawing. Large, complex portions of a structure can be broken into integrated components, which can be fabricated anywhere in the world and brought together for final assembly. All of the parts, joints, and corners are suffused with structural information and design constraints and can be viewed from multiple points of view. All of this information allows for a higher degree of control and technological sophistication within each element.

The defining feature of architecture, of course, is that it is somehow tied to the earth. Thus, the labor needs to be broken up into off-site fabrication and on-site assemblage. The traditional sequential construction model is supplanted by a simultaneous prefabricated process, where integrated components are delivered for on-site assembly. Coupled with the geometric and technical certainty of the parametric model, all of this happens with little to no error.

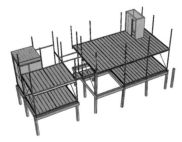  

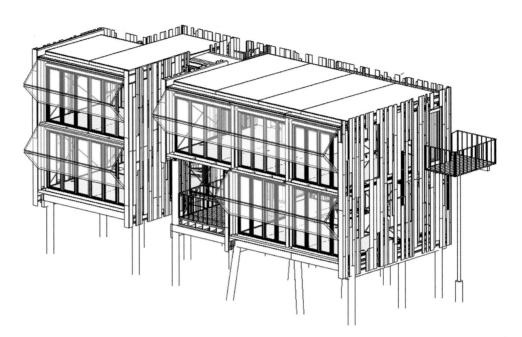

KieranTimberlake divided Loblolly
House into six critical elements: scaffold,
cartridge, block, fixture, furnishing, and
equipment. The 40,000 parts of a conventional house were collapsed into these six
elements. This, the architects say, can eliminate the current wasteful system, "where
fifty divisions of materials and equipment
classify tens of thousands of products
into a confusing array of disjointed parts."
Furthermore, the potential for specialization and refinement within each individual
component—say, to meet stringent environ-

mental standards, or incorporate high-tech
materials—could potentially serve a broad
spectrum of the housing market and "redefine the housing supply chain in the U.S."

A team made up of an off-site crew
from Bensonwood Homes, an on-site crew
from Arena Program Management and
Bensonwood Homes, and project architects
from KieranTimberlake was able to work
simultaneously on different components
of the design and construction process and
communicate efficiently through Loblolly's
single parametric model.

KieranTimberlake likens this prefabricated method of assemblage to quilting, versus the piece-by-piece weaving in the current system. "We propose to simplify, merge, and unify these materials and environmental systems—structures, windows, doors, and finishes—into integrated assemblies, which we consider to be the elements of a new architecture," the architects wrote in their book *Loblolly House*.

The information available to designers using BIM can provide new insight into areas outside of construction. "Our research on Loblolly House and Cellophane House suggests that the embodied energy in the materials and the making of a house is far more than most would like to believe," Kieran says, referring also to a related, off-site-fabricated house built for a show at New York's Museum of Modern Art. "Practically forty years' worth of operating energy is embedded in a house before it is even occupied, even in an energy-efficient home. That is an awful lot of embodied energy. Our position is that we as designers need to assume ethical responsibility and control of the life cycle of the materials going into our building. We can do this by creating mechanisms that allow them to be disassembled rather than demolished, so that we can recover those materials whole and bear the cost of reconstituting them." Loblolly's aluminum scaffolding frame, which uses dry joints (bolted as opposed to welded fastening), holds great potential in this regard. Instead of demolishing it, the house and its framing components can be broken down and reassembled elsewhere. The same BIM tools used for its design and construction will also be essential for its efficient disassembly.

The technology can be applied to a variety of projects, not only ground-up endeavors. "The more accuracy one has in the model, the more you can start to change the way we are actually building things," explains Kieran. He gives the example of a renovation the firm recently completed for Silliman College at Yale University. The architects created a parametric model of the preexisting structure, which included the miles of conduit and wiring stuffed into

The house's major systems were integrated off-site in "cartridges" designed to be lifted and fitted into the aluminum frame.

THE SAME BIM TOOLS USED FOR THE HOUSE'S DESIGN AND CONSTRUCTION WILL ALSO BE ESSENTIAL FOR ITS EFFICIENT DISASSEMBLY.

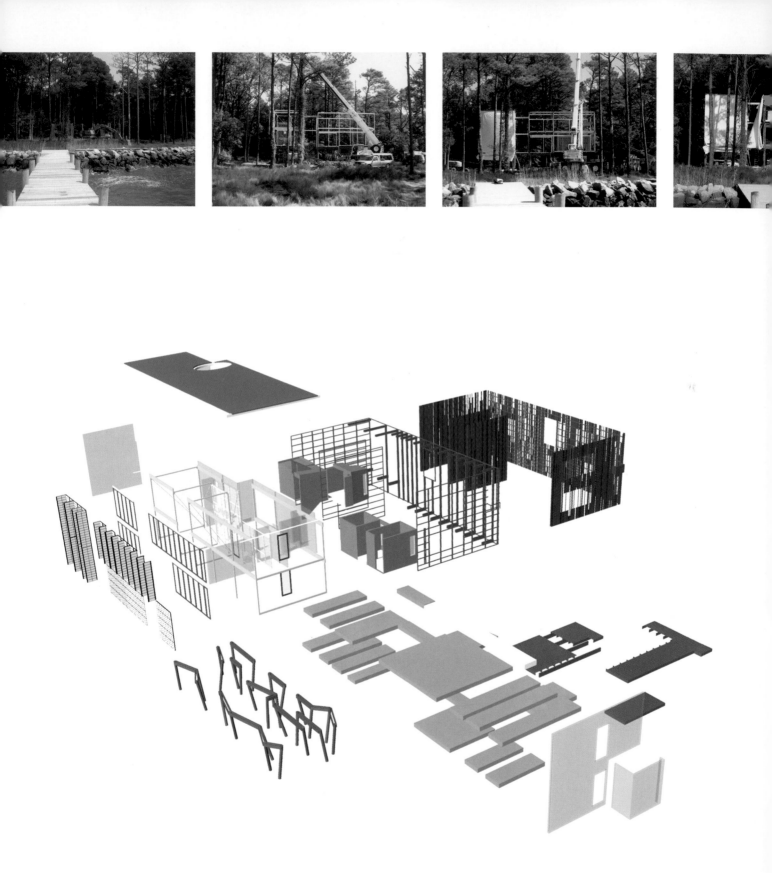

ACCORDING TO STEPHEN KIERAN, GOOD ARCHITECTURE IS THE "FUSION OF SHELTER WITH PLACES AND THE PEOPLE THAT NEED TO USE THEM, AND THE TECHNOLOGIES AVAILABLE TO US TO BUILD THEM."

—

In less than nine weeks, the house went from plan (left) to pile installation (above left) through aluminum frame building (third from left) to the finishing touch of airplane hangar doors (right). The finished home opens up directly to the Chesapeake Bay via folding doors (following pages).

the old and complicated structure. "All of the clashes were figured out in advance and laid to the framework of that existing digital model, as opposed to in the field. The contractors had so much confidence in the model that they built long racks of piping—which might contain up to twenty different types of piping woven into it—all off-site," explains Kieran. "There is a tremendous amount of work going on through the agency of digital design to basically change

construction in all of our projects."

According to Kieran, good architecture is the "fusion of shelter with places and the people that need to use them, and the technologies available to us to build them." This criteria certainly applies to Loblolly House, which is, first, a singular architectural expression deeply sensitive to its environment. But Loblolly House is also proof that the potential for change is great as we embrace new technologies. Ⓐ

EXPERIENCE

HOW DOES DESIGN MAKE US FEEL?

DESIGN USED TO BE ASSOCIATED WITH THE CREATION OF OBJECTS, BUT INCREASINGLY, THE FOCUS HAS SHIFTED FROM "OBJECT" TO "EXPERIENCE." THIS EVOLUTION HAS BEEN DRIVEN BY THE GROWING RECOGNITION THAT GOOD DESIGN DOES NOT EXIST MERELY WITHIN THE THREE-DIMENSIONAL CONFINES OF A MADE OBJECT.

—

previous spread: **Production designer and immersive-design guru Alex McDowell's work includes Tim Burton's psyche-delic update to** *Charlie and the Chocolate Factory.*

Experience design is not about the thing itself, but about all that happens when people begin to interact and engage with that thing. How does the design make them feel? Does it somehow improve or enrich their lives? Does it anticipate and adapt to needs that may change over time?

Designing an intangible experience can be more complex than designing a solid object. In fact, technically speaking, it's an impossibility: One cannot actually design an experience for others—the perception of an experience happens inside each individual's head. But what designers can do is shape and orchestrate the many variables likely to inform the human experience of interacting with a product, a film or other media, or a service. When designers get all the bits and pieces of experience design just right, the results can delight and amaze.

One of the key questions that designers must answer is: What causes us to be fully and completely engaged with a design? For video-game designers at Ubisoft, the challenge was to combine compelling drama and meticulously choreographed gamesmanship with hyperrealism—and to do all of this so well that the activity could continuously capture a user's imagination for a hundred hours. For Alex McDowell, production design allows for a new kind of storytelling: one that employs digital design tools, along with talent and imagination, to create a more immersive filmgoing experience.

Experience design is not limited to the realm of games and entertainment—it is rapidly becoming an important way of thinking about design throughout the business world. Companies are coming to understand that the overall experiences they create for consumers are the ultimate determinant of success today.

At the same time, a growing awareness of and emphasis on experience design is impacting everything from the buildings we live and work in to the way our kids play and learn.

Experience design requires more of designers—more planning, more analysis, more anticipation of user needs, more richness and high fidelity in output. As IDEO cofounder David Kelley has observed, the creation of rich and rewarding experiences "represents a higher level of design." Ⓐ

NATHAN SHEDROFF

An experience-design pioneer describes the elements of experience, the need for deeper research, and the payback of great design.

Let's start with the obvious. What is experience design?
On one level, it's really simple: designing experiences for other people. Obviously most people want successful, wonderful, and delightful experiences.

The next question is, What do you mean by experience? The design part isn't the big problem. It's the experience part that's challenging because it's abstract. That's why I call experience design an approach, not a discipline. It's not its own category like fashion design, or interaction design, or car design. Experience design is how you approach design of anything.

Some people will say that you don't design experiences, you design for people having experiences. Is that a worthwhile distinction?
The reality is, we design amazing experiences every day. We design weddings, and dinner parties, and birthday parties. In the commercial realm, we design everything from theme parks to operas to products and services. Go to Cirque du Soleil. You are having an amazing experience that is highly

designed. We design experiences all the time. So it becomes an academic distinction without much value.

Designers' inspiration has always been around experience, or has had elements of experience. This isn't something that we just started doing. But because we've never been taught a vocabulary about it, it ends up being called "intuitive." We haven't been deliberate about it, or had a way to tangibly put it into the design process. That's what we can do now.

What are the elements of experience design?
There are six dimensions of experience that we've identified: Duration, or how time flows through the experience. The level of interaction. The level of intensity of engagement. The level of significance—that's where meaning lives. The breadth of touch points in the experience. And the last one is triggers.

What do you mean by triggers?
How designers practice today is more as curators. It's not about what you do and don't like. It's about how you curate design decisions to trigger the effects that you want in your customers. Should I use natural wood? Does that trigger the reaction of more human, more natural, or more organic? Or maybe I want to trigger feelings of industrial machine

—

"It's not about what you do and don't like. It's about how you curate design decisions to trigger the effects that you want in your customers.... It's my job as a designer to make choices that trigger the right responses."

tolerance and high precision. In that case, I might use aluminum, or steel, or plastic. But I can't make these decisions until I know what reactions I want to trigger in my audience, and how those decisions actually trigger those reactions. (Which may not be the same as *my* reactions.)

Every choice that I make creates the foundation of an experience. It triggers meaning. And it's my job as a designer to make choices that trigger the right responses so that they have the experience that my client wants them to have, or I want them to have.

What do we need to learn in order to design better experiences?

As a designer, I need deeper, broader research so that when I go into the design process (ideation, brainstorming, and prototyping), I know I'm curating the right triggers for a particular user or customer within a particular context. I need to figure out what makes this person feel proud of the work they've done, or feel happy, or feel connected to other people. And when I go to test that to see if it's actually working, I now have a set of things to test against.

There's more to be aware of and to work with. For instance, how many Web designers even consider sound? Sound is always in the environment, even for online experiences. Most product design doesn't take into account smell or taste. Much of it doesn't even take into account touch. We have the opportunity to consider more than just the obvious and, as a result, build better solutions that are differentiable from everything else.

We need to understand and consider these other senses because experiences are not just about surface, color, texture, and material. As an example, Singapore Airlines has branded itself with a smell. It's one way they've chosen to differentiate themselves. It's in the soap on the plane. It's in the aroma in the first-class lounge. For some, that may be subtle, but for others it might be very powerful.

What do you think is the future of design?

I think design is getting richer. This approach allows us to design wider and deeper and, therefore, better and more interesting experiences as well as new things that we've never thought of before or we've never drawn together before.

Design also needs to reach more people. We need to teach design to everyone. More people need to know design thinking and integrative thinking. Everyone needs to be exposed to whole-mind thinking. If you want to be pragmatic, you can call it better problem-solving.

"This approach allows us to design wider and deeper and, therefore, better and more interesting experiences."
—

It's hard for me to remember how, as a child, I could look at the world and not realize that I could change the world. Designers learn that they don't have to wait for someone else to make changes, and that's very powerful.

We need 6 billion people that think like this, because everything needs to be improved. In the context of sustainability and resource scarcity, we no longer have the luxury to assume that just a few people are going to make positive change. We need everyone thinking about these challenges.

We need to add the design process to education, in kindergarten on up. Kindergartners are great at this already, by the way. They don't know that they can't change the world. They don't know that they can't make a solution that's funny and wonderful. Somewhere between kindergarten and twelfth grade, we tell people that they can't do this anymore. That has to change. Ⓐ

Nathan Shedroff is the chair of the MBA in Design Strategy program at California College of the Arts (CCA) in San Francisco.

SPLINTER CELL: CONVICTION

The creators of Ubisoft's first-person shooter found that dispensing with gaming conventions and focusing on an immersive experience empowered players to feel like true action heroes.

One of the most important qualities in a first-person shooter game like Ubisoft's *Splinter Cell: Conviction* is engagement: A player should feel completely immersed in the world and action of the game.

DEEP INTO THE DEVELOPMENT OF THE FIRST *ASSASSIN'S CREED*, a Ubisoft video game that would go on to sell more than 7 million copies, the game's design director, Maxime Béland, sat behind two-way glass. He watched a player heavily involved in playing the game's enchanting sequences for test purposes. The teenager appeared riveted, enmeshed in the game.

In the role of a twelfth-century assassin, the player prepared to execute his next target; he calmly wiped his sweaty hands together and repositioned his controller. "I thought, *We've totally got him,*" recalls Béland. "The only thing closer would have been for him to enter the TV." But minutes later, as the gameplay paused temporarily and rolled into cinematic sequences, something happened.

Unglued from the action in the game, the young man removed his headphones, looked around, and took a leisurely sip of his Coke. By playing an in-game movie to establish the game's backstory, gameplay switched from interactive to passive, and player turned to watcher. The very game that had first taken the player deep within its immersive layers simply cut him loose. Béland vowed to find a way around such *disengagement* in favor of *immersion* in his next project.

Designing immersive experiences is the cornerstone of good video-game design, but putting all the right pieces in place to provide a truly new and nuanced gaming experience is no easy task. Though video-gaming company Ubisoft stands at the forefront of designing these fully immersive experiences, designing to yield full immersion remains a moving target. Developers who follow tried-and-true techniques and stick to formulas don't produce memorable and singular experiences; what *does* is making a range of creative decisions and experimental moves with the launch of every single new game.

Soon enough, Béland, based in Ubisoft's Montreal offices, was assigned to direct *Tom Clancy's Splinter Cell: Conviction. Conviction* would be the latest game in a strong franchise created by Ubisoft in the Tom Clancy universe. *Splinter Cell* first launched in 2002 as one of the pioneers of the stealth/action genre (along with *Metal Gear Solid*) but had developed a problem in its previous iterations. Many players had not finished the series of missions, or maps, that comprise the video game and were frustrated by their gameplay experiences.

"We had a lot of data about how many people bought our game, versus how many finished it," says Béland. "And the numbers were kind of sad." Much of the reason for the low completion rate was that the game was too hard; the players that did succeed did so by dying and starting over. To Béland, "learning by dying" was no way to gain adherents to a game.

In January 2008, Béland, along with producer Alexandre Parizeau, took over as director of *Conviction,* the fifth title in the *Splinter Cell* lineup. Their first job was to focus the project after an initial two years of creative development. Béland and Parizeau's overarching mission was no small task: to redefine the franchise in part by cranking up its immersive elements. In short, their task was to design a new gaming experience that would raise the bar in terms of engagement and immersion.

"We are in a world where everything is competing with everything. You want to watch a movie, but if it gets boring, you are going to send an SMS. Or tweet about how the movie sucks," says Béland. In the new gaming world exploding with options, a successful game must draw a gamer in for an extended multiple-hour experience or he will simply look around to replace it with a better one.

In their quest to build an immersive new sequel, Béland and Parizeau rolled up their sleeves to conduct wide-reaching research before they set about rejiggering the title. They read the online forums to see what was loved and what was hated in past games.

Splinter Cell is an intricate stealth game with a deep narrative, the gameplay of which is filled with ambushes, sneaking, lurking in shadows, and evasion of enemies. The game is a story of a splinter cell—a one-man National Security Agency special-operations officer who takes on impossible military tasks. And *Splinter Cell* games had long been associated with one character, the elite stealth agent Sam Fisher. In the new incarnation, none of this would change. Light and shadow would remain a key part of gameplay.

Games live and die by differences in action and story line, and *Splinter Cell* and its Sam Fisher character had succeeded in many respects. Fisher was the much-loved hero of a franchise that had sold in excess of 19 million games between 2002 and 2009. Voiced by Hollywood cult action hero Michael Ironside, Sam Fisher would be going rogue in the latest installment; ejected by the U.S. government and its top-secret Third Echelon outfit, he was seemingly on his own. That was a different story line, but much about Sam Fisher would stay the same. What would change in the next *Splinter Cell* would be a far-reaching push into new levels of immersion.

"There is something we call the 'player fantasy,'" says Béland. If you are playing *Madden,* you want to feel like an invincible NFL player—that is your game fantasy. "To me, the *Splinter Cell* fantasy is that you want to feel like the best stealth special agent in the world," he says. As a character, Sam Fisher shares a lot with *24's* Jack Bauer, James Bond, and Jason Bourne, all of whom are ex-military, or ex–special forces. One of the problems Béland identified early on with *Splinter Cell* was that the players he polled could not easily connect with the game fantasy of *Splinter Cell,* the fantasy of being a clandestine operative who can go anywhere, do anything, and get away with it. Béland could sympathize: "I never felt like the guy on the box," he says.

"Sam Fisher is the kind of agent who sleeps in a sewer pipe somewhere in North Korea for a week until the time is right to strike," says Béland's colleague Patrick Redding, who led the development of the game's cooperative multiplayer modes.

As his team set about rebooting *Splinter Cell,* the Coke-drinking kid stood as a talisman of sorts for Béland. He knew that he had to keep players immersed, otherwise they would bail out. *Splinter Cell*'s creator and publisher, Paris-based Ubisoft, strives to ensure that its triple-A blockbuster games like *Splinter Cell* have mass appeal.

Founded in 1986, Ubisoft employs more than six thousand people and takes gameplay seriously; classes in game-design

One strategy for full immersion was to communicate with players within the game; instead of breaking for a movie sequence or using subtitles, game goals were projected within the gaming space.

DEVELOPERS WHO FOLLOW TRIED-AND-TRUE TECHNIQUES AND STICK TO FORMULAS DON'T PRODUCE MEMORABLE AND SINGULAR EXPERIENCES—WHAT <u>DOES</u> IS MAKING A RANGE OF CREATIVE DECISIONS AND EXPERIMENTAL MOVES WITH THE LAUNCH OF EVERY SINGLE NEW GAME.

—

theory are compulsory for high-level creative managers, and the company runs state-of-the-art game-testing facilities in many of its global studios, including the one in Montreal. "We are competing at an Olympic level, where everything we mess up costs us a hundred thousand players," says Redding. "We are really vulnerable, but the rewards are very high."

As part of the review of the game and how to best move forward for the new *Splinter Cell* title, Béland and Parizeau decided to not force stealth on the player not because he was afraid and weak, but because he was powerful and it was an intelligent tactical decision to hide and wait for the proper moment. "It was magical. As soon as I talked to the developers about the concept of being a panther and not a grandmother, I was getting sparks in their eyes," says Béland.

Béland and Parizeau decided to embrace stealth, but they did want to change the mechanics of the gameplay—how the player operates and maneuvers in the game environment, the literal actions of the player.

—

BÉLAND WANTED A PLAYER TO FEEL LIKE A FELINE PREDATOR IN THE GAME— STEALTHILY AND CUNNINGLY WALKING AMID THE GAME'S SHADOWS UNTIL HE FOUND THE RIGHT TIME TO ATTACK.

—

as a type of inferior mode of competition, but to fully embrace stealth. "We decided to make stealth something that is appealing for the player, something that makes him feel strong and like a predator," says Béland.

Béland further developed a metaphor of Sam Fisher as a panther to explain to his team that he wanted a player to feel like a feline predator in the game—stealthily and cunningly walking amid the game's shadows until he found the right time to attack. The panther worked because Sam Fisher was to be a character who used stealth and hid

As producer for *Conviction*, Parizeau served as the guardian of the main objectives for the game. To get where they wanted to with the new mechanics, there was a lot of team experimentation and idea prototyping, overseen by him. "The ideal situation for a game is when you have a really strong vision, or philosophy, so you can communicate to the team what the game is about," explains Parizeau. "And you have a feedback loop where the team is allowed to contribute other ideas and influence the core vision through prototyping."

Game conventions called for traditional changes: If a player, as Sam Fisher, is using a human shield, say, classic game design calls for him to navigate slower and only shoot one-handed weapons. For every positive, the player gets a minus. But Béland overturned this notion. "If our hero is supposed to be the best stealth agent in the world, well, what does that mean? It means that when he has a weapon, he can shoot it better than anyone else," says Béland. "We had to stop thinking about balancing and more about delivering experience." This new thinking led the team to create two new game styles, which they named "mark and execute" and "last known position," two counterintuitive ideas that, while unlikely as true fighting techniques in the real world, greatly enhanced gameplay.

Béland called for two overarching ideals that would build player immersion—no noticeable loading of game data, and no cuts in the action. The first idea, to avoid interruptive sequences in the game when new maps loaded, proved impossible to achieve with the technology but was simulated by playing full-screen high-definition video during loading.

Building a game with no cuts, à la Hitchcock's film *Rope*, was something they did achieve through much trial and error. Traditional games use cinematics to help flesh out the all-important story for players. To show why a killer is trying to execute the game's hero, a game will show some form of video backstory. But when a player is watching such a clip, he feels like nothing can happen to him; he mentally shuts down and falls out of the state of disbelief that he is in during gameplay. That's what happened to Béland's Coke-sipping kid.

Action genre games like *Conviction* are typically either first- or third-person "shooters." Game "cameras" are either focused forward from the eyes of the player (first person) or show the player from some remove

BÉLAND CALLED FOR TWO OVERARCHING IDEALS THAT WOULD BUILD PLAYER IMMERSION—NO NOTICEABLE LOADING OF GAME DATA, AND NO CUTS IN THE ACTION.

"I DON'T WANT TO FORCE THE STORY DOWN THE PLAYER'S THROAT. THAT IS PART OF SHARING THE AUTHORSHIP WITH THE PLAYER. WE HAVE A TWO-WAY DISCUSSION WITH OUR AUDIENCE."

SARAH

(third person). The in-game camera with third-person shooters usually cuts from the main character to other action surrounding the character. But in the latest iteration of *Splinter Cell*, Béland sought to never cut Sam Fisher in the game's single-player mode. This camera-induced tension would create a real-time feel that invoked a sense of urgency for the player. "Our cameras in *Conviction* are related to, and inspired by, the TV show *24*," says Béland.

"We want the players to be the instruments of action," says Redding. Echoes Béland: "I don't want to force the story down the player's throat. That is part of sharing the authorship with the player. We have a two-way discussion with our audience. The player is an actor, and the player is the cameraman in a way. That is part of the challenge, but also part of what we have to embrace."

Modern video games have evolved into ambitious works of narrative fiction in which

presenting a story is critical to pass on information to the gamer. How to do so without cutting from play to backstory video is a challenge. In *Conviction*, the game's creators had to tell a story to players that did not always revolve around the main character. The solution to avoid cutting away from the real-time action to backstory was solved when Béland saw the Denzel Washington film *Man on Fire,* which showed video sequences within the real environments of the film, pictures inside pictures.

Conviction's presentation editor, Jean-Philippe Rajotte, went on to design an innovative style that used the game's environment as a canvas. Instead of removing the texture of in-game walls, he found a way to use dynamic film-esque light and project movies on walls. "Because it is an actual light in our world, the characters are affected by the light," says Béland. These new projections allowed the *Conviction* team to avoid cuts in action by projecting movies in the

A subtle but key visual design tactic was to keep the player at the center of the action at all times. There is no cutting away, no shifts in perspective that might break the engagement with the game.

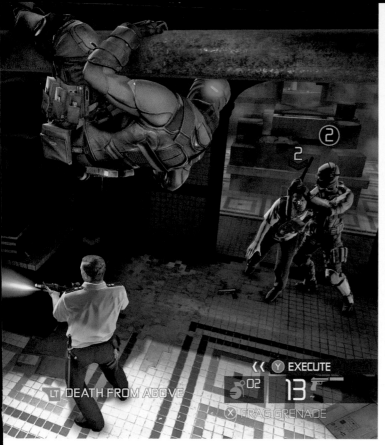

LT DEATH FROM ABOVE
<< (Y) EXECUTE
02 13
(X) FRAG GRENADE

<<< (Y) EXECUTE
03 08
(X) FLASHBANG

game world. The same went for instructions: Players viewed projected words and directions within the game world ("Move and cover," say) instead of seeing messages pop up on top of their screens. That move also avoided the traditional heads-up display, a common strategy for giving the player information, but one that also pulls the player out of the game.

All of these changes in game mechanics had to add up to an immersive experience for them to be worthwhile. But there is no real metric for measuring the level of gamer immersion. Says Redding: "Immersiveness for us is always done relative to other game experiences. Choosing to make an immersive game means that we may let go of a few features that would make the game easy to understand in favor of making the players feel as if they are in a real world, where they have to apply their human instincts. That line between immersive and nonimmersive is very heavily connected

to accessibility and learnability."

After four and a half years of development and six thousand hours of testing in Ubisoft's Montreal lab, *Splinter Cell: Conviction* shipped in April 2010. Three months after the launch, Ubisoft had sold almost 2 million copies of the game and found that more players than ever for the franchise had completed the game—some 46 percent. *Conviction* became the game with the highest finishing rate in Ubisoft's stable of titles. And, not only did gamers finish in higher numbers, many felt that the game took them two hours shorter than it actually did—a genuine measure of immersion.

The numbers, if nothing else, seemed to answer affirmatively the big question that had preoccupied Béland early on: "When you look at the box and see Sam Fisher and then you play, do you feel like the guy on the box?" Ⓐ

"CHOOSING TO MAKE AN IMMERSIVE GAME MEANS THAT WE MAY LET GO OF A FEW FEATURES THAT WOULD MAKE THE GAME EASY TO UNDERSTAND IN FAVOR OF MAKING THE PLAYERS FEEL AS IF THEY ARE IN A REAL WORLD, WHERE THEY HAVE TO APPLY THEIR HUMAN INSTINCTS."

MEASURING EXPERIENCE

How does *Cloudy with a Chance of Meatballs* create emotional engagement?

Sony Pictures Imageworks' *Cloudy with a Chance of Meatballs* creates an engaging experience through its use of plot devices, pacing, and color. The Galvanic Skin Response chart below visualizes subconscious reactions, the Emotion Graph shows subjective responses, and the Camera Cuts convey rhythm and action. The Color Script illustrates the emotional tone of each scene, revealing another important tool designers use to develop and accentuate the experience of the movie.

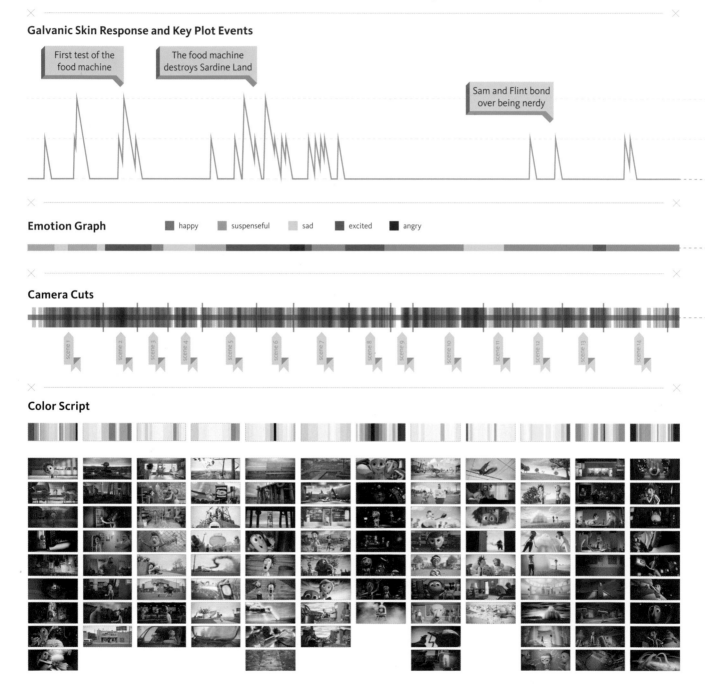

Galvanic Skin Response and Key Plot Events

First test of the food machine

The food machine destroys Sardine Land

Sam and Flint bond over being nerdy

Emotion Graph

happy   suspenseful   sad   excited   angry

Camera Cuts

scene 1 scene 2 scene 3 scene 4 scene 5 scene 6 scene 7 scene 8 scene 9 scene 10 scene 11 scene 12 scene 13 scene 14

Color Script

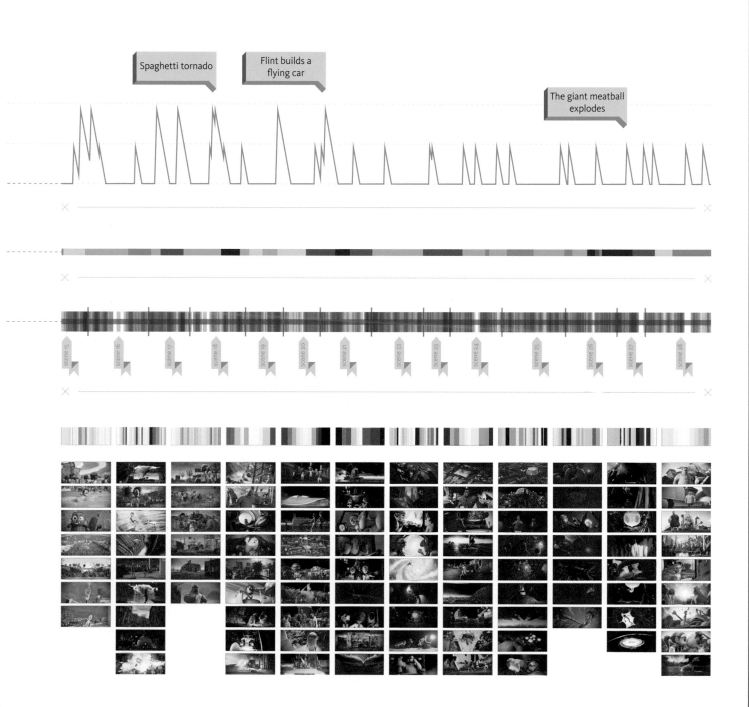

Spaghetti tornado

Flint builds a
flying car

The giant meatball
explodes

scene 15 scene 16 scene 17 scene 18 scene 19 scene 20 scene 21 scene 22 scene 23 scene 24 scene 25 scene 26 scene 27 scene 28

EXPERIENCE

SCENES THAT TELL STORIES

Production designer Alex McDowell's immersive pre-visualizations give his elaborate film worlds an active role in storytelling.

AFTER STEVEN SPIELBERG INVITED HIM TO JOIN THE TEAM MAKING THE SCI-FI THRILLER *MINORITY REPORT*, Alex McDowell started work on the same day as the script writer, Scott Frank. As a production designer, McDowell's job is to give a film its distinctive look and feel—a task that embraces every aspect of the production, from building sets to choosing props to creating computer-generated visual effects. Once upon a time, McDowell wouldn't have been brought in until after the script was written. But in today's environment, that no longer makes sense.

"We're used to the idea that a film starts with a script, but that's not very logical, because film is a visual medium," says McDowell. The start-with-the-script approach might have worked for the dialogue-driven films of an earlier era, but when it comes to the kind of action-packed movies that Hollywood produces today, the look and logic of the on-screen world are as important to a film as the script. In fact, they can do much to inform it.

Minority Report demonstrates that. Set in Washington, D.C., in the year 2054, *Minority Report* was a hit film about a small group of psychics called "precogs," who can foresee murders and help police arrest the perpetrators before the crimes occur. Although it was released in 2002, *Minority Report* has endured as a cultural touchstone ever since, in no small part because it envisioned a number of technologies—including gesture-based computing interfaces and personalized, location-based advertising—that have since become reality.

But in 1999, when McDowell joined the project, none of those ideas existed yet. So McDowell and his team started with the big picture—what would Washington, D.C., look like in 2054? A mind-spinning two-day think tank with scientists and futurists from MIT and Silicon Valley provided insight into demographic trends and emerging technologies like retinal scanning and maglev transportation. With a clearer picture of what life might be like in fifty years, McDowell's team started to map the world.

This kind of conceptual world-building isn't meant to replace the script-writing process, McDowell says. But by preempting it—by envisioning the world the story will inhabit, and understanding its social and physical structure—he seeks to help the writer carve a linear narrative through that space. "The work you do to embed a story into a space and an environment directly correlates to how convincing the film will be for the audience," McDowell says. The result is a more efficient creative process and a more interesting, coherent movie.

McDowell has an impressive track record of building coherent fictional worlds. He designed the dark, decaying spaces of *Fight Club*, David Fincher's psychological twister. He dreamed up the surreal wonderland of Tim Burton's *Charlie and the Chocolate Factory*, not to mention his memorable designs for *The Watchmen*, *Cat in the Hat*, and *Corpse Bride*. For *The Terminal*, he even constructed a full-scale replica of an airport concourse inside a 97,000-square-foot (9,000-square-meter) hangar that was originally built to serve as an assembly plant for U.S. Air Force bombers.

"The best design is often that which the audience never notices," says McDowell. That

Minority Report **was a pivotal film for production designer Alex McDowell. Using digital pre-visualization techniques allowed him to bring the production's most important spaces, like the precog chamber (left), into focus early in the process. That let the physical aspects of the film become important parts of the plot, too.**

WALL 4

AGATHA IN LIQUID

TANK

ANDERTON

may be why production designers are seldom household names and production design is poorly understood beyond the confines of the film industry. Yet the role of production designers is critical. Although production designers were traditionally part of a creative triumvirate that included directors and cinematographers, with the introduction of computer-generated special effects during the 1980s and 1990s, their influence declined. "The technology allowed the director to defer creative decisions about design, and post-production became the star," says McDowell, who points to *The Perfect Storm* as an example of that trend: "Industrial Light and Magic can probably claim credit for the look of the film more than the production designer, who may have created the boat."

McDowell is part of a nascent movement to reassert the influence of production designers by creating visual spaces that play an active role in the storytelling. Along the way, he's helped introduce technologies to the design process that have changed the way Hollywood approaches storytelling.

Trained as a fine art painter but surrounded by friends in bands, McDowell—a Brit who split his childhood between his parents' home in South Asia and boarding school in England—got his professional start designing album covers for punk rock bands in the late 1970s. When Iggy Pop asked him if he knew anyone who could make a music video, McDowell jumped at the new challenge. It was an experimental era, when bands themselves had creative control over music videos, with little input from their labels. For McDowell it was also an opportunity to explore filmmaking by gaining technical experience in an environment with few creative limits. After a decade spent making music videos, McDowell earned his first film credit in 1992, with *The Lawnmower Man*, followed two years later by *The Crow*.

"It is a stunning work of visual style— the best version of a comic book universe I've seen," film critic Roger Ebert wrote of

McDowell's ideas for the precog chamber (left) and other spaces in *Minority Report* helped shape the action of the film. His "immersive design mandala" (right) describes the emerging nonlinear process of digital design and filmmaking, though its details are relevant to many other creative fields.

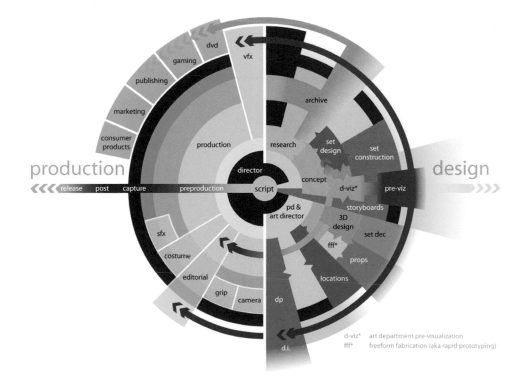

the latter. Ebert was impressed by the visual consistency of the movie, and the seamless experience it created, adding, "It's not often that movies can use miniatures and special effects and sets and visual tricks to create a convincing place, rather than just a series of obvious sets."

McDowell's work on *Fight Club* further boosted his reputation for creating sets that capture and amplify a film's central themes. Take *Fight Club*'s Paper Street House: Once a grand Victorian, the house has fallen on hard times. The wallpaper is peeling, the faucets run brown, and the basement floods when it rains. The decrepit house becomes a metaphor for mental breakdown and the end-of-the-millennium philosophy espoused by Brad Pitt's character, who believes society itself has decayed under the corrosive influence of corporate interests and cheap commercialism.

Fight Club was where McDowell had his "aha moment." That's when he saw how director David Fincher used software to visualize scenes he wanted his special-effects team to create. "Right around then, for the first time, you could put $2,000 worth of software on a Mac and have the rough equivalent of the $100,000 workstations that the special-effects team used in post-production," McDowell says. Using similar technology, he began building visually rough but detail-rich digital versions of sets known as pre-visualizations, or "pre-vis." His pre-vis sets provided a way to explore potential spaces and think through the practical elements that might make a scene more immersive.

"Visualization has created the most dynamic, creative, collaborative space that has ever existed," says McDowell, who calls this collaborative approach "immersive design." (He has since cofounded the 5D: Immersive Design conference.)

Minority Report was a pivotal project for McDowell's use of the new technology and an opportunity to fully exploit its potential.

For McDowell, architecture is a key element to a film's narrative. The complex layout of the Precrime headquarters—a visual echo of the immersive design mandala—tracked with the plot intricacies that happened there, while the abundance of glass alludes to the radical transparency of precognition.

Consider the film's Hall of Containment, a subterranean room that serves as a sort of jail for those arrested by the Precrime unit for murders they were about to commit. For the scene, Steven Spielberg "had this image of Arlington National Cemetery, and digital gravestones, stored vertically, that contained each person's data," recalls McDowell. He imagined a jailer in the center of the vast space, traveling on a movable platform to access individual gravestones. "It was a great visual, but it was hard to figure out how to contain it."

Using pre-vis, McDowell developed the mechanics of the scene: Pre-perps are stacked one atop the other in columns that slide up and down. The set is part panopticon (the eighteenth-century prison design that allows jailers to watch every prisoner) and part cathedral (with its connotations

of an omnipotent God). The sheer number of gravestones, extending row after row in three dimensions, packs a profound psychological punch. The Hall of Containment doesn't get a lot of screen time in *Minority Report*, but it is a powerful space, and it sparks an awakening of sorts for the main character, John Anderton—and for viewers of the film. "I never knew there were so many," says Anderton, suddenly aware of the inhumane reality of the seemingly enlightened idea of capturing people before they commit a crime. In the brilliant design of this one space, McDowell captured the central idea of the movie: That *Minority Report*'s seemingly utopian world has a dark and troubling core.

As a planning tool, pre-vis also proved invaluable for *Charlie and the Chocolate Factory*, a production that had more sets than

The dark, decaying house in David Fincher's film *Fight Club* constituted another character with a distinct personality. The decrepit structure became a metaphor for mental breakdown and the nihilistic philosophy espoused by Brad Pitt's character.

MCDOWELL IS PART OF A NASCENT MOVEMENT TO REASSERT THE INFLUENCE OF PRODUCTION DESIGNERS BY CREATING VISUAL SPACES THAT PLAY AN ACTIVE ROLE IN THE STORYTELLING. ALONG THE WAY, HE'S HELPED INTRODUCE TECHNOLOGIES TO THE DESIGN PROCESS THAT HAVE CHANGED THE WAY HOLLYWOOD APPROACHES STORYTELLING.

—

McDowell had ever created for a single film. McDowell's pre-vis models provided the information he needed to determine exactly how many gallons of fake chocolate was needed to fill the 120-foot Chocolate River, for instance, and how many blades of plastic grass would be needed to cover the rolling hills. "The grass was coming from China, and it took six weeks to deliver," he says. "We didn't have time to order more had we come up short."

For *The Terminal*, Spielberg used McDowell's pre-vis models to explore potential camera angles long before the airport set was built. That advance work gave the designer early warning if, say, an escalator or window needed to be relocated—changes that would have been expensive or even impossible to make after the set

was built and film crews were standing by. Likewise, when set construction costs threatened to skyrocket, McDowell and art director Chris Burian-Mohr also used *The Terminal*'s virtual set to identify elements that could be modified to save money without sacrificing the story. A rear staircase was eliminated, a Starbucks kiosk was modified, and the airport concourse shrank slightly, but the changes didn't detract from the realism of the scene.

The practical advantages of pre-vis are obvious, but McDowell prefers to focus on the creative advantages of immersive design and how it can improve storytelling. "Visualization has liberated the imagination. There is no constraint on the worlds we can create," he says, pointing to the Harry Potter films and *Avatar* as projects that studios

wouldn't have even attempted decades ago.

Just as important, however, McDowell believes that visualization enables a richer collaboration between the people who are actually producing a film. "Think about the origins of storytelling, with a group of primitives sitting around the campfire, trying to make sense of the world around them," McDowell explains. Fast-forward to Hollywood, where a script writer goes off to his room and writes a story that reflects his experience—a story that is then broken apart and reassembled by dozens of others who have a creative hand in a movie. With immersive design, McDowell argues, "the storyteller, the designer, the cinematographer, the director—everyone can sit around that campfire, experience the same environment, and start shaping the story around it." Ⓐ

Fight Club was where McDowell had his "aha moment," when he saw how director David Fincher used software to visualize scenes he wanted his special-effects team to create. After that experience, he began building visually rough but detail-rich digital versions of sets known as pre-visualizations, or "pre-vis."

"THE BEST DESIGN IS OFTEN THAT WHICH THE AUDIENCE NEVER NOTICES."

By the time McDowell worked on Tim Burton's *Charlie and the Chocolate Factory* (2005), digital special effects and pre-visualization techniques had become part of the standard workflow. When he designed the scenes around a chocolate river, though, he did not know whether the scene would be "real" or computer generated.

WITH IMMERSIVE DESIGN, MCDOWELL ARGUES, "THE STORYTELLER, THE DESIGNER, THE CINEMATOGRAPHER, THE DIRECTOR— EVERYONE CAN SIT AROUND THAT CAMPFIRE, EXPERIENCE THE SAME ENVIRONMENT, AND START SHAPING THE STORY AROUND IT."

—

McDowell used pre-visualization extensively when he worked on Steven Spielberg's *The Terminal*. As in *Fight Club*, the space itself served as an important character in this film about a man without a country, trapped in an airport.

Immersive design is total design—every detail must be considered, because everything contributes to the overall experience. Above, two views of chocolate-sucking pipes from *Charlie and the Chocolate Factory*.

—

"VISUALIZATION HAS CREATED THE MOST DYNAMIC, CREATIVE, COLLABORATIVE SPACE THAT HAS EVER EXISTED," SAYS MCDOWELL, WHO CALLS THIS APPROACH "IMMERSIVE DESIGN."

IRENE AU

The director of user experience at Google discusses how speed, objectivity, and research shape the search giant's design approach.

Google's design can seem very neutral. Does Google have a design philosophy?
Very much so. It ties back to our values as a company. We value objectivity. At Google, we use powerful algorithms, rather than human editors, to find the best of the Web. We value openness, so we often allow interconnectedness with third parties through APIs (Application Programming Interfaces). We also value speed. We want the Internet as a whole to be faster, and we want our products to perform extremely quickly. Those three values translate into a set of design principles that inform the design of all our products.

How are those values manifested in Google's products?
Google's machine-driven look and feel is very deliberate. We don't want our designs to look too handmade, because then they will look editorialized. It's also minimal because we want to be fast, and any kind of adornment added to a page contributes to longer load times—even if it's 4 milliseconds. We're all about getting people to the information

"We value objectivity. We value openness. We also value speed. We want the Internet as a whole to be faster, and we want our products to perform extremely quickly. Those three values translate into a set of design principles that inform the design of all our products."

—

that they're looking for very quickly; this is our point of view.

Also, especially in search results, we use high-contrast color schemes—black text or dark blue links against a white background. We reference human interface research that shows that black text against a white background is optimal for on-screen reading and scanning.

Our interfaces are often dense. We're constantly looking at how much information we put "above the fold." If you're looking at your Gmail inbox or your Docs list, we try to get as much of that content above the fold as possible. We care about speed, not only in terms of page latency but also the speed of information retrieval via human perception and cognition. Those principles are overarching across all of Google's experiences.

Of course, how you execute on those principles evolves over time and varies depending on whether you're building a search experience, a content-driven site like News, or a highly interactive Web application like Gmail. Ultimately, we aim to create an experience that is distinctly and uniquely Google.

You mentioned objectivity. Design tends to be a personal exercise, but objectivity suggests taking the designer out of the process.

We definitely have a point of view. All of these values and principles—that is our design strategy. Our design challenge is figuring out how to achieve the appearance of objectivity through interface design.

Google was born out of search, so that's the most relevant example. There, we strive to show the best of the Web and the results that are most relevant. We rank results in order of what's the best result. And you can see that in the design. We treat all results equally.

—

"Google was born out of search, so that's the most relevant example. There, we strive to show the best of the Web and the results that are most relevant. We rank results in order of what's the best result. And you can see that in the design. We treat all results equally."

So objectivity is the shortest distance between two points for the user?

Yes. Any kind of adornment on the page is going to express a personality. The reason for Google's minimalist look and feel is to create a fast experience, and to have the user focus on the content. The content is the interface.

How do you approach new design problems?

The first place we start is to look at our users, by looking at how people use technology. What's the context? What do people with high information needs do in their daily lives? We use insights about our users throughout the product-development cycle to inform the overall product design and interface design. These insights may come from a variety of methods, whether through surveys, diary studies, field studies, or usability studies.

How does that research turn into real-world products?

Here's one example. There are parts of the world where people don't use desktop computers at all; most of their interaction with the Internet is on mobile devices. So how do we bring information to people when they aren't in front of a computer?

We did field research in Uganda where we looked at people with high information needs, and we simulated an SMS-based search service. Through this simulation we understood what information people most needed, and we identified three major categories of interest: health, agriculture, and weather. As a result, we focused on these three areas when we launched our SMS-based search service in Africa.

How do you define good design? What does that mean today?

Good design is an experience that makes the mundane delightful. It's beautiful, useful, enduring, and simple. **Ⓐ**

Irene Au is director of user experience at Google.

THE ESSENTIALS OF PLAY

In translating its iconic bricks into a massively multiplayer game, the LEGO Group extended the joys of physical play into an online social experience.

WHEN GAME CREATIVE DIRECTOR RYAN SEABURY SPOTTED A LEGO PIECE he hadn't seen since 1982—a rocket fin from a set he owned long ago—tears nearly came to his eyes. "The rush of nostalgia hit me hard," he says. "Instantly I was six years old, in the basement, playing with my outer-space set." The long-lost piece, however, wasn't in his hand but on his PC screen, one of twenty thousand virtual bricks brought back from the dead by the LEGO Group for its new game.

There has always been something enchanting about the tangible *snick* of ABS plastic bricks locking together—something that forms the essence of play. A few years ago, however, the LEGO Group realized that its beloved building sets would not carry the day alone. In 2005, with sales down and a possible bankruptcy looming, the $2 billion firm risked losing not only its business, but a distinct and oddly innocent corporate culture that made the toy one of the most popular of the last half century.

The company commenced a dogged fight for its future, and in so doing embarked on a quest to discover nothing less than the future of play. Tempered by the crisis, executives at the LEGO Group sought advice from university professors and game developers to somehow broaden their understanding of the topic. They knew, of course, that children will always build stuff on the basement floor, but there were other sides of play that executives had neglected. For instance, kids love becoming entangled in the type of overheated story lines that jolt the imagination. They also want a community of like-minded builders to share their experiences and creativity.

The way to bring these elements to play turned out to be a massively multiplayer online game. It may seem a little strange that in the midst of a deep restructuring, the LEGO Group's new CEO poured resources into a sprawling and expensive video game—clearly outside the core business of plastic bricks. But the resulting title, *LEGO Universe,* which debuted in October 2010, is actually the culmination of a series of these hard-won lessons. After a decade of development and the efforts of LEGO Group employees, contractors, and the staff of gaming partner NetDevil, *Universe* is no mere flash-animated outpost among other companies with a toy and a Web presence. *Universe* allows fans around the globe to build projects together from virtual LEGO bricks, show them off to one another, and then take them into battle against the forces of the "Maelstrom." "*Universe* is a very important step for our future," says game senior director Mark William Hansen. "We need to find ways to make physical play more relevant and exciting and innovative all the time."

When Seabury heard that his company, NetDevil, in Louisville, Colorado, was asked by the LEGO Group to make a pitch for an online game in 2005, he literally jumped out of his seat. But, he says, he then grew a bit wary. Translating LEGO toys to the online world could potentially result in something "really tedious." Existing PC-based LEGO building games had

The LEGO Group discovered that one of the most important things kids did with its bricks and figures was create stories around them. This insight is at the core of the scenarios and action of the massively multiplayer game *LEGO Universe.*

KIDS LOVE BECOMING ENTANGLED IN THE TYPE OF OVERHEATED STORY LINES THAT JOLT THE IMAGINATION. THEY ALSO WANT A COMMUNITY OF LIKE-MINDED BUILDERS TO SHARE THEIR EXPERIENCES AND CREATIVITY.

—

enjoyed success but reached a limited market; networking them online wouldn't add much. "We said to them right up front that we don't want to just make a literal interpretation of what it is to build with LEGO bricks in real life," Seabury recounts from his office chair while fiddling with a multicolored penguin he constructed from the random bricks strewn across his desk. "There will always be this nice reward of snapping the bricks together—the sound it makes, how it feels in your fingers. You can't replicate that on a computer screen—not even with haptic devices [that give tactile feedback] or the new motion capture devices for gamers. It's always going to feel disconnected."

The game would feature building stuff, but it would surely need something more. Seabury pointed executives to the brilliance of the LEGO Group's bestselling licensed

LEGO Universe comes with a large backstory—about protecting Imagination from a dark force known as the Maelstrom. That simple setup allows for a nearly endless series of quests as well as a wide variety of characters for the game's players to identify with.

NetDevil, the Colorado company that developed the game with the LEGO Group, immersed itself in the culture of LEGO bricks. Clockwise from top left: The brick repository; a LEGO Death Star was one of many large-scale LEGO brick creations built for research; the game underwent extensive kid-testing, by groups and individuals; NetDevil developers spent years perfecting the look and feel of the game, as well as its sophisticated brick-building simulation.

titles such as *LEGO Star Wars* and *LEGO Indiana Jones*. While those games lack an open building component, they successfully translated playing with bricks into the imaginary realm. "Look, when you play with minifigures in real life," says Seabury, "you imagine them doing stuff—putting on strange gear and doing cool moves in your mind. The computer's job is to allow your imagination to come to life visually in front of you."

Hansen got it right away. "The story is the emotional hook," says the manager, who originally came up with idea of *Universe* and now runs the partnership with NetDevil. Hansen says that each year, the LEGO Group brings hundreds of kids in for focus groups in Colorado and Denmark to test play scenarios. Their research shows that after playing LEGO video games, children often hop back on the floor with their real LEGO bricks, exploring the scenarios they left behind on the screen. In fact, almost 60 percent of LEGO toy sales is tied to licensed properties. "You can extend your physical play into the computer," says Hansen, "and you can bring it back out again and play with your LEGO toys on the floor."

Seabury's insight convinced Hansen. They would mix building and gameplay in the same title. At first, Seabury liked the open possibilities of an urban landscape—

"like *Grand Theft Auto* without the bad stuff"—so the first iteration was a big city where friends could play games and make stuff together. But how did these functions work together? Why play the game if all you want to do is build, and vice versa. The Danes were pressing the group to come up with the "red thread"—a Scandinavian phrase for a defining element that pulls everything together.

The group hired Dungeons and Dragons gaming guru Keith Baker to help them with a more mythic story line and then honed the story to the point where it is now—a universal conflict as compelling as it is earnest. The conceit? Some LEGO minifigures got too curious about Imagination's fountainhead and accidentally released the "Maelstrom"—an evil force of bad imagination. To fight the Maelstrom, you smash up the soldiers of the dark imagination and build LEGO models to push back the Maelstrom and restore order to LEGO Universe. It basically sounds like an abridged version of *Paradise Lost* for middle schoolers. Explains Seabury: "It sets up a creative loop where you go through the game, build stuff on your property with the bricks you earned, then do more gameplay when you need more bricks." The universal conflict also neatly pulls in scenarios like pirates, jungles, spaceships, and other kid eye candy.

AFTER PLAYING LEGO VIDEO GAMES, CHILDREN OFTEN HOP BACK ON THE FLOOR WITH THEIR REAL LEGO BRICKS, EXPLORING THE SCENARIOS THEY LEFT BEHIND ON THE SCREEN.

EXPERIENCE

THE DEVELOPERS WERE PRESSED TO COME UP WITH A "RED THREAD"—A DEFINING ELEMENT THAT PULLS EVERYTHING TOGETHER.

In a marquee image for *LEGO Universe*, the Maelstrom Cavalry faces off with game players, who are represented by iconic LEGO minifigures.

With the red thread in place, the engineering challenges of actually creating the universe pressed to the fore. This was no ordinary online game. Over five years, NetDevil quadrupled its staffing, putting more than 140 people on the game. (Compare that with a sixty-person team and nine months of development for a typical console game. Seabury says, "Our head count is equivalent to a triple-A Hollywood movie.") An army of animators began drawing the backgrounds and props used in the battles. They roughed out spaceships and pirate ships using the Autodesk SketchBook application on an iPad, or they sketched directly on a PC. The objects were then poured into Autodesk Maya, which has a direct link to the LEGO factory's internal database of thousands of brick shapes currently in production.

Making LEGO bricks look real on the screen became the next engineering stumper. It turned out that a single 2-by-4 brick required more polygons than a *World of Warcraft* avatar—the tiny studs and surfaces contain a lot of detail. The solution turned out to be "hidden surface removal," which preserved the integrity of each brick while a player manipulated it onscreen, but removed the polygons once the piece snapped into place in a user's creation. It took forty engineers four years to build code so that a computer could understand when and where to remove surface detail without harming the look of the model.

The visuals were only a small portion of the engineering work necessary to accommodate a massive number of players. To appreciate this, think about stomping around the virtual LEGO landscape and slipping an object in your minifigure's backpack. The server has to make note of the object in your pack until you take it out again a few minutes—or a few months—later. To accomplish this, engineers constructed a giant database on the back end of *Universe* to keep track of the assets and creations of tens of thousands of minifigures for as long as their human users were registered.

To prepare for the hordes to populate the site, engineers devised a number of technical measures to ensure user safety. LEGO customers have long included around 8 percent of adult fans, but the presence of kids and adults in the same online world justifiably raises questions from parents. To address these, the team designed measures to check the appropriateness of content at several points. When you build a new object out of bricks, the object goes to a team of roughly one hundred live moderators, who evaluate it before making it visible to other members.

The chat functions are moderated twenty-four hours a day, seven days a week. To further keep the talk clear of bullying or predatory behavior, the team employs a combination of filtering systems to automatically block inappropriate content in various languages. Cutting-edge software solutions are used to detect inappropriate behavior and content and alert the moderation team. Users can't type numbers, making it difficult to share phone numbers and other personal information. Behind the scenes, a server assigns a "goodness score" based on a user's behavior and efforts to build and share their creations, or a "badness score" to flag users who need to be moderated more closely.

Hansen says that all the cautionary measures serve a major philosophical goal for LEGO toys—playing well with others. "Demonstrating your creativity is a fundamental power of the LEGO experience," he says. *Universe* is simply a tool that makes it possible to have a lot more playdates. "Every child is creative, but if they just build in their room and never see what other people do, it may be limiting. Your imagination gets fed when you witness the creativity of thousands of others." ⒶA

The imagination-saving quest of *LEGO Universe* is populated with other scenarios, such as pirates, jungles, spaceships, and, at left, ninjas.

SYSTEMS

HOW DO WE DESIGN DESIGN?

CAN GOOD DESIGN BE...DESIGNED? THE ANSWER IS THAT IT NOT ONLY CAN, IT MUST. FOR DESIGN TO FULFILL ITS POTENTIAL TO ADDRESS OUR BIGGEST, MOST DIFFICULT CHALLENGES, WE NEED NEW SYSTEMS FOR IT THAT WILL ENCOURAGE DESIGNERS TO THINK BIG, TO MAKE MAXIMUM USE OF AVAILABLE RESOURCES AND SOURCES OF INSPIRATION, AND TO APPROACH PROBLEMS IN AN INTEGRATED OR HOLISTIC MANNER.
—

previous spread: **The Empire State Building recently underwent an energy retrofit, led in part by Amory Lovins and Rocky Mountain Institute.**

Better systems for designing can be based on emerging technology or on established laws of nature; they can be rooted in new frameworks that provide inspiration and incentive to break new ground or that encourage designers to think and act in a more efficient, integrative manner.

Starting with technology, a potentially revolutionary new system of design that is just now coming to the fore is "design computation," discussed in Chapter 3 by technologist Robert Aish. It uses computing to create a framework within which designers can explore alternatives as they ask, "What if I try this?" It promises to change the process of design in profound ways—designers will set up the parameters and design the actual framework, but the computer can generate the various alternatives as well as take care of the drudge work.

Contrast this with the system designed by Peter Diamandis of the celebrated X Prize initiative. Nothing high-tech or complicated about this approach: Diamandis relies on good old-fashioned monetary prizes and the spirit of competition as a means of inspiring people to take on the biggest, toughest challenges our planet faces today. And, as he explains in this chapter, the X Prize system is carefully designed to elicit the widest range of entrants and solutions, and allow those solutions to get to market.

Amory Lovins is known for pioneering a whole-systems design approach geared toward integrated, high-efficiency design that is also sustainable (though don't use that s-word around Lovins). The key, he notes, is to be able to convene all the key players on a design project in a "disciplined framework that fits all the moving parts together" in the most cost- and energy-efficient ways. That, says Lovins, is at the core of integrative design.

Of course, if we're looking for systems and frameworks for integrative design, we can do no better than to look to nature—which has been solving design problems this way for a few billion years. The biomimicry pioneer Janine Benyus suggests that nature offers a ready-made system that designers can tap into by asking the fundamental question, "How would nature design this?" The answers to that question can provide critical lessons and principles that can then be applied to man-made design projects.

From high-tech to all-natural, these are radically different systems for designing, but the common element is this: They all provide designers with new methodologies and ways of approaching the complex and difficult design challenges of today and tomorrow. Ⓐ

THE X PRIZE

This carefully crafted system for encouraging design has brought innovation to space travel and automotive efficiency—with more to come.

SOME TIME IN LATE 2011, AT A NEWLY ERECTED SPACEPORT IN LAS CRUCES, NEW MEXICO, six passengers and two pilots will board a sixty-foot-long rocketplane called *SpaceShipTwo*. A much larger, four-engine carrier craft will haul the smaller vessel halfway up into the stratosphere, to fifty-two thousand feet. Here, *SpaceShipTwo* will release itself from the underbelly of its mother ship, ignite a hybrid engine that burns a potent cocktail of synthetic rubber and nitrous oxide, and accelerate to twenty-five hundred miles per hour. It will hurl itself to an altitude of seventy miles, where for six glorious minutes its passengers will experience zero gravity, floating weightless in the cabin as they skirt the boundary of outer space. And then *SpaceShipTwo* will begin a silent free fall until, at an altitude of eighty thousand feet, its tapered wings will pivot horizontally and glide its passengers and crew gently back to terra firma.

Space-industry old-timers long scoffed at the feasibility of safely ferrying well-heeled tourists to suborbital altitudes in a reusable spacecraft. Some claimed it was technologically impossible, others bemoaned its prohibitive cost, and many regarded it as just plain silly. But as Peter Diamandis loves to tell naysayers, "The day before something is truly a break-through, it's a crazy idea." Diamandis is the Brooklyn-born forty-nine-year-old founder and chairman of the X Prize Foundation, a nonprofit institute that establishes lucrative incentive prizes to spur groundbreaking innovation.

SpaceShipTwo and its carrier craft, *WhiteKnightTwo*, owned by billionaire entrepreneur Richard Branson, are anomalies of aviation. Their designs depart radically from the paradigm of conventional aerospace engineering. Both vessels are offspring of the first X Prize: In 1996, Diamandis offered $10 million to any privately funded group that could send a manned vehicle into space twice in two weeks.

The Ansari X Prize was the first test of the X Prize as a system for encouraging design. The prizes—there are now four, with more under development—are Diamandis's strategy to alter the course of design and engineering, and to do it with carefully crafted, highly visible com-petitions. The prizes are intended to thrust research and design in a direction they wouldn't ordinarily go. Diamandis succeeded unequivocally with the first X Prize. For decades, aero-space innovation had languished amid a handful of government agencies, where the pace of development was glacial. Today, many credit the Ansari X Prize with single-handedly hatching what is now a flourishing commercial space industry. "Humans have a tendency to be stuck in the way they think," Diamandis says. "We talk about change, but people really don't want change. This is where the X Prize has potential value, because the best way to cause people to change is through a very bold, big, dramatic demonstration that flips a switch in their mind."

Some twenty-six teams stepped up to compete for the Ansari X Prize. The lure of fame and $10 million—and the chance to reinvent an industry—spawned a dazzling fleet of one-of-a-kind spaceships. Not since the moon landings had there been such a flurry of fresh ideas for

THE GENIUS OF THE X PRIZE IS THAT THE SYSTEM IS DESIGNED TO PRODUCE A WIDE RANGE OF ENTRANTS AND SOLUTIONS. "HUMANS ARE GENETICALLY ENGINEERED TO COMPETE," SAYS DIAMANDIS.

—

Finland's RaceAbout electric vehicle (left) took second place in the competition to reach 100 mpg. The X Prize is the creation of Peter Diamandis (right), who regards it as an efficient and important method for creating breakthroughs.

space travel. The X Prize attracted plenty of garage loonies, compulsive inventors, engineering prodigies, serial entrepreneurs, and lofty dreamers. And that was just fine with Diamandis. "You don't want to turn away those pesky bicycle mechanics from Dayton, Ohio," he says. It was precisely this amalgam of eccentricity, practicality, and drive that he hoped would finally pry the floundering space industry from the prosaic claws of big government.

"In large corporations, you worry because of the embarrassment and what it could do to your stock price," says Diamandis. "But true breakthroughs often come from sequestered labs at small companies, where the failures won't cause public harm." The X Prize, he believes, "allows for crazy ideas to come into existence—real breakthroughs that require high levels of risk and great risk of failure. Incentive prizes are a mechanism to get people to take that level of risk and try those crazy ideas."

At the moment, there is a $10 million X Prize offered to the first team of scientists that can sequence an entire human genome in ten days or less. Send a robot to the moon, get it to roam at least 1,640 feet (500 meters) from its landing site while

it beams data to Earth, and you'll win the $30 million Lunar X Prize. Up for grabs in 2010 was a $10 million purse for building a production-capable automobile (either electric or hybrid) that got the energy equivalent of 100 miles per gallon. And there are X Prizes in development to address the need for clean energy to end our dependence on fossil fuels, eliminate poverty, cure cancer, and heal dying coral reefs.

DIAMANDIS CONTENDS THAT THE ELABORATE AND SOMETIMES DRACONIAN RULES ESTABLISHED FOR X PRIZES ARE ESSENTIAL TO MEET HIS ULTIMATE GOAL: CULTIVATING DISRUPTIVE TECHNOLOGIES.

—

While the X Prizes seem tailor-made for a media-saturated, reality-show-friendly time, Diamandis notes that this kind of system for spurring design has a long history. In 1714, the British government established the Longitude Prize, one of the earliest incentive awards. It sought a technique to determine a ship's longitude while under sail. Today's marine chronometer is based on the invention of the English carpenter who won the £20,000 prize—the equivalent amount today is in the range of an X Prize. Trying to figure out how to feed his far-flung troops, Napoleon sponsored a prize to devise a way to preserve food. You can thank the winner for that twelve-year-old can of Chef Boyardee ravioli in your pantry.

It was the Orteig Prize that most inspired Diamandis. In 1919, New York hotelier Raymond Orteig offered $25,000 to the first pilot who could make a nonstop flight between New York and Paris. Eight years later, Charles Lindbergh completed the 33.5-hour crossing in the *Spirit of St. Louis* and as a result jumpstarted the modern aviation industry.

Diamandis earned a master's degree in aerospace engineering and for a long time dreamed of becoming an astronaut. But he didn't pursue either field. Instead, he fashioned himself into the world's leading cheerleader for private space travel. Diamandis knew that his chances of blasting into orbit on the space shuttle were slim. His ticket to the final frontier would be onboard some yet-to-be-conceived private spacecraft. Using the Orteig Prize as a model, Diamandis scrounged for cash and eventually managed to cobble together $10 million, with a hefty chunk coming from telecom entrepreneur Anouseh Ansari. He renamed the challenge the Ansari X Prize, and the competition quickly blossomed into a global race to the cosmos—or the edge of our atmosphere, to start. The genius of the X Prize is that the system is designed to produce a wide range of entrants and solutions. "Humans are genetically engineered to compete," says Diamandis. "We have it in our genes, in our ethos." The result is invariably a fertile and diverse field of players working within very particular limits and rules.

Diamandis has a clear framework for designing an X Prize. It has to offer a real incentive, typically $10 million or more. "That gives people an excuse to dream big, assemble teams, and raise capital," he says. Often competitors will pour up to forty

times more cash into their efforts than they stand to gain from winning the prize. The aim is "to bring forward dozens of different designs and consequently a new industry rather than a single solution backed by venture capitalists."

An X Prize must focus on an area where there is a market failure—such as in the aerospace and automotive industries. The Prize's goal must be clear and measurable: 100 miles per gallon, or flying to an altitude of 100 kilometers twice in two weeks. The goal has to be achievable in three to eight years. Too short is too easy; too long and no one cares anymore. Finally, Diamandis says, "it must be a competition that the public gets excited about, and one that creates heroes."

On October 4, 2004, aerospace pioneer Burt Rutan, leading a team backed by Microsoft cofounder Paul Allen, won the Ansari X Prize. "On that day, two things happened that were significant," recounts Diamandis. "One was that Richard Branson committed a quarter of a billion dollars to develop *SpaceShipOne* into *SpaceShipTwo* and launch Virgin Galactic. That was critical, because rather than just having the prize result in a museum piece hanging in the Smithsonian, it launched an industry, which was our objective goal. The other thing that

THE AUTO-PRIZE RULEBOOK NUMBERED A WHOPPING 137 PAGES. "THE PEOPLE WHO WROTE IT DID A GOOD JOB OF ENSURING SOMETHING NEW WOULD APPEAR," SAYS RON MATHIS.

—

"WE HAD TO DO THINGS QUICK, RATHER THAN SPENDING TIME TESTING AND ANALYZING," SAYS SAMI ROUTSALAINEN. "THERE WERE LITERALLY INNOVATION AND DESIGN CHANGES HAPPENING ON THE TRACK."

—

One of Diamandis's requirements for an X Prize is that it attract a lot of attention. The combination of cars, racetracks, high technology, and prize money helped keep the Progressive Insurance Automotive X Prize in the headlines for many months.

happened is Northrop Grumman purchased Scaled Composites, the company that had built *SpaceShipOne*."

Next up was the Progressive Insurance Automotive X Prize, announced in April 2007. The auto-prize rulebook numbered a whopping 137 pages. "The people who wrote it did a good job of ensuring something new would appear," says Ron Mathis, chief of design for the Edison2 team, one of the seven finalists. "The requirements were really at the very edge of what was possible."

The performance parameters led competitors to scrap everything they knew about cars. "You had to start from scratch," continues Mathis. "There was no way to stretch a normal production car to achieve that sort of efficiency. I deliberately decided not to be very organized about our design process, because if it were too formalized we'd lose originality and spontaneity." Gary Starr, whose ZAP team designed a three-wheeled vehicle, says, "The rules helped create something that was low-cost

and affordable, that people would actually want to buy and feel safe in." They also forced teams to think on the fly. "We had to do things quick, rather than spending time testing and analyzing," says Sami Routsalainen, who led a team from Finland. "There were literally innovation and design changes happening on the track."

Diamandis contends that the elaborate and sometimes draconian rules established for X Prizes are essential to meet his ultimate goal: cultivating disruptive technologies that challenge conventional wisdom and smash entrenched archetypes. "For me, good design is being clear about the boundary conditions, clear about where you are heading, even when you're not sure about the realm of possibility. But because we're interested in the realm of breakthroughs, we're very careful to not overconstrain the problem." He cites the Ansari X Prize as a benchmark. "None of the detail was specified, to keep the options for experimenting wide open. As a result, we had literally

SYSTEMS

Another stated aim of the X Prize is that the technology developed for competition be adapted for the market. The Finnish RaceAbout team shared that goal, developing a powertrain made primarily from Finnish technology.

twenty-six different designs tackling the problem. It was extraordinarily fulfilling to see this sort of Darwinian evolution taking place. We wanted to set up a structure that would allow for really exciting, surprising, and unexpected solutions with unexpected benefits."

Diamandis has said of the X Prize approach: "One of the precepts that I'm learning is, fail often and fail early, until you make it happen right." Of the twenty-four teams that initially enlisted for the Automotive X Prize, all but seven had been eliminated by the final stage of the competition. The high knockout rate is typical—a challenge's stringent rules ensure what Diamandis calls the "proper balance of audacity and achievability."

In 2009, Diamandis set forth his convictions in a self-published paper. "The prize rules should define a problem to be solved, not a specific solution to be implemented,"

he wrote. "An incentive prize can support a wide variety of approaches/solutions to come into existence to address a challenge, thereby creating an entire industry." Market research and consulting firm McKinsey & Company recently sought to quantify whether incentive awards like the X Prize make a meaningful impact on advancing innovation. They cite a study from Harvard and the Norwegian School of Economics and Business Administration that examined prizes offered between 1839 and 1939. Winners, it turned out, had a far better chance of getting their inventions patented, and even the losers applied in record numbers to protect their creations.

The Orteig Prize had similar repercussions: Within eighteen months of Lindbergh's flight, the number of airline passengers soared from 6,000 to 180,000. The population of pilots tripled, and there were four times as many airplanes buzzing the

The Edison2 team took an unconventional approach, entering four different cars, each with varying bodywork and characteristics but using the same drivetrain.

THE X PRIZE ATTRACTED PLENTY OF GARAGE
LOONIES, COMPULSIVE INVENTORS, ENGINEERING
PRODIGIES, SERIAL ENTREPRENEURS, AND
LOFTY DREAMERS. AND THAT WAS JUST FINE
WITH DIAMANDIS. "YOU DON'T WANT TO TURN
AWAY THOSE PESKY BICYCLE MECHANICS
FROM DAYTON, OHIO."

—

PETER DIAMANDIS LOVES TO TELL NAYSAYERS, "THE DAY BEFORE SOMETHING IS TRULY A BREAKTHROUGH, IT'S A CRAZY IDEA."

—

DIAMANDIS IS "EXCITED ABOUT THE FUTURE OF DESIGN....ALL OF US WILL HAVE WHAT MIGHT BE CONSIDERED GODLIKE POWERS TO CREATE, TO MANIFEST OUR DREAMS IN A WAY THAT IS MAGICAL."

---

skyways of the United States as there had been before. Soon after *SpaceShipOne* made its historic suborbital flights, and Branson spun off the technology into Virgin Galactic, private spaceflight companies with names like Armadillo, Blue Origin, Rocketplane, and SpaceX, among dozens of others, gathered momentum, kindling further investment and attracting new talent. Diamandis explains, "We insist that the competition's design has a back-end business model, meaning that when the prize is won, the teams are able to take their technology to market." Of the Auto X Prize, Mathis says, "if the intent was to introduce new solutions and fresh thinking to the world of car design, the organizers succeeded hands down. They recognized the possibility for small groups of people to do uncommon things—and created an arena to make that happen. They should be commended for it, and we should thank them."

For his part, Diamandis is confident that the X Prize will continue to evolve in sync with advancing technology—artificial intelligence, robotics, nanotech, biotech— enabling the awards to take on increasingly ambitious feats. He points out that "creat-ing the future is all very hard, and you will likely have multiple failures along the way." Even so, Diamandis is "excited about the future of design. It's all about the ultimate personalization, where the design tools fade from perception and empower us to turn our whimsy into reality. All of us will have what might be considered godlike powers to create, to manifest our dreams in a way that is magical." Ⓐ

The Ansari X Prize, the first such competition, awarded $10 million for a vehicle (right) that could enter low-space orbit three times. The winning entrant has become Virgin Galactic's *SpaceShipTwo* (preceding pages).

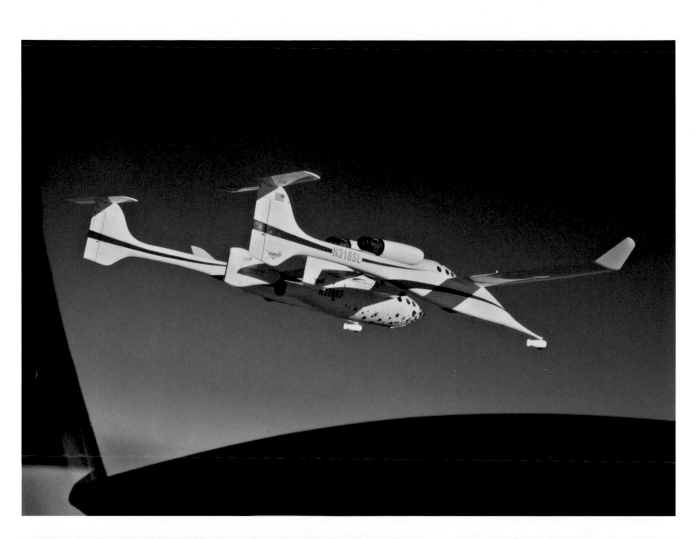

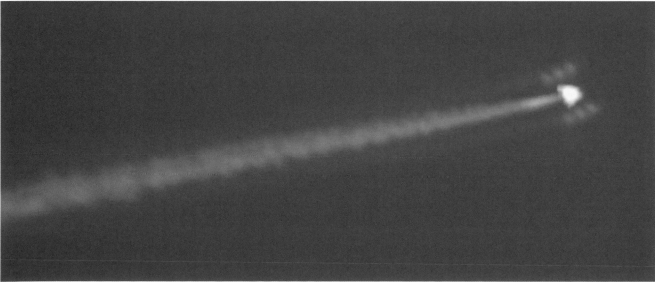

SYSTEMS

JANINE BENYUS

The renowned biomimicry expert homes in on life's design principles and lessons.

What is biomimicry? Why is it important?
Biomimicry is the process of learning from and then emulating life's designs. It's innovation inspired by nature. We look at form. We look at processes: strategies, relationships, how photosynthesis works, for instance, or green chemistry. And at the ecosystem level, we look at how you put all the pieces together in a framework that has a consistent criteria for success. How do ecosystems actually work? What are the principles?

Can you elaborate on these three areas that you focus on in biomimetic design?
Form is mimicking nature's physical designs—shape and to-pography. That might include mimicking the tubercles on the fin of a humpback whale to reduce turbulence, or solar cells that mimic photosynthesis. Mimicking process is everything from green chemistry to mimicking natural selection in a genetic algorithm. So, once you create a fan based on that form, how do you manufacture it? What kind of chemistry do you use? What kind of materials do you use? What energy source do you use to manufacture it?

The third level is taking a whole system as a model. So that's where you get into looking at a native ecosystem in a region and saying, "This is a model for how to run our city, or to run an economy."

Can you describe a successful design based on these principles?
One is Pax Scientific's water mixer—a device that sits at the bottom of the big, million-gallon water tanks that you have in many municipalities. It is a logarithmic spiral, the Fibonacci spiral, which you find in so many places in the natural world. It runs on a very small amount of energy—it's nature's perfect flow structure.

The mixer creates a kind of tornadic form, and it starts the water moving after a few minutes. The entire thing starts to circulate, and it's beautiful. The important thing is that a well-mixed water tank means that you can use less chlorine to purify the water.

What was the inspiration for the water mixer?
[Pax Scientific CEO] Jay Harman's initial inspiration was a giant kelp in Australia, which he saw when he was eight.

A kelp looks like a ribbon. And when it gets pulled by the current, that flat ribbon spirals into a tube—the same thing that leaves do. If you watch leaves in a storm, large leaves will fold with the wind to create a Fibonacci sequence spiral that wind goes through very easily. What that means is that very powerful winds can't yank the leaf off or powerful currents can't yank the kelp out.

Jay was sitting at the shore as a little kid, and he was able to pick up the holdfast [where the kelp is anchored

—

"Biomimicry is the process of learning from and then emulating life's designs. It's innovation inspired by nature."

> "Life uses a subset of safe materials and then uses very elegant recipes for things like enzymes to get that sort of specificity and that economy to make very, very strong materials, but without the need for really toxic chemicals and without the need for really horrific processes: heat, beat, treat."

—

from the same recipe that the coral reefs use. They're sequestering CO_2 rather than emitting it in the manufacture of concrete. That's a big deal.

Six to eight percent of all CO_2 emissions comes in the manufacture of concrete. What Calera's CEO Brent Constantz has done is he's realized that coral reefs have a way of mineralizing CO_2 and calcium and carbonate in a way that glues it all together without the need for Portland cement. With Portland cement, you have to heat the limestone up to enormous temperatures for fourteen hours to make clinkers, which are ground up and are the glue that holds it all together.

Biomineralization, on the other hand, is an organic process that can make ceramic. You and I do it in our bones; we do it in our teeth. All the hard critters you see in the ocean obviously are doing it, and even the creation of glass—silicas, silicate—is a biomineralization process.

People are trying to make layered cement that's very, very tough. They're trying to design computer chips using silicon, not in the normal process by which we make glass or silicon ingots, but rather having the silica self-assemble in a biologically mediated way, the way diatoms do. Diatoms are little critters that make glass underwater. Mimicking that, we could make everything from lenses to windows to chips.

What are some of the larger implications of using chemistry inspired by nature?

The difference between industrial chemistry and nature's chemistry is that industrial chemistry uses every element in the periodic table, and uses very simplistic and very unsophisticated reactions—brute force. Life uses a subset of safe materials and then uses very elegant recipes for things like enzymes to get that specificity and that economy to make very, very strong materials, but without the need for really toxic chemicals and without the need for really horrific processes: heat, beat, treat.

It's inherent in bio-inspired chemistry that the costs come down and that it becomes safer. If you really want to get into what's world-changing about biomimetic design, it's that you have safe chemical processes for manufacture. Suddenly you can think about doing it on a 3D printer, just sending designs through.

So suddenly you enable a local economy. You enable people to make things where they live. You're talking about a systems change, not just talking about technology. You're talking about a technological system or a product system that is also an economic system and a social system.

to rock] and pull it out easily. He said to himself, *If I can do this, why is the tide not ripping all of these kelp up?*

It's a really good question. Then he noticed the spiral pattern. It was creating a flow structure for water to move through. And he began to notice Fibonacci spirals in everything. Water coming out of a faucet describes this Fibonacci sequence. So does a hurricane cloud. He has spent his lifetime mimicking that shape.

What biomimetic design projects are you most excited about now?

I'm interested in life's ability to take CO_2, make it into cellulose, or make it into coral reefs or ceramics—seashells. How does life do that? How does life make CO_2? What's the chemistry? You've got Novomer, which makes plastics out of CO_2, and you've got Calera, which is making concrete

What are you exploring at the third level of biomimicry, the systems level?

We began our consultancy in 1998, thinking that we were going to go in and give people ideas about how to lightweight products by changing the shape, how to change packaging, how to solve technical problems. We were just going to keep our heads down and solve engineering problems.

What happened was that once we got into companies, they were interested in the solutions. They might say, "Oh, a new way of doing water repellency. Now we can get away from Teflon. That's terrific. Now, what can you tell us about running our company differently?"

That brought us to the systems level. Managers would begin to come down and say, "Tell us about biomimicry." And of course, they were interested in something at a systems level, and so they said, "Are there ubiquitous principles in the natural world?" I mean, you can mimic the bumps on the Namibian beetle's back, and you can harvest fog water out of it. That's amazing. But that's one beetle. Is there something that all living creatures have in common? Are there principles? And indeed there are, and they're quite informative.

—

"We came up with this list and taught it as an eco-checklist of sorts. Is my design locally attuned, and what does that mean? Does it use local, raw materials wherever it possibly can? Is my design self-healing?"

—

"Once we got into companies, they were interested in the solutions. They might say, 'Oh, a new way of doing water repellency. That's terrific. Now, what can you tell us about running our company differently?'"

—

So we began to gather. It was actually very difficult to find life's principles—to find the general rules. We're trained to find the exception to the rule rather than the general rule. We're rewarded for *disproving* someone's theory.

What these principles are is a systemic framework. There are very technical things, like life does chemistry in water rather than organic solvents. There are also very large concepts like life banks on resilience, and there's a very deep scientific basis for what we mean by "resilient."

Life's principles have all of these levels, and we began to teach these as a system of best practices that were pulled from the biological and ecosystem literature that happened to be relevant to this complex, adaptive system called a company.

We came up with this list and taught it as an eco-checklist of sorts. Is my design locally attuned, and what does that mean? Does it use local, raw materials wherever it possibly can? Is my design self-healing?

What surprised us was that a lot of companies would take the word *design* in that sentence and put the word *company* in: Is my company locally attuned? Is my company self-healing? Ⓐ

Janine Benyus is a natural sciences writer, innovation consultant, and the author of *Biomimicry: Innovation Inspired by Nature*.

LIFE'S PRINCIPLES

Design lessons from nature

According to Janine Benyus and her colleagues, organic life forms survive and thrive by developing strategies that are optimized, rather than maximized. These patterns can offer designers powerful insights and opportunities for innovation.

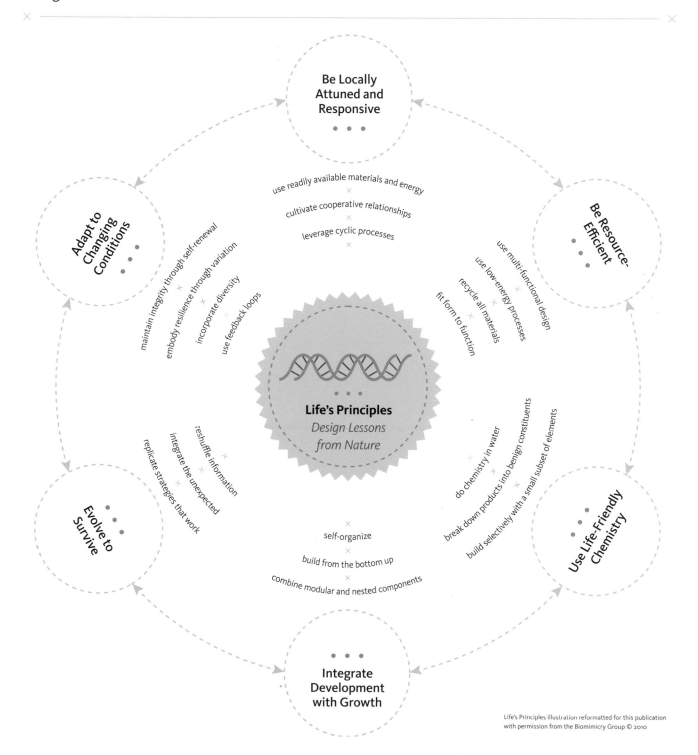

Be Locally Attuned and Responsive

use readily available materials and energy

cultivate cooperative relationships

leverage cyclic processes

Adapt to Changing Conditions

maintain integrity through self-renewal

embody resilience through variation

incorporate diversity

use feedback loops

Be Resource-Efficient

use multi-functional design

use low-energy processes

recycle all materials

fit form to function

Life's Principles
Design Lessons from Nature

Evolve to Survive

reshuffle information

integrate the unexpected

replicate strategies that work

Use Life-Friendly Chemistry

do chemistry in water

break down products into benign constituents

build selectively with a small subset of elements

self-organize

build from the bottom up

combine modular and nested components

Integrate Development with Growth

Life's Principles illustration reformatted for this publication with permission from the Biomimicry Group © 2010

AMORY LOVINS'S INTEGRATIVE DESIGN

Lovins describes how to enable integrative design—and how it has helped modernize the world's most famous skyscraper.

AMONG OTHER THINGS, AMORY LOVINS IS AN OPTIMIST, A PRAGMATIST, AN EFFICIENCY GURU, AND A BELIEVER IN THE POSSIBILITIES OF A UTOPIAN TECHNO-FUTURE. At the core of Lovins's work is a zeal for reducing the use of nonrenewable resources like oil and coal. This overarching passion to find efficiencies and save resources in creative ways has brought Lovins and his nonprofit "think-and-do-tank," Rocky Mountain Institute (RMI), into the boardrooms and offices of industrial companies around the globe—from the largest automobile companies to the biggest energy production companies to the developers of the tallest office buildings.

An efficiency retrofit of the Empire State Building is an example of what Amory Lovins calls "integrative design"—an approach that optimizes a system as a whole, instead of focusing only on components.

These days, the unifying factor in the work Lovins and his firm do is something he calls "integrative design." Another name for "whole system design," the main idea of integrative design is that even when each component of a system is independently optimized, this tends to lead to complete systems that are nonoptimal. By contrast, integrative design, as practiced by Lovins, tends to throw out many assumptions as part of the process of uniting disparate systems into new, better, less-resource-consuming, optimized solutions. Integrative design is part engineering, part design, part number crunching, and a good deal of rethinking standard operating procedures.

Lovins first gained national recognition during the 1970s energy crisis with an essay asserting that the United States could eventually cut all use of fossil fuels, and do so at a profit. In the thirty-plus years since then, Lovins has continued to extol the deep possibilities of energy efficiency and has remained a prolific writer of books, articles, and industry reports.

One of the first scientists to recognize the dangers of global warming, Lovins has maintained a pragmatic approach throughout his long career. In 1982 he cofounded RMI as a nonprofit research and collaborative organization. As chairman and chief scientist of RMI, Lovins and a staff of eighty work toward a stated goal of driving "the efficient and restorative use of resources to create a world thriving, verdant, and secure, for all, forever." RMI, in work with clients as diverse as the U.S. Department of Defense and Coca-Cola, is largely dedicated to working with clients and helping them apply free-market economics to the looming energy challenges society faces.

Recently, RMI took part in an efficiency retrofit of the Empire State Building that promises to save up to 38 percent of current energy use and some $4.4 million in annual operating expenses. The retrofit design is a real-world example of RMI's integrative design process, which Lovins describes in the interview below.

THE MAIN IDEA OF INTEGRATIVE DESIGN IS THAT EVEN WHEN EACH COMPONENT OF A SYSTEM IS INDEPENDENTLY OPTIMIZED, THIS TENDS TO LEAD TO COMPLETE SYSTEMS THAT ARE NONOPTIMAL.

—

You work with big issues within large, complex systems. How does RMI approach these kinds of challenges?

At Rocky Mountain Institute, we start with the proposition that there are three main foci of power and action in the world—business, civil society, and government—and those are generally in order of decreasing effectiveness. I tend to look for solutions that not only make sense but also make money so that they can be pursued by the private sector in its coevolution with civil society. They can then spread those ideas through "Aikido politics" and "institutional acupuncture" to figure out where the busi-ness logic is congested and not flowing properly. We do solutions, not problems; practice, not theory; transformation, not incrementalism. At the core of our practice is integrative design.

When designing a new car today, for example, is there a system or set of rules that car designers are working with to make a more efficient car? In previous years, was there as much thought about making a car that could drive farther on less gas?

There was quite a lot of thought about it. And powertrains even got about a third more efficient, although that was all

One of the foremost examples of Lovins's integrative design approach is his residence in Snowmass, Colorado (left and far right). The superefficient house uses components with more than one function, such as the atrium, which collects energy in five different ways.

swallowed up in faster acceleration and higher mass. But the design paradigm in that industry, which I know well, supposed that efficiency and emissions were goals set for regulatory compliance.

The mode of design in the automobile industry has been very dis-integrated; that is, specialized groups design one piece of the platform and then toss it over the transom to the next group. It's so dis-integrated that the question of how much lightweighting you can pay for by downsizing the powertrain to get the same acceleration was only seriously asked by an American automaker in the past few years. But this is a very elementary level of design integration.

Is it fair to say that from an energy-saving, planet-saving perspective, we would want all cars to be designed as systems that would work at their ultimate efficiency?

Probably not, unless you very carefully define efficiency. You can get five thousand miles a gallon in a little capsule that you lie down in and hope you don't hit anything. So cars have a variety of objectives, some of which conflict. And automakers meet those with great skill. But without integrative design, they end up supposing that high efficiency and low or zero emissions will

raise the cost or compromise the safety or performance of their cars. None of these things need to be true—but to [achieve the objectives] you need a different way of organizing people.

Ten years ago, my team worked with a couple of European car-engineering companies. We designed a midsize SUV that got sixty-seven miles a gallon. The extra sticker price would be $2,500 at midvolume production. That's a one-year payback. And the vehicle's uncompromised in all respects.

To do that, we had seven people design the car over several months instead of having, say, a thousand people working on it over several years. The secret sauce was to use Skunk Works rules and to organize the people in a very different way. Toyota asked how we had done that, and we told them. And they then did something, I dare say, quite similar to get the 1/X concept car in 2007, which has the interior volume of a Prius with half the fuel use and a third the weight.

Is this a good way to spread positive change in larger industries?

We have a much more direct method than that. We work with automakers all over the world. We have worked intensively, in recent

"THE COEVOLUTION OF BUSINESS WITH CIVIL SOCIETY IS VERY POWERFUL AND ACTIVE AS A LEARNING PROCESS. IT IS ALSO [FOR US] ESSENTIAL TO ENGAGE WITH COMMERCE. THE CHOICES THAT HAVE LANDED US IN THIS MESS ARE BILLIONS OF INDIVIDUAL DECISIONS."

—

years, with an American automaker to good effect. But what I did was, first of all, invent a new way to design cars, which we called Hypercars, back in 1991. And we spent a couple of years working mainly with GM hoping they would adopt this concept for strategic advantage. It turned out they were not culturally ready to do so.

So in 1993, I open-sourced the concept and, working with automakers worldwide, got them all worried that their competitors would do it first. And that simple technique leveraged our $3 million R&D investment into about $10 billion of industry commitments. Three-thousand-fold leverage suited me just fine. And we're continuing to work in that way. We're also getting better at relating the technical opportunity to a breakthrough competitive strategy.

Can you explain a bit more about this strategy?

There are four boxes in which one must play to transform big, complex systems like the energy or automotive industry. The ones people normally talk about are technology and policy. The other two, which may be even more important, are design and strategy—or, if you like, business innovation. And if you play with a full deck, with all four of those, you reach your goals a lot faster, make more money, have more fun, and have less risk.

The example you just shared, how you open-sourced that concept and then saw the industry follow suit, do you have a name for the steps you took to do that?

It's part of a broader strategy we've always used at RMI. And that is to use competition to do our work. We typically use soft money—grants and donations—to develop valuable new concepts. We then work with early adopters in the private sector who have a real problem they're highly motivated to solve, and we have a solution for it. So together we learn rapidly. This gives us precious hands-on implementation experience, unrestricted revenue, and buzz. But more important, it gives us teachable cases and

Empire State Building Retrofit

In 2008, the Empire State Building consumed as much energy as forty thousand single-family homes each day. Standing in an iconic position in the New York skyline, the Empire State Building was the perfect type of project for Rocky Mountain Institute to achieve both a substantial local and global effect. Lovins and RMI were a vital part of the planning process that led to a $20 million comprehensive energy-efficiency retrofit of the landmark midtown-Manhattan office building. During a complex two-year planning process, RMI served as the design partner and peer reviewer along with three partners: project advisor Clinton Climate Initiative, project manager Jones Lang LaSalle, and energy service company Johnson Controls. The partners had multiple goals: to reduce the eighty-year-old building's carbon footprint and shrink its $11 million annual utility bill while also demonstrating the business case for green retrofits of older buildings. The resulting solution would yield projected savings of 38 percent of the building's energy, reduce carbon dioxide emissions by 105,000 metric tons over the next fifteen years, lower building costs by $4.4 million annually, and recoup its incremental costs within three years.

The greatest cost savings will come from the ability to refrofit the chiller plant rather than replace it, achieved by reducing the cooling load by 1,600 tons. One of the more creative solutions was to refurbish—on-site—the building's 6,514 windows, instead of replacing them. The windows were removed, upgraded with a third pane and low emissivity (low-E) film, and reinstalled, all of which led to improving the thermal resistance of the glass from R-2 to R-6.

In addition to solving the challenges of the Empire State Building, the group created a replicable modeling and measurement process to determine the cost benefit of energy-reduction retrofits on commercial buildings with practices and processes applicable worldwide, and shares its model and practical tools so that other building owners can use and replicate them. Empire State Building Company president and building owner Anthony Malkin has sought to share every aspect of it freely with competitors and is a champion of the systemic approach in which all the building elements—the lights, the cooling tower, the insulation—work together. Ⓐ

competitive pressure for emulation. That is, we help early adopters become so conspicuously successful using advanced energy and resource efficiency and other tenets of natural capitalism that their competitors are forced to follow suit or lose market share.

The Empire State Building retrofit that RMI was part of—does this work fit into that approach? Getting a large office building to adapt and change, with the idea that other buildings in Manhattan and elsewhere will follow suit?

Yes. We agreed to do the project precisely because of that kind of leverage. The owner, Tony Malkin, is a very demanding and aggressive developer who will not hesitate to walk up to his peers at a cocktail party—a very competitive crowd—and say, "Hi, I made more money than you did last year. Let me tell you how. It's called integrative design for advanced energy efficiency."

Moreover, we got to work with a major energy service company and a major property manager—Johnson Controls and Jones Lang LaSalle—in ways that may motivate them to switch their business model toward deep retrofit to gain competitive advantage. And that's a way to drive their respective sectors in the same direction.

So the Empire State Building wasn't just another client.

We don't have "just other clients." We choose them strategically to get that kind of leverage. We don't just do whatever job comes in the door.

Is there a phrase you use to describe the ideal types of clients and how they'll have this cascading effect on other members of their industry?

We might call that "leverage" or "influence."

"WITHOUT INTEGRATIVE DESIGN, THEY END UP SUPPOSING THAT HIGH EFFICIENCY AND LOW OR ZERO EMISSIONS WILL RAISE THE COST OR COMPROMISE THE SAFETY OR PERFORMANCE OF THEIR CARS. NONE OF THESE THINGS NEED TO BE TRUE—BUT...YOU NEED A DIFFERENT WAY OF ORGANIZING PEOPLE."

—

The Empire State Building's thousands of windows were upgraded within the building, saving time, money, and energy. The result of that upgrade was savings of $4.4 million, up to 38 percent of current energy use.

As an example, we agreed to work with Wal-Mart on a number of important initiatives, not just because they're so big and they can move a market all by themselves, but also because they buy most of their stuff from China. We saw an opportunity to influence Chinese development strategy, which is the future of the world, by influencing Wal-Mart's upstream purchasing and manufacturing practices.

There are, of course, many other attributes we look for in a client. They have to be ripe for radical change; that is, they must have the right leadership, management, and cultural attributes. They have to have high integrity and curiosity and be culturally ready to work in unusual ways with a small nonprofit. And there are other attributes: We like to work with really smart people who are open to fundamental innovation and can spread it through their organization and then to their industries via competition.

The influence RMI gains is often from taking on singular clients who can influence their competitors. If you look at the changes and decisions that individuals can make in their own lives versus larger industrial changes, is there one or the other that leads us to a more hopeful future? Or do both need to happen?

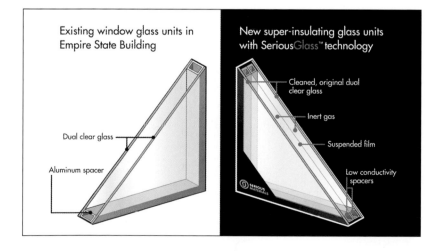

Existing window glass units in Empire State Building

Dual clear glass

Aluminum spacer

New super-insulating glass units with SeriousGlass™ technology

Cleaned, original dual clear glass

Inert gas

Suspended film

Low conductivity spacers

INTEGRATIVE DESIGN

Rocky Mountain Institute's Factor Ten Engineering Principles

The Rocky Mountain Institute's Factor Ten Engineering Principles underpin the practice of integrative design, which can yield radical resource efficiency. Integrative design optimizes a system as a whole, rather than its parts in isolation. Teams apply the Factor Ten Engineering Principles throughout a collaborative design and build process, divided into three stages: Ready, Set, Go.

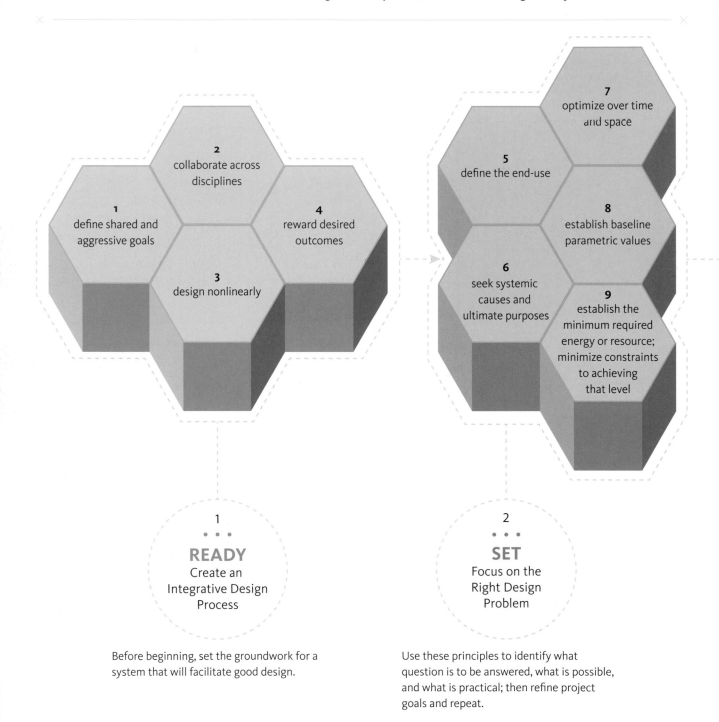

2 collaborate across disciplines

1 define shared and aggressive goals

3 design nonlinearly

4 reward desired outcomes

7 optimize over time and space

5 define the end-use

8 establish baseline parametric values

6 seek systemic causes and ultimate purposes

9 establish the minimum required energy or resource; minimize constraints to achieving that level

1
• • •
READY
Create an Integrative Design Process

Before beginning, set the groundwork for a system that will facilitate good design.

2
• • •
SET
Focus on the Right Design Problem

Use these principles to identify what question is to be answered, what is possible, and what is practical; then refine project goals and repeat.

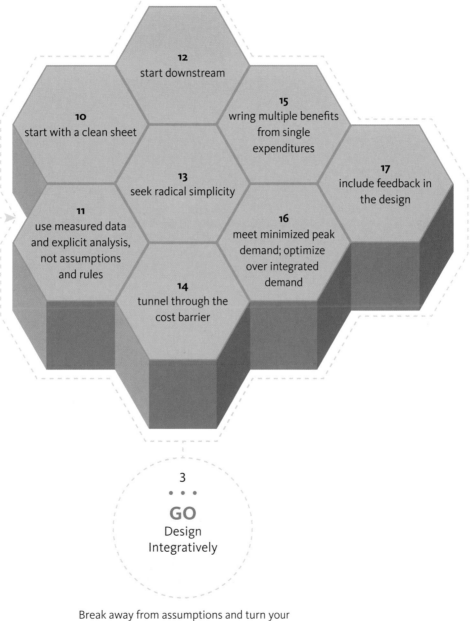

12
start downstream

10
start with a clean sheet

15
wring multiple benefits from single expenditures

13
seek radical simplicity

17
include feedback in the design

11
use measured data and explicit analysis, not assumptions and rules

16
meet minimized peak demand; optimize over integrated demand

14
tunnel through the cost barrier

3
• • •
GO
Design
Integratively

Break away from assumptions and turn your design intent into action. Keep improving through a process of analysis and iteration.

It's both. Indeed, they're different faces of the same decision, because if you vote with your wallet, as we all do, business is exquisitely sensitive to what you do or don't buy and why they think you do or don't buy stuff. The coevolution of business with civil society is very powerful and active as a learning process both ways. It is also essential [for us] to engage with commerce.

The choices that have landed us in this mess are billions of individual decisions. More mindful, better-informed individual decisions in the billions can lead us out of this mess. So you need both of these: individual choices of what to do or refrain from doing and the ability of business to provide solutions in a way that none of us has the individual capacity to make and market.

Your work at the Empire State Building is an example of a project that changed a whole system. Is the consulting work that you did largely creating metrics that will allow a client to believe in making the changes proposed?

Understanding metrics is an important part. But we mainly work with designers of record in buildings, vehicles, and industry to help them do what they didn't know how to do or didn't even realize they could do. When we went into the Empire State Building project, we worked on the conceptual design and early phases of the schematic, and design development after that. The conventional wisdom was that you could save about 7 to 10 percent of the energy with a few years' payback. We're ending up saving 38 percent of the energy with a three-year payback, even though it's a very difficult building and the windows had already been switched from single- to double-pane glass.

In the case of the Empire State Building, 38 percent savings with a three-year payback was considered quite exceptional. And it arose from integrative design.

Basically, we were remaking the windows, in an improvised temporary window factory on-site, into superwindows that blocked winter heat loss three times better and summer heat gain twice as well. And that, combined with better lights and some other improvements, cut the peak cooling load by a third. This enabled us to save $17.4 million versus renovating and redesigning, rather than replacing and expanding, the chillers. Then we used that savings to help pay for everything else.

In working with the other stakeholders in the project, such as Johnson Controls, were you serving as an efficiency consultant for each of those designers, and then bringing all of them together?

Our most important role is in convening everybody in a disciplined but imaginative framework that fits all of the moving parts together in a new way, yielding bigger savings and lower costs. That's integrative design. Ⓐ

Some finished retrofit floors of the Empire State Building (right) have been transformed into full, green office space (above).

"PEOPLE NORMALLY TALK ABOUT TECHNOLOGY AND POLICY. THE OTHER TWO, WHICH MAY BE EVEN MORE IMPORTANT, ARE DESIGN AND STRATEGY—OR IF YOU LIKE, BUSINESS INNOVATION."

—

"I had access to senior executives in influential organizations, but I wasn't taking advantage of the opportunity to have an impact."
—

VALERIE CASEY

The founder of the Designers Accord is leading a new generation of designers who are determined to be part of the solution.

What was your inspiration for the Designers Accord?
I have been a designer for sixteen years. Four years ago, I was working for several *Fortune* 50 companies, traipsing back and forth across the country, and designing products without accounting for the environmental impact they would have. I was creating consumer electronics and fast-moving consumer goods—disposable cell phones, disposable diapers, and disposable packaging—but even then I knew that none of them were truly disposable. I had access to senior executives in influential organizations, but I wasn't taking advantage of the opportunity to have an impact—to change the course of my products and their portfolios.

Personal responsibility prompted me to investigate environmental issues more seriously, but I also had a professional motivation. I knew my clients would expect me to have expertise in sustainability, just as designers are now called upon to integrate brand, technology, and business acumen in the things we create.

The backbone of my design work has always been about finding new ways to collaborate and solve problems.

I decided to apply some core principles—leveraging distributed intelligence, learning through experimentation, and exciting cooperative competition—to the question of sustainability, and that culminated in a "Kyoto Treaty" of design, which is now known as the Designers Accord. The basic idea is to enable designers and creative firms to share perspectives, experiences (good and bad), and sustainability case studies, so others can learn from them, build on them, and share their results within the Designers Accord community. It's about encouraging collaboration among competitors to develop our collective environmental intelligence, and it's led to smarter and more-efficient innovation.

What are the goals of the Designers Accord?
It's a five-year project with three goals. One goal is to increase awareness about the principles of sustainability throughout the professional design community and in design education. About seven hundred design firms, forty universities, and forty corporations across one hundred countries have adopted the Designers Accord guidelines. The second goal is to help shape the values of practicing designers by enabling practitioners all over the word to share strategies and stories. The last goal is aspirational: We want designers to have a seat at the table with lobbyists, economists, and scientists when it comes time to develop policy and influence regulation. If a designer's greatest strength is the ability to generate new kinds of solutions, then shouldn't designers use those skills to address problems we all face? I don't expect design thinking to save the world. But I know it can be an important part of the solution.

The Designers Accord has ended up being about more than environmental issues. How did that evolve?

The conversation around sustainability three or four years ago was focused on environmental issues. The discussion was either highly technical—centered on green chemistry and material selection—or incredibly depressing because it was all about reduction and sacrifice. We wanted to bring designers into this conversation to add creativity and optimism. Over the years, the discussion has evolved and broadened. Personally, I came across the work Dana Meadows did on applied systems thinking. It is an integrated approach to understanding how systems that include social, cultural, economic, and environmental factors work. My work with the Designers Accord stresses that systems approach. These days, I rarely use the word *sustainability*. Instead, I speak more about celebrating relationships and interconnections.

You've spoken about the myopia that surrounds a lot of design decisions. Decisions can have profound implications that are not necessarily obvious at the time of creation. What are some of the causes of that?

Traditional design education teaches designers to focus on things they have immediate control over but not what they influence. It's a niche mind-set, rather than an integrated mind-set. Another cause is that the design process is usually mapped to a typical corporate structure, which is often fragmented and siloed. Designers end up working in corporate territories that have impermeable boundaries. Only now are designers starting to question how we work, and why we design the way we do.

Has your work on the Accord changed your perspective on sustainability?

My perspective has changed radically. I've shifted from creating products to creating services, and from driving consumption to creating experiences. I have a sense of responsibility for the recommendations I make to my clients. I recognize the imperfection of a design-centric approach and the value of multidisciplinary teams. I work on a different time frame; I've shifted from the usual three-week or three-month design contract to structuring design engagements over longer time frames where I can adapt to industrial, cultural, and economic change.

What kind of tools facilitate systems-oriented thinking?

When people talk about sustainability "tools," they're often asking for a silver bullet—a magical thing to transform a dire situation. But there is no silver bullet. It's silver buckshot—multiple interventions, adapted constantly to actually generate change.

In a way, that question is the problem. It supports the false expectation that one tool can solve extraordinarily complex challenges. It supposes we can design a thing that will alleviate our responsibility to think. A tool is only as strong as the systems that make it successful—the behavior of its users, the economic model that sustains it, and its measurable cultural effects.

A better question is, What promotes better thinking? The answer is more collaboration and greater understanding of interdependence. Honoring the natural environment as our primary educator for creating living, thriving solutions. Realizing the limitations of current business models. Recognizing the fallibility and limitations of design, and embracing its extraordinary potential to create the conditions for change. We can have hopeful, delightful, creative, optimistic lives, but that means designers need to really think and act differently about how we apply our craft and our passion.

—

"My definition of good design has changed. But more important, my definition of good designers has changed, too."

—

In light of all of this, has your definition of good design changed?

It's not an accident that this movement is called Designers Accord, not the Design Accord. We want to advance the evolution of designers' value systems—not just the things we create. So yes, my definition of good design has changed. But more important, my definition of good designers has changed, too. **A**

Valerie Casey is a design consultant and founder of the Designers Accord.

WHERE WILL DESIGN TAKE US
NEXT?

PREDICTING THE FUTURE IS NOTORIOUSLY HARD, ESPECIALLY IN THE MIDST OF THE BLIZZARD OF CHANGE SWIRLING AROUND US TODAY. BUT ONE THING WE CAN BE SURE OF IS THAT THE REMARKABLE DESIGN ADVANCES OF THE PAST FEW YEARS—MANY OF THEM CHRONICLED HERE—ARE JUST A PRELUDE TO THE REVOLUTION JUST AHEAD.

—

previous spread: **The undulating "living roof" of Renzo Piano's design for the California Academy of Sciences.**

The growth and rapid change in technologies such as 3D printing, network connectivity, bioinformatics, genomics, artificial intelligence, nanotechnology, robotics, and mobile computing, among others, will accelerate the evolution of design in the coming years. Fundamental shifts in how we work together, already emerging in our always connected, socially networked lives, are also altering the practice of design. Deep collaboration and crowdsourcing are becoming part of our everyday workflow. And the ever-increasing consciousness of how architecture, engineering, manufacturing, and other design professions affect our environment, culture, and social fabric are also changing the basic requirements and goals of design. It is becoming essential for design to make positive changes in the world, rather than to simply make the things we create "less bad." In that and many other ways, it is the mind-set of designers that is changing, as well as their toolset.

Five trends in particular promise to transform design as we know it.

1. Infinite Computing will make essentially unlimited processing power and bandwidth available to designers, giving them the power to create virtually anything they can imagine.

2. In this new environment, and as the boundaries between our analog and digital worlds continue to blur, we will see **Reality, Digitized,** enabling designers to bring real-world data and environments into the virtual world with surprising ease. This will help all of us do a better job of "designing for the real world."

3. That really does mean "all of us," because we are rapidly entering a world in which **Everyone Is a Designer**, thanks to technologies that are inspiring design self-reliance *and* crowdsourcing, as well as widely distributed, inexpensive tools for design and fabrication.

4. It is also a world that increasingly will be characterized by **Amazing Complexity**—where more information, more connections between design elements, and faster change will force design professionals to adapt with new tools, techniques, and mind-sets.

5. The complexity and urgency of the **Global Challenges** facing designers today—such as climate change, economic uncertainty, and resource scarcity—will require them to call upon all of these new capabilities and more.

Our world will increasingly be shaped by the degree to which designers are able to create smart, effective, and elegant solutions that improve what that world looks like, how well it functions, and what it's like to live in it. The future surely will transform design— but it's just as certain that design will transform the future, by visualizing, optimizing, giving shape to, and ultimately creating a world that, for now, we can only imagine. ⒶΑ

INFINITE COMPUTING: AMPLIFYING OUR IMAGINATIONS

WHAT WOULD YOU BUILD IF YOU COULD BUILD ANYTHING YOU WANTED?

The rising power, increasing ubiquity, and decreasing cost of computing are giving designers the chance to answer that question. "Infinite computing" will make it more practical for us to design and create virtually anything we can imagine—and more quickly and cheaply than ever before.

This is the result of several technology trends coming together, including the advances in processing, storage, and bandwidth accompanying the rise of "cloud computing." It's astounding that each year more computing power is produced than in the sum total of all prior years. What may be even more important than the sheer *amount* of computing power is its widespread accessibility. Increasingly, designers have access to amazing amounts of power, and the ability to access variable amounts of power as their needs dictate.

Infinite computing will be one of the forces bringing about a profound change in the relationship between the designer and the computer. Computer-aided design, or CAD, will, for the first time, truly live up to its name and begin to *aid* in the creation of designs. Designers will rely on the computer—or on the widely dispersed network that is the "cloud"—to generate dozens or even hundreds of design alternatives in the time it once took to create one or two options. This increased "speed of exploration" will allow designers to extend their creative reach.

Invention (the creation of something new) and innovation (the successful integration of something new into society) will both be enhanced by this new capability—because both require the generation, development, evaluation, and selection of new ideas in large numbers. And, of course, designers won't just need more ideas and options—they'll need the *right* ones, ones that meet the criteria and fit the parameters of each design challenge. This is one of the benefits of the field of computational design: the generation of multiple options in quantities and complexities that outstrip our natural human abilities. The computer's exploration and analysis becomes an integral part of the overall design process and a valuable augmentation of human speculation and judgment.

Infinite computing will allow more and more designers to take advantage of an "always-on analysis" capability—enabling the designer to delegate real-time analysis to the computer, thereby ensuring that the options that are being pursued have been vetted by the technology to ensure those ideas make sense and will actually work in the real world.

The new paradigm is one in which the computer analyzes and optimizes the design *while* the designer is working. Want to test every possible window size to see which one will best reduce energy usage? Or test many different rotations of the building's positioning relative to the sun? With the speed and power of infinite computing, it's possible to run all these possibilities through a simulation, or even to run hundreds of simulations in parallel. The information needed will be out there in the cloud, and it will be searchable based just on visual data ("I want something that looks like this").

Having so much more power, information, and options to choose from, the question

With high-speed computers on every designer's desk, the massive data facilities that form the "cloud," and ever-more-powerful mobile computing devices present at all times, there is no practical limit to the processing power designers can use.

HAVING SO MUCH MORE POWER, INFORMATION, AND OPTIONS TO CHOOSE FROM, THE QUESTION ARISES: IS MORE ALWAYS BETTER?

—

arises: Is more always better? If designers can avoid being overwhelmed by the onslaught of massive data and complexity, there is good reason to believe that the quality of design will be enhanced. Because instead of just creating a design and then hoping that it passes the test of acceptability and practicality, the new methodology will be about trying as many options as possible in order to get to an optimal result.

Moreover, by having the computer do some of the drudgery of constant analysis, the designer frees himself to focus more on creative exploration and the art of design—while being less burdened by technical demands. Consider the Centre Pompidou in Metz, France, as an example. The roof structure is based on a complex surface inspired by a traditional Chinese hat and

was constructed using custom-fabricated "glue-lam" wood beams. Figuring out the complexity of the support beams for each shape change would have been impractical as design options were explored. But by using scripted computer languages to generate and optimize the structure's geometry, the architect didn't have to work out construction details with the fabricator; nor did those details have to be drawn or modeled. They were computed each time the designer changed the overall form. With the computer doing instantaneous calculations on every change of the shape, it ensured the designer would only spend time exploring shapes that could actually be built.

Which takes us back to that question: *What would you build if you could build anything you wanted?*

Shigeru Ban's design for the Centre Pompidou in Metz, France, includes a highly complex system of wooden supports that create the museum's distinctive shape. That complex system would have been impractical without a smart, scripted design approach that calculated the buildability of the design.

REALITY, DIGITIZED: CREATING FOR THE REAL WORLD

DESIGN IS ABOUT APPLYING OUR IMAGINATIONS TO THE REAL WORLD—creating things that have value not only in and of themselves but also in terms of the environments in which they will exist. Traditionally, designers have often had to "leave out the context" because they didn't have access to the data that represented that context. For example, buildings were often built as if they were all going to exist on the same spot on the planet, with little regard for their specific location. And products have often been designed without taking into account the impact that their manufacture, and subsequent obsolescence and disposal, would have.

So how can designers bring more of the "real world" into the design process, ensuring that their projects are developed with regard for the context in which they will exist? The solution is to bring more of the real world into the digital realm where designers' work is shaped. As it becomes easier to simulate real-world conditions and environments, designers will be better able to think and work "in context" and create designs that are better suited for real-world conditions.

Bringing everything they know about a project's surrounding environment into a digital model allows designers to experience a project before it is real, and as a result, create a finished design that will be more effective and efficient. For example, a digital model that includes weather data and daylighting information can show us what the natural lighting of a room will be like at different times of the day, and allow us to measure its energy efficiency.

We can also incorporate new types of data into our digital models—data that we're just beginning to be able to capture as sensors become cheaper and easier to install, and that is helping us to create "smart grids" that aggregate all the information about a given project, system, or geographic area.

The speed and ease with which we can capture reality—in the form of a rich 3D image representing an environment or object—makes it much easier to digitize the real world, work with those models, and eventually reshape the real world.

As 3D scanners become cheaper, it will become common practice to take an object like a coffee mug, digitize it, customize it in some way, and then print it out again on an affordable 3D printer. This process, known as "scan, modify, print" or "personal manufacturing," will radically change the processes, economics, and dynamics of the manufacturing industry.

But coffee mugs are just the start. Soon, we'll be scanning and creating digital models of not just objects, not even just buildings, but of entire cities. How long will it take to scan and digitally model a whole city? Already, using the latest technology, we can scan a whole building in about three hours. It's going to get much faster. "Point cloud" scanning technology is making it possible to quickly capture millions of data points—a snapshot that captures not just color but also form. That data can then be imported into digital design tools, making it much easier, for example, to retrofit an existing building for energy efficiency. Infinite computing will play an important role in helping us move between the real and digital worlds, because the kind of photorealistic rendering that once took many hours can be done in seconds when you have the power of thousands of computers at your disposal. Want to digitize your kitchen in 3D and remodel it online? It'll be a snap.

Point cloud 3D scanning allows designers to quickly digitize real-world objects, such as the Cathedral of Pisa (left), in very precise detail.

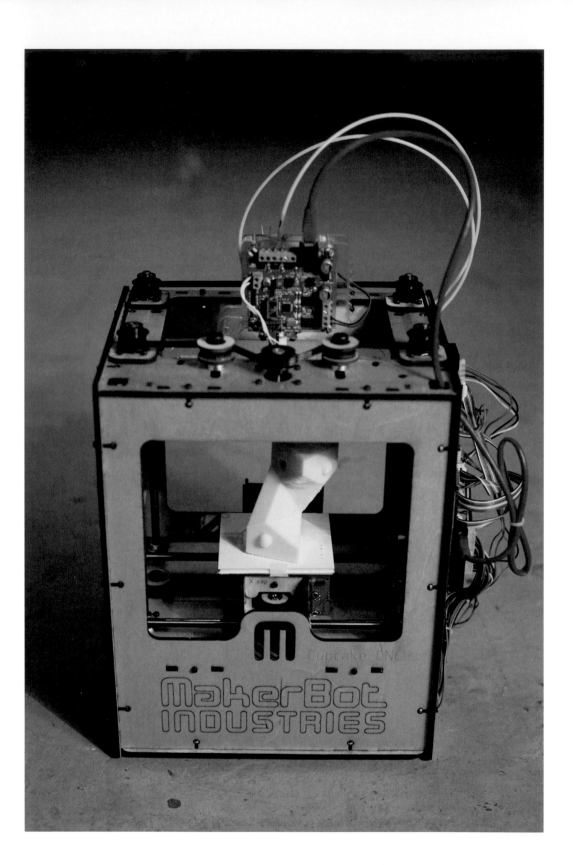

But the trend of being able to increasingly move from analog to digital (and back) involves more than merely speed and convenience: it means designers will no longer be designing in isolation. In the past, the design for a building lived in the head of the designer, for the most part disconnected from the real world until it was actually built there. Now, armed with high-resolution information about that real-world environment, the designer can connect with and incorporate every condition and detail that will affect that building in its future life. Designers: Welcome to the real world.

EVERYONE IS A DESIGNER: DIY (DESIGN IT YOURSELF) AND DIT (DESIGN IT TOGETHER)

THE DEMOCRATIZATION OF DESIGN IS NOT A NEW DEVELOPMENT. Various innovations and advances over the past quarter century have tapped into the innate human urge to design and have given people the means and opportunities to do so more artfully and effectively. Examples of this include Apple's introduction of the Macintosh, Autodesk's creation of CAD design tools that gradually have become more affordable and accessible, and the rise of the Internet and the accompanying boom in DIY (do it yourself) Web design.

But now the democratization of design is about to take a big leap forward. New tools, techniques, and communities are developing that will have a two-pronged effect: First, they will allow people to take a greater role in designing more things on their own; second, they will enable each of us to reach out to an infinite number of collaborators who can give us the support and expertise needed to take on more difficult design projects.

The simultaneous growth of "design self-reliance" on the one hand, and design crowd-sourcing on the other, promises to revolutionize manufacturing, architecture, and design across disciplines—as well as the daily lives of tomorrow's "citizen designers."

Here, too, emerging technology, such as low-cost 3D scanners and printers, will make it easier for non-designers to shape and manufacture everyday objects at home, feeding the already growing desire for more design control and customization. Instead of design that is mass-produced, we'll see personalized creations designed for "production units of one." In some ways, this represents a return to the pre-industrial, handcrafted approach to making things, albeit with much more sophisticated tools.

While this trend might seem to be focused on individual acts of design, i.e., the making of "one-offs," one of the most interesting effects of DIY design is the diversity it creates. The movement is most apparent today in popular culture where, for example, hundreds of fans might make their own videos based on an Eminem song and publish them on YouTube. As other people see these "homemade" videos, they'll get to work on their own, and the creation of content becomes part of a social cycle, rather than a discrete, individual act. As people try to top one another, the iterations can get more and more interesting. This kind of "hive mind" productivity is already producing things that are more sophisticated and of a higher quality than any single entity or organization can produce.

Twenty-five years after desktop publishing democratized graphic design, 3D printers—like the sub-$1,000 open source MakerBot—are bringing fabrication to the desktop, too.

NEXT

DESIGNERS WILL PROVIDE THE GUIDANCE THAT WILL ENABLE OTHERS TO DESIGN WELL.

—

This is all very exciting, but it also leads to a question: If "everyone is a designer," where does that leave all of the professional architects, engineers, product designers, and filmmakers? To put it simply, they'll be leading the revolution: Highly trained, talented designers will provide the inspiration, knowledge, and guidance that will enable others to design well. They'll be able to understand, and sometimes actually establish, the constraints that the citizen-designers will work within. But while designers will be guiding the way toward good design, it doesn't necessarily mean that they'll be creating rigid templates, because there will be plenty of room for designing parameters that still allow the layperson to be highly creative en route to the finished design.

Meanwhile, professionals can expect to get something back from the amateurs—in the form of information, and even inspiration. If more people are designing and doing so digitally, the professional designer can capture that information and learn from the experiments and variations that work or don't work—which in turn can lead to design choices that are more informed. There will be a near-infinite supply of creative influences to draw from—more components with which to build.

The design community of tomorrow will be as big as the world itself. It will be more competitive, for certain, but also more cooperative. The DIY and DIT (do it together) movement is inspiring and enabling designers and innovators to band together in trying to solve problems. This "extreme collaboration" approach often involves opening up design challenges to a wider community and inviting the members of that community to work together (or compete with one another) to find the best design solution. This movement toward open innovation and open-source design will continue to grow because it offers the irresistible benefit of having many minds working on a single problem at the same time. But there are inherent pitfalls, too—including the temptation for companies to undercut professional designers by trying to get low-cost or even free design "from the crowd." One of the challenges ahead will be to find ways to tap into the mass creativity of tomorrow's citizen designers while still respecting the perspectives and abilities of more experienced and knowledgeable practitioners. Because even in a world where "everybody is a designer," not all designers are created equal.

The burgeoning DIY (do-it-yourself) and DIT (do-it-together) movements are inspiring new generations of professional and amateur designers, engineers, and inventors.

NEXT

"Technology will give us many more tools for exploration at the conceptual stage. Designers will be more able to explore different alternatives." —

CARL BASS

Autodesk's CEO discusses the roles and skills of future designers, the rise of an "Internet of things," and the changing way we make things.

How will the nature of what a designer does change? What do you expect a future designer to be able to do more of, or need to do less?
Designers will document less and explore more. Technology will give us many more tools for exploration at the conceptual stage of a project. Designers will have more power to explore different alternatives involving aesthetic and functional choices right from the start.

Part of the design process is analytical. I have an idea—what are the implications of it? What does it look like? How does it fit together? Does it bump into something else that already exists? How does the light reflect off it? Based on these questions, I'm going to decide to change the idea to make it better. That kind of feedback is much more immediate in a technology-based design process. So there will be less analysis that we have to do ourselves and more synthesis of the data that comes back to us more quickly and easily.

Much of what's going on technologically is enabling better prototyping, so that people can experience their ideas before they are real and improve them accordingly. The better our tools are at helping them do that, the more they can focus on exploring and creating.

What else is changing about the practice of design?
Well, first of all, it's good to keep in mind that some things never change; I'm reminded of what my old boss used to call "the problem of the computer," the systematic generation of useless alternatives. Even with a really great computer, you can still manipulate the digital model in a way that does not provide useful information or insight.

But on the plus side, the increasing power of computers creates entirely new areas of exploration for people who design and create things. One example: We're accustomed to the idea of design as the human brain making decisions. But now there's the new question of "meta-design": You have to design a process, or write a script, or parameterize a problem space, within which the design problem will operate.

Over time, I think we're going to be delegating parts of complex design problems to these kinds of automated processes so that we can focus on the stuff that we really care about. Imagine if a digital model would just automatically tell you that something you were doing was a code violation. It'd say, "Hey, dummy, that's a dead-end corridor." Or, "Hey, that staircase isn't wide enough!"

Another example: Our director of software development, Robert Aish, has talked about the new roof over the British Museum's Great Reading Room. The idea was to create a faceted glass surface where none of the facets were larger than *this* in area, and the angle between any two adjacent pieces was no more than *that*. It's a meta design, in other words. You create a problem space or script and generate the answer. Without that advanced technology, the designer never would have considered that solution, because the complexity would have made it impossible, or at least impractical.

What are some of the trends affecting the end products of design?

Mobility and sensors are changing the way people interact with their designs. Soon everything that you design and create will actually be an IP device, because it will have sensors that generate an ongoing stream of information. Sometimes this is called "the Internet of things." If I design a chair, sensors will let me know how often the chair is used, how many people sit in it, how often it gets moved, where it's located right now, and so on.

You can imagine "smart" buildings, bridges, tunnels, and consumer products all being able to be monitored, and in some ways take on—I don't know if "life" is the right word—but you end up with a system that can change in response to its environment because it can sense things in an effective way. A designer or engineer of these systems will be better able to understand how these things are used.

We're moving from communicating about the design to communicating *with* the design. During the design process, you can now interact with very high-resolution information, and, later, you can understand and interact with the way the thing actually behaves and performs out in the world. The line between reality and design abstraction is getting really fuzzy.

So new tools and processes are changing our relationship with the things we make?

The way we interact with our designs is becoming very different from when we worked in isolation, in functional silos, producing a blueprint that someone would use to manufacture the thing, and so on. We're getting better at creating design processes that let us think about multiple functions and disciplines all at once, which prevents some of the problems you usually see when you go from one phase to the next.

One example of that kind of problem can be seen in the awkward connection between the worlds of design and fabrication. I was at a construction site recently, watching some builders try to prepare the concrete forms needed to execute some very complicated shape that had been done with parametric modeling software. These forms should have been milled and assembled off-site, brought on-site, and then put together. Instead, I watched as laser-cut molds were used

"The way we interact with our designs is becoming very different from when we worked in isolation, in functional silos." —

to guide the bending of plywood, and a guy worked with a jigsaw and a file. The building had a wild interior shape. It had a pattern of ridges that was specified algorithmically or parametrically. And yet the guy building it was using very traditional carpentry techniques. He was sitting there filing and holding up a traced outline. I thought, *It's unfortunate that form generation has progressed so far, but fabrication hasn't.*

But one interesting thing I'm seeing happening today in manufacturing and architecture is that a designer can now fabricate most of the things he can conceive of. And in the next five to ten years, we will not only have widely available 3D printing but some existing techniques, such as computer numerically controlled (CNC) equipment, will be more connected to the overall design process.

So I think we will start seeing a unification of these different functional realms. There's enough sophistication on both sides. There's enough technology. We are able to connect up the modeling to some of the documentation in an automated way. The next step will be to improve that automated connection to the point that it makes it trivial to fabricate those forms and all the matching parts.

What are your hopes for the future of design?

That's a little bit like asking, "What is your hope for mathematics?" My hopes are not around design, specifically. I look at design as a method of solving problems and bringing new objects into the world. So, what I hope is that we end up with better designs, more people capable of doing design, and that the ideas of design are more broadly accessible and understood. I also hope that we'll be able to solve problems that we couldn't solve before. ⓐ

Carl Bass is CEO of Autodesk.

AMAZING COMPLEXITY: AN OVERWHELMING OPPORTUNITY

WANT TO GET A SENSE OF HOW COMPLEX THE WORLD IS NOW? According to Google, every two days we create as much information as we did from the dawn of civilization up until 2003.

The hyperconnected world that has produced that remarkable statistic is also spawning a complexity greater than we've ever faced. That complexity is being amplified by the three aforementioned trends—infinite computing, the ability to digitize the real world, and the fact that more people are continuing to design more and more *stuff*—as well as by countless other factors, having to do with technology, shifting global conditions, increased specialization of disciplines, and more. That these conditions are also tightly interconnected further contributes to the "radical complexity" of a world where seemingly every task (even one as simple as making a pencil) requires global collaboration, and seemingly every action has far-reaching effects and consequences. For designers, whose job is to build, innovate, simplify, and make sure the world works and its parts mesh together smoothly, dealing with massive complexity is a major challenge already, and one that will only intensify in years ahead.

A map of the Internet reveals the density and complexity of our digital interconnections.

This will make it all the more critical that designers are able to distill clarity from complexity. As they sift through the blizzards of data that swirl around us, their challenge will be to take maximum advantage of all that data without becoming overwhelmed by it. The key will be to turn *data* into *valuable information*—a task that will require both advanced technology, including search capabilities that can leverage the massive amounts of information in the cloud, and sophisticated information design and visualization skills. More than ever, good design will be needed to organize information, to simplify and streamline it, to bring it to life through simulations and storytelling and, ultimately, to give it meaning and clarity.

As all that massive data is tamed, organized, and made instantly accessible, it has the potential to help simplify complex design tasks that could otherwise be overwhelming. A designer trying to balance structural issues, environmental concerns, building codes, cost analyses, questions about material properties, and countless other interlocking factors will be able to use this massive amount of data to do simulations and analyses that address all of these matters, simultaneously—allowing him to remain focused on the actual design. In this new way of working, complexities like "computational fluid dynamics" and "earthquake simulation with finite element analysis" will be simplified by a system that simply tells you, in effect, "You need a stronger I-beam over there."

Technology is only part of the solution; designers will also have to adopt processes and working approaches geared to dealing with this radical complexity. We can expect to see more and more emphasis on "systems design," which attempts to take all disciplines and perspectives into account from the outset of a design project. This holistic approach can help designers tackle the kind of problems where solving for one aspect actually worsens another, and can lead to "big picture" solutions that couldn't have been envisioned using a more traditional "siloed" approach to design. It is the combination of better technology and better design practices—a tool set change and a mind-set change—that will make incredibly

complex challenges more addressable.

To get the most out of holistic design, bringing together different disciplines is critical. From architects to structural engineers to the people who deal with parking, utility hookups, and city planning—if all of these different specialists can be brought together on a project, it avoids the now-common problem of people working at cross-purposes on projects. And it can bring important and useful new perspectives into the design process. For example, if you're designing an airplane, wouldn't it make sense to have the cabin crew—the people who practically live on that plane and deal with its design on a daily basis—be part of the design process? Breaking down the walls between disciplines will, again, require both a change in toolset (new technologies) and a change in mind-set (the way we think about and do things). By using information-rich digital modeling and prototypes that are centralized and accessible to multiple design partners in a variety of disciplines and locations, we can enable a community of people, with different skills and expertise, to work together effectively on the same project. This kind of multidisciplined collaboration will be a key to tackling the interconnected design challenges we'll face in the radically complex world of the future.

GLOBAL CHALLENGES—AND THE DESIGN RESPONSE

ARE DESIGNERS READY TO TAKE ON THE WORLD'S GRAND CHALLENGES?

Environmental and other challenges are redefining what design success is. If no one can see the CCTV tower in Beijing, is it still a great building?

In the years ahead, as increasingly complex global issues become more urgent and approach tipping points, the world's designers, architects, engineers, and digital artists are likely to find themselves right there on the front lines. They'll be armed with dazzling technology, massive information, and, above all, their own creativity and ingenuity—and they'll need every bit of it.

Some of the grand challenges that will loom large in months and years ahead include climate change—which in turn contributes to the growing need for sustainable design and clean, renewable energy—and the need for clean water, better education, improved health services, and a better quality of life for most of the world. These are just a few of the many issues that will require innovative design as part of the overall strategies to address them.

How can the discipline of design respond to such daunting challenges? In the most general sense, design can help bring a systematic, iterative way of thinking and problem-solving to bear on many of these issues. Designers can also apply the latest technology to change the ways we create products, buildings, and even cities. When we use advanced digital simulations to test thousands or even millions of scenarios during the design process, it becomes increasingly possible to achieve the best real-world results. It will also become more and more feasible for design to apply advanced problem-solving approaches—everything from algorithmic design to biomimicry—to some of our oldest and most entrenched problems.

While new technology and new systems of thinking will be of great importance, ultimately it will be up to the designers themselves—working as individuals or within companies

INFINITE COMPUTING

Computers will have greater awareness of a design's real-world context, accessibility to computing power will spread, and processing power will increase significantly, enabling designers to generate dozens or even hundreds of design alternatives in the time it once took to create only a single option.

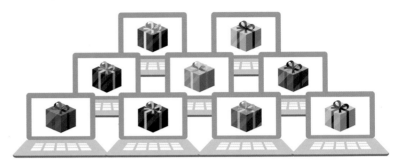

From: creating a single design option

To: creating numerous design options in the same amount of time

REALITY, DIGITIZED

The speed and ease with which we can capture reality—in the form of a detailed 3D model representing an environment or object—makes it more and more feasible to virtualize the real world. Once an object or place is virtualized in the form of a digital model, we can reshape it—and eventually reshape the real world.

From: meticulously hand-drafting and constructing our designed objects

To: scanning real-world objects, modifying and printing them and their components at will

EVERYONE IS A DESIGNER

Low-cost, widely distributed design tools make it easy for non-designers to shape, manipulate, and manufacture everyday objects at home, fulfilling the growing desire to have more control over the objects in our lives. Instead of design that is mass-produced, we'll see personalized creations designed for production units of one.

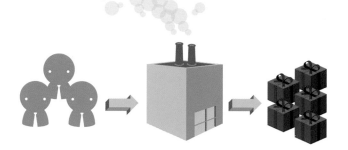

From: teams of professionals designing manufactured objects for mass consumption

To: amateur designers customizing their own creations through democratized design tools and 3-D printing

AMAZING COMPLEXITY

As we create and consume more information, and the elements of our lives become increasingly connected, we face unprecedented levels of complexity. For designers, that massive complexity is a major challenge that will intensify in years ahead, making it critical for them to distill clarity from chaos.

From: designed objects existing with little consideration for any connections beyond the consumer

To: designed objects existing in endlessly complex systems, connected to countless other objects, environments, and people

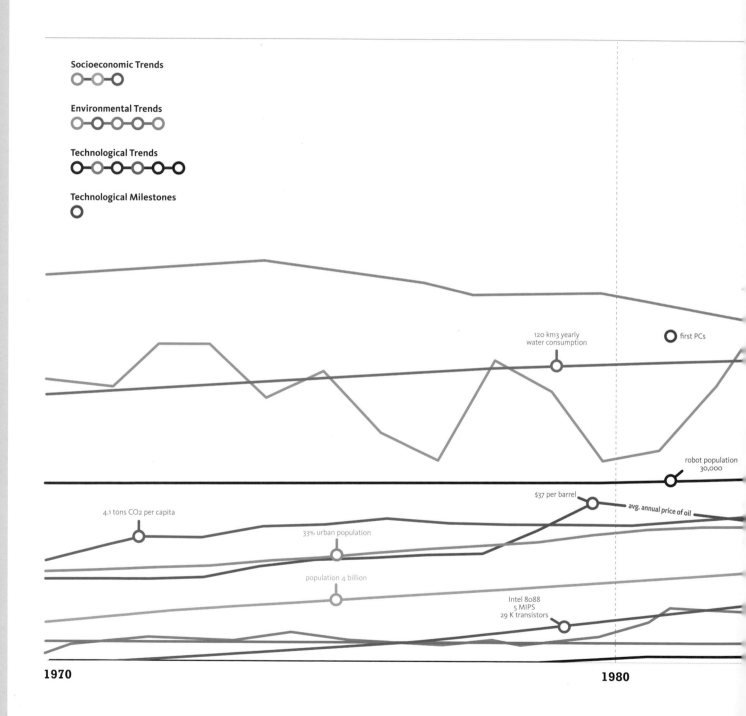

Socioeconomic Trends

Environmental Trends

Technological Trends

Technological Milestones

120 km3 yearly
water consumption

first PCs

robot population
30,000

$37 per barrel

avg. annual price of oil

4.1 tons CO2 per capita

33% urban population

population 4 billion

Intel 8088
5 MIPS
29 K transistors

1970

1980

THE FUTURE OF DESIGN

How will design shape our changing world?

Disruptive technologies like the PC and the Internet have transformed design, and the future promises even greater changes at a more rapid pace. Increased bandwidth and processing power will help make "infinite" computing accessible. Together with widely

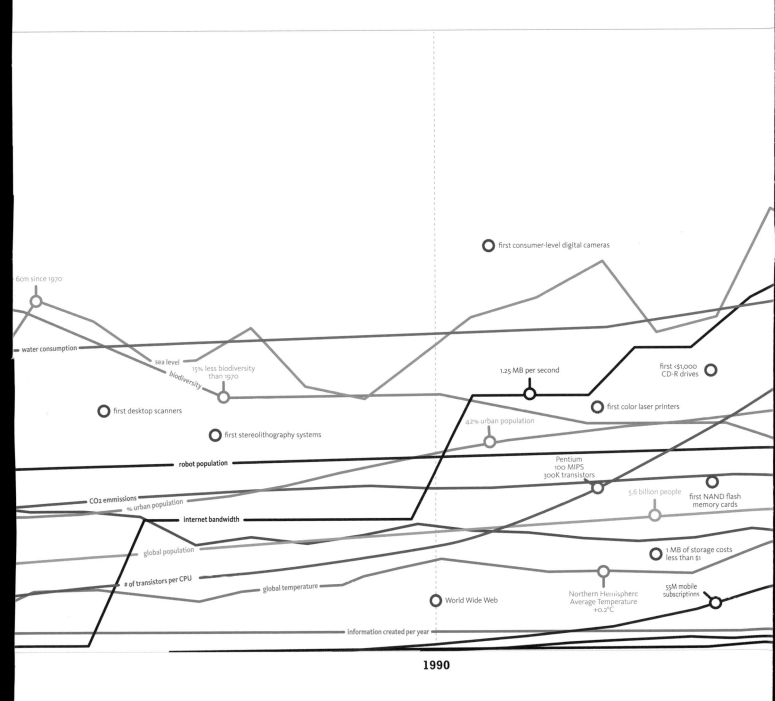

6cm since 1970

water consumption

sea level

15% less biodiversity than 1970

biodiversity

first desktop scanners

first stereolithography systems

robot population

CO2 emmissions

% urban population

internet bandwidth

global population

# of transistors per CPU

global temperature

information created per year

first consumer-level digital cameras

1.25 MB per second

first <$1,000 CD-R drives

first color laser printers

42% urban population

Pentium
100 MIPS
300K transistors

5.6 billion people

first NAND flash memory cards

1 MB of storage costs less than $1

World Wide Web

Northern Hemisphere Average Temperature +0.2°C

55M mobile subscriptions

1990

available tools like 3D printers and scanners, these trends will democratize the ability to digitize, model, and create more of the real world. With that will come a rapid increase in complexity and the amount of data generated—from exabytes today to zettabytes in the very near future. Along with continuing urbanization, climate change, energy scarcity, and numerous other global challenges, the world in 2020 will pose new problems and opportunities that will change what it means to design.

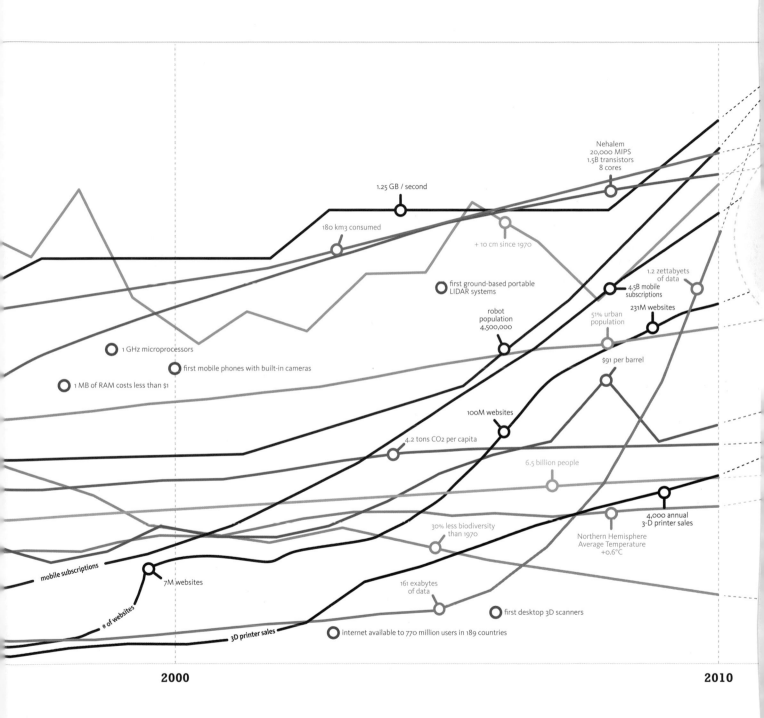

1.25 GB / second

180 km3 consumed

Nehalem
20,000 MIPS
1.5B transistors
8 cores

+ 10 cm since 1970

first ground-based portable
LIDAR systems

1.2 zettabytes
of data

4.5B mobile
subscriptions

robot
population
4,500,000

51% urban
population

231M websites

1 GHz microprocessors

first mobile phones with built-in cameras

$91 per barrel

1 MB of RAM costs less than $1

100M websites

4.2 tons CO2 per capita

6.5 billion people

4,000 annual
3-D printer sales

30% less biodiversity
than 1970

Northern Hemisphere
Average Temperature
+0.6°C

mobile subscriptions

7M websites

161 exabytes
of data

first desktop 3D scanners

# of websites

3D printer sales

internet available to 770 million users in 189 countries

2000

2010

Reality, Digitized
Designers will soon be able bring more of the analog world into the digital realm, allowing them to create designs that are better suited for the real world.

Infinite Computing
When computers can give us any solution we want, the designer's role will be to ask the right questions.

These five trends promise to dramatically change the work of designers in the next decade, and, to a great extent, determine what tomorrow's world looks like, how well it functions, and what it's like to live in.

• • •

the *future* of
design

Everyone Is a Designer
New design tools, opportunities, and communities will allow anyone to tap into the natural human urge to design.

Global Challenges
Our increased capacity to create and evaluate design solutions will allow us to build resilience and confront the complex global challenges ahead.

Amazing Complexity
In a hyper-connected world, it will be all the more critical that designers be able to distill clarity from complexity.

2020

and collectives—to take the initiative in tackling these grand challenges. Design professionals must move from thinking of themselves as doing "only" design to intentionally engaging in a broader range of activities with a mind-set geared toward innovation.

For example, some leading-edge companies have begun to apply principles of sustainable design to the challenge of minimizing the harmful environmental impact of what they make, spurred on partly by consumers who are beginning to demand more sustainable and responsible approaches from the companies they do business with. At the center of this burgeoning movement are individual designers such as Valerie Casey, founder of the Designers Accord (which encourages business to design products and practices far more sustainably), as well as companies such as Autodesk, which has developed a new approach that corporations can follow in setting targets to reduce greenhouse gas emissions. If all companies were to adopt this approach, private sector emissions would be on track to help stabilize the climate by 2050.

In the quest for clean energy, companies like Tesla Motors and Green Ocean Energy are using innovative design to create groundbreaking products that reduce our dependence on oil. Tesla Motors' Roadster and Model S cars are proving that electric automobiles can compete not just on the moral high ground but also on the high-speed freeway. Green Ocean Energy, located in Scotland, has created a remarkable technology that harnesses energy from ocean waves in an entirely new way, using huge devices—usually around 50 meters long and weighing 300 tons—that must be able to survive harsh ocean storm conditions. Designing and building these machines would be virtually impossible without using digital modeling and advanced simulations.

In the educational realm, designers such as Yves Behar and the team at Nicholas Negroponte's One Laptop Per Child (OLPC) group have demonstrated that it's possible to apply innovative design to the challenge of bringing affordable laptop computers to children in developing nations. Although the OLPC project has encountered political and cultural roadblocks along the way, it has nonetheless helped more than 2 million children in poor, often remote areas to connect with the resources of the Internet. Meanwhile, designer Emily Pilloton is redesigning classrooms and learning approaches geared to at-risk children. Pilloton is an example of one designer who crosses over into various areas of need: Before focusing on education design, she had left the practice of product design to create a traveling road show of design objects that improve people's lives.

The sophistication of our design tools, and the sources of design inspiration, will continue to grow as we harness everything from the power of algorithms to the wonders of nature to make it increasingly possible to design and create almost anything we can imagine. And as design's ability to do more increases, it will become ever more important to design thoughtfully, elegantly, and ethically.

And while many of the aspects of design will undergo radical change over the next few years, the *timeless* aspects of design—and our instinctual desire to imagine, design, and create a better world—will be with us as long as someone is around to ask the question, "What if?"

The challenge of building a clean, sustainable energy infrastructure is already inspiring new design approaches, such as this tidal generator by Marine Currents Limited.

ARE WE READY TO EMBRACE THE CHALLENGE?

THE TECHNOLOGIES DESCRIBED HERE SUGGEST THAT WE NEEDN'T WORRY ABOUT HAVING THE TOOLS REQUIRED TO DESIGN A BETTER FUTURE. Armed with unlimited processing power, vast amounts of information, greater connectivity, and widespread manufacturing capabilities, the toolset will be there. But what about the mind-set?

Design is, in essence, a way of thinking. It is dependent on the ability and willingness to explore ideas and options, to question what is and what might be, to experiment, and to consider multiple viewpoints and potential outcomes. These are the mental and emotional activities that will be increasingly critical to navigating a world of complex, interconnected challenges. So here's the question: Do we have what it takes?

Judging by the insightful and innovative designers, problem-solvers, and thinkers profiled here, there is good reason to be hopeful. The challenge is to foster this way of thinking and problem-solving, this mind-set, among the many, not just the few.

That may require bold changes in the way we educate and encourage tomorrow's designers—including both professionals and motivated amateurs empowered by accessible, inexpensive tools. As Sir Ken Robinson and inventor Dean Kamen have both pointed out, it all starts with nurturing the creative spark in people when they're young—teaching them that there is usually no single right answer, encouraging them to experiment, to be open to all possibilities, and to let their imaginations roam.

When these students leave academia, they will be entering a realm where complexity is the norm and innovation is critical to success. While there is no shortage of inventive minds coming out of universities, there is a considerable gap between invention (creating something new) and innovation (introducing something new into the world). And because design is often the bridge that connects one to the other, it behooves everyone to know how to think like a designer. That means knowing how to generate and synthesize ideas; to develop those ideas over time; to learn the subtle skills of evaluating, analyzing, and making choices; and knowing how to work across disciplines and collaborate with a wide range of people. It involves listening, communicating, empathizing, and myriad other "soft" skills that are so essential to solving the hardest problems.

Adopting this mind-set, this way of thinking, is a lifelong undertaking. Fortunately, the "classroom" now is all around us; through social networking and crowdsourcing, today we can get answers and feedback, and find expert partners to help on our most important projects.

It's an ideal environment for the bold and the brainy, the curious and the flexible and the people who thrive on improvisation and love nothing more than the feeling of amazement when they surpass even their own high expectations with a great idea or a brilliant execution. We'll still need the elite thinkers, the experienced craftsmen, the bright-eyed newcomers, and just about everyone else to pitch in as we confront the immense challenges ahead.

Designing this new world is no solitary pursuit, but rather one that demands the very best of our collective imagination and effort. We'll need to share our ideas and our visions in an ongoing conversation about tomorrow that, hopefully, begins now. That conversation—and the ideas and innovations it will generate—is the first step in the next chapter of the timeless story of design, as we work together to imagine, design, and create a better world. **Ⓐ**

The Masdar Headquarters building in Abu Dhabi, designed by Adrian Smith + Gordon Gill Architecture, will be the world's first large-scale positive-energy building

CONTRIBUTORS

Michael Behar is a freelance writer based in Boulder, Colorado, who covers adventure travel, the environment, and innovations in science and technology. His articles have appeared in several publications including *Outside*, *Wired*, *Men's Journal*, *Mother Jones*, *Popular Science*, *Backpacker*, *Discover*, and *Air & Space* magazines. Michael's work has been nominated for a National Magazine Award and the Grantham Prize for Excellence in Reporting on the Environment, and featured in the *Best American Travel Writing* and *Best of Technology Writing* anthologies.

Warren Berger is the author of *Glimmer: How Design Can Transform Business, Your Life, and Maybe Even the World* (Penguin Press) and the editor of *Glimmersite.com*. He's served as a longtime contributing editor at *Wired* magazine and a business columnist for the *New York Times*. He writes and lectures about (among other things) design thinking, innovation, advertising, and gangsters in old Detroit.

Amber Bravo is a freelance writer and former senior editor at *Dwell* magazine. Her work has appeared in various publications like *I.D.*, *Ready-Made*, *Grafik*, and the book *3D Typography*. Amber's most recent project is developing the editorial and creative direction for *Mantle*, a collaborative fashion, design, and art journal.

Brian Ford is an artist, illustrator and designer with a passion for storytelling and creative collaboration. Brian is a cofounder of coLab, a collaborative design consultancy, and has worked on a range of projects in healthcare, entertainment, sustainability, and education. He lives in Toronto and can be found online at *www.brianford.net*.

Based in San Francisco, **Alex Frankel** is the author of two books that examine business, marketing, and popular culture: *Punching In* and *Wordcraft*. Alex has written for *Fast Company*, *Outside*, *Wired*, and the *New York Times Magazine*. Alex is the founder of Ground Level Research (*www.grdlvl.com*), which conducts journalistic research for corporate clients.

Mark Freeman is a Toronto-based writer, filmmaker and digital media artist. He is a cofounder of coLab, and is currently writing a book on the role of anxiety in the workplace.

Suzanne LaBarre is a senior editor at Co.Design, *Fast Company*'s design blog. Her work has appeared in *Metropolis*, *I.D.*, *Fast Company*, and many other publications.

Based in southern Vermont, **Bob Parks** is author of the book *Makers* and contributes to the magazines *Wired*, *Make*, and *Popular Science*. This year, he won an honorable mention in a local Lego contest for a clock that he built with his 9-year-old son. He is currently working on a book about the daily lives of contemporary inventors.

A former editor at *Wired* and *Business Week*, **Jessie Scanlon** has a passion for design and technology. She has written for the *New York Times*, *Slate*, *Popular Science*, and *Dwell*, among others. Scanlon lives in Cambridge, Massachusetts.

Tom Wujec is a Fellow at Autodesk and works at the intersection of digital technology, team creativity, design thinking, and visual collaboration. He is author of three books on creativity and innovation and has brought several award-winning design software applications to market. In his position at Autodesk, Wujec helps companies work in the emerging field of business visualization—the art of using images, sketches, and infographics to help teams solve complex problems as a group.

ACKNOWLEDGMENTS

At Autodesk, thanks to the leadership of Carl Bass, Chris Bradshaw, Jeff Kowalski, and Jon Pittman. This book depended on the help of many Autodesk staff, including a core group of advisors: Phil Bernstein, Maurice Conti, Jonathan Knowles, Brian Mathews, Bill O'Connor, Dave Rhodes, and Kelly Rupp. Special thanks to Tim Eischens for his skillful organization and management of the project. And thanks to the producers of this book, Charles Melcher and David Brown at Melcher Media.

Others at Autodesk who helped make the book possible are Dan Ahern, Robert Aish, Lynn Allen, Lyne Arsenault, Karen Brewer, Lynelle Cameron, Dawn Danby, Mark Davis, Doug Eberhard, Christina Gialluca, Susan Gladwin, Roxie Hecker, Clay Helm, Mary Hoadley, Erin Rae Hoffer, Shaan Hurley, Christine Kalb, Jake Layes, Carol Lettieri, Kerry Ann Levenhagen, Gonzalo Martinez, Amy McKee, Jason Medal-Katz, David Morin, Maurice Patel, Brian Pene, Chris Ruffo, Craig Schnabel, Rob Schrack, Angela Simoes, Efrat Stark, Emma Stewart, Melissa Thomas, Matthew Tierney, Lisa Turbis, Robert Vizza, and Dan Zucker.

Thanks to the many people who shared their time and insights with us, including Irene Au, Google; Raymond Bakker, ADEPT; Max Béland, Ubisoft; Janine Benyus; Gabrielle Berger, SOM; Gary Blakesley, FIRST; Frederick Brooks; Tim Brown, IDEO; Bill Buxton, Microsoft Research; John Cary, Next American City; Valerie Casey; Sally Cohen, Heatherwick Studio; Alex Cohn, KieranTimberlake; Roger Collier, FIRST Team 2550 Oregon City Pioneer Robotics Organization; Isabella Conti; Peter Diamandis, X Prize Foundation; Hugh Dubberly, Dubberly Design; Nils Fischer, Zaha Hadid Architects; Flemming Binderup Gammelgaard, the LEGO Group; Gretchen Hartley, Marriott; John Hoke, Nike; Rohan Kandlur, FIRST Team 640, Quixilver; Kevin Kelly; Jon Landau, Lightstorm; Don Levy, Sony Imageworks; Chris Luebkeman, ARUP; Alex McDowell; Patty Mack; Ron Mathis, Edison2; Jay Mezher, Parsons Brinckerhoff; Nolan Murtha, Lightstorm; Jeff Nowak, Ford; Lisbeth Valther Pallesen, the LEGO Group; Alexandre Parizeau, Ubisoft; John Parman, Gensler; Emily Pilloton, Project H; Leah Ray, Gensler; Pam Raymond, SOM; Patrick Redding, Ubisoft; Alexandre Remy, Ubisoft; Sami Routsalanien, Electric RaceAbout; Sarah Sandercock, Heatherwick Studio; Ryan Seabury, NetDevil; Nathan Shedroff; Peter Skillman, Nokia; Gary Starr, Zap World; Hayden Walling, Ubisoft; Carin Whitney, KieranTimberlake; and John Wolf, Marriott.

Melcher Media thanks Colin Berry, William Bostwick, Chris Cowans, Glenn Derry, Max Dickstein, Amelia Hennighausen, Zane Holsinger, Heather Hughes, Todd Lappin, Brett McFadden, Lauren Nathan, Cheryl Della Pietra, Holly Rothman, Julia Sourikoff, Maureen Spitz, Shoshana Thaler, Anna Thorngate, Scott Thorpe, Jason Wachtelhausen, Megan Worman, and Matthew Wright.

INFOGRAPHIC SOURCES

P. 78 — CREATING IMPACT

Emily Pilloton, *Project H Design Process*, October 2010. Available at: *projecthdesign.org/about.html*

P. 102 — SPHERES OF INFLUENCE

Prince McLean, *The Inside Track on Apple's Tablet: A History of Tablet Computing*, www.appleinsider.com, January, 2010.

Edwin Tofslie, *Apple Form Factor Evolution*, 2007. Available at *www.core77.com/blog/object_culture/apple_form_factor_evolution_6722.asp*

Bill Buxton, *Multi-Touch Systems That I Have Known and Loved*, October 2009. Available at *www.billbuxton.com/multitouchOverview.html*

P. 148 — SIX DESIGN PROCESSES

Hugh Dubberly, *[Beta] How Do You Design?* Dubberly Design Office, 2005. Available at *www.dubberly.com/articles/how-do-you-design.html*

P. 206 — THE EVOLUTION OF CAD

Micro Processor Cost per Transistor Cycle, www.singularity.com, 2004. Available at *www.singularity.com/charts/page62.html*

Processor Performance (MIPS), www.singularity.com, 2004. Available at *www.singularity.com/charts/page64.html*

P. 238 — MEASURING EXPERIENCE

Cloudy with a Chance of Meatballs, directed by Phil Lord & Christopher Miller, Sony Pictures Imageworks, 2009. Images used with permission.

P. 296 — INTEGRATIVE DESIGN

Factor Ten Engineering Design Principles Version 1.0, Rocky Mountain Institute, 2010. Available at *rmi.org/rmi/10xe%20principles*

P. 322–327 — THE FUTURE OF DESIGN

Baltimore Tide Gauge Data, Permanent Service for Mean Sea Level, ID 148, 2010. Available at *www.psmsl.org/data/obtaining/*

Roger E. Bohn, James E. Short, *How Much Information?* 2009, Global Information Industry Center, University of California, San Diego, 2009.

"CO2 Emissions Per Capita," World Bank, World Development Indicators, October 2010.

John F. Gantz, et al., "The Diverse and Exploding Digital Universe: An Updated Forecast of Worldwide Information Growth Through 2011," IDC, 2008. Available at *www.emc.com/collateral/analyst-reports/diverse-exploding-digital-universe.pdf*

Global Mobile Cellular Subscriptions, International Telecommunication Union, 2010. Available at *www.itu.int/ITU-D/ict/statistics/*

HadCRUT3: Global surface temperatures, Met Office, 2010. Available at *www.metoffice.gov.uk/climatechange/science/monitoring/hadcrut3.html*

Alastair Halliday, "Timeline: March of the Machines," www.technologyreview.com, May/June 2010.

Jeff Hecht, "Internet Backbone Breaks the 100-Gigabit Barrier," www.newscientist.com, Reed Business Information Ltd., January 2010.

"Historical Crude Oil Prices," www.inflationdata.com, July 2010.

"Internet Backbone Bandwidth," www.singularity.com, 2004. Available at *www.singularity.com/charts/page81.html*

John C. McCallum, "Memory Prices (1957–2010)," 2010. Available at *www.jcmit.com/memoryprice.htm*

Igor A. Shiklomanov, *Industrial and Domestic Consumption Compared with Evaporation from Reservoirs*, UNESCO, 1999.

The 2010 Living Planet Report, WWF International, 2010. Available at *wwf.panda.org/about_our_earth/all_publications/living_planet_report/*

IMAGE CREDITS

Produced by

MELCHER MEDIA

124 West 13th Street
New York, NY 10011
www.melcher.com

President and Publisher: Charles Melcher
Associate Publisher: Bonnie Eldon
Editor in Chief: Duncan Bock
Executive Editor: Lia Ronnen
Production Director: Kurt Andrews

Editor: David E. Brown
Production Coordinator: Daniel del Valle

Design by MacFadden & Thorpe